MATHEMATICS 10
Applying the Concepts
Student Workbook

Authors
Steve Etienne, B.Sc., B.Admin., Ed. Cert.
Kernahan Park Secondary School
Niagara District School Board

John Gardiner B.Sc., B.Ed.
Virtual Learning Centre
Trillium Lakelands District School Board

McGraw-Hill Ryerson

McGraw-Hill Ryerson
Toronto Montréal Boston Burr Ridge, IL Dubuque, IA Madison, WI New York San Francisco St. Louis Bangkok Bogotá Caracas Kuala Lumpur Lisbon London Madrid Mexico City Milan New Delhi Santiago Seoul Singapore Sydney Taipei

The McGraw·Hill Companies

McGraw-Hill Ryerson

COPIES OF THIS BOOK MAY BE OBTAINED BY CONTACTING:

McGraw-Hill Ryerson Ltd.

WEB SITE:
http://www.mcgrawhill.ca

E-MAIL:
orders@mcgrawhill.ca

TOLL-FREE FAX:
1-800-463-5885

TOLL-FREE CALL:
1-800-565-5758

OR BY MAILING YOUR ORDER TO:
McGraw-Hill Ryerson
Order Department
300 Water Street
Whitby, ON L1N 9B6

Please quote the ISBN and title when placing your order.

Student Workbook ISBN:
0-07-094776-7

Mathematics: Applying the Concepts 10 Student Workbook

ISBN 0-07-094776-7

http://www.mcgrawhill.ca

1 2 3 4 5 6 7 8 9 10 MP 0 9 8 7 6 5 4

Printed and bound in Canada

National Library of Canada Cataloging in Publication Data

Etienne, Stephen Aimé, 1960-
Mathematics: applying the concepts 10. Student workbook/Stephen Aimé Etienne, William John Gardiner.

ISBN 0-07-094776-7

1. Mathematics—Problems, exercises, etc. 2. Mathematics—Study and teaching (Secondary) I. Gardiner, William John, 1948- II. Title.

QA39.2.M33 2000 Suppl. 4 510 C2003-907274-6

PUBLISHER: Diane Wyman
DEVELOPMENTAL EDITOR: David L. Peebles
SUPERVISING EDITOR: Susan Morton Stewart
COPY EDITOR: Rosina Daillie
EDITORIAL ASSISTANT: Erin Hartley
PRODUCTION SUPERVISOR: Yolanda Pigden
PRODUCTION COORDINATOR: Janie Deneau
COVER DESIGN: Greg Devitt
ELECTRONIC PAGE MAKE-UP: VISU*TronX*
COVER IMAGE: Gandee Vason/Stone

Acknowledgements

Reviewers of *Mathematics: Applying the Concepts 10 Student Workbook*
The authors and editors of Mathematics: Applying the Concepts 10 Student Workbook *wish to thank the reviewers listed below for their thoughtful comments and suggestions. Their input has been invaluable in ensuring that this text meets the needs of both students and teachers.*

Advisors

Jeff Brosseau, B.A., B.Ed.

Krysta Brosseau, B.Sc., B.Comm., B.Ed.

Lillian Kovachis Perivolaris, B.A., B.Ed., M.A.
Toronto District School Board

Donna Kotsopoulos, B.A., B.Ed., M.Ed.
Thames Valley District School Board

Reviewers

David Furlong
Toronto District School Board

John Di Vizio
Durham Catholic DSB

Emidio DiAntonio
Dufferin Peel Catholic District School Board

Raymond Kennedy
Toronto Catholic District School Board

David Lovisa
York Region District School Board

Angela Van Kralingen
Niagara Catholic District School Board

Alexis Galvao
Dufferin-Peel Catholic District School Board

Natasha Sudy
York Region District School Board

Contents

CHAPTER 4

Piecewise Linear Functions

CHAPTER 5

Systems of Linear Equations

CHAPTER 6

Similar Triangles

CHAPTER 7

Trigonometry

CHAPTER 8

Quadratic Functions

CHAPTER 9

Algebraic Expressions

CHAPTER 10

Solve Problems: Quadratic Functions

Features of This Workbook

Warm-Up Guide

This two-page guide lists hints and techniques to help you answer the **Warm-Up** questions at the beginning of each numbered section.

Succeed on the Chapter Tests

This section outlines a number of methods you can use to study more effectively and improve your results on the chapter tests.

Get Set

At the beginning of each chapter, a page of questions reviews key skills from other mathematics courses and from previous chapters.

Numbered Sections

Warm Up

Each section starts with eight **Warm Up** questions, which provide an ongoing review of the major topics of the course. Often, these questions include prerequisite skills for the next topic.

Practise

The **Practise** pages give you a chance to apply and extend the concepts you have just learned. Often, the first questions outline the steps in the solution to help you understand the mathematics used to answer the question. Then, you advance to answering similar questions without guidance.

Chapter Review

The **Chapter Review** has a set of questions covering all the numbered sections in the chapter. As you work through these questions, you can identify the topics for which more study and practice will help you do your best on the chapter test.

Rich Problem

Each chapter has a rich problem with questions that use concepts from the various sections in the chapter. Some of the rich problems also involve topics from earlier chapters. These problems let you practise using the concepts together and help you understand how they are related.

Key Equations

A convenient list at the back of the workbook gathers together all the equations for the key concepts of the course.

Warm-Up Guide

1. Number Sense

Common sense is the key to solving most Number Sense problems.

- Read each question carefully. Re-read the question if you are not sure what is being asked.
- When looking for a pattern in a sequence of numbers, consider the increments between successive numbers. If the increments are not constant, check for a constant multiplier.
- Ask yourself, "Does this answer make sense?"

2. Mental Math/Estimating

Resist the temptation to use a calculator for Mental Math/Estimating questions. These questions let you practise methods for checking your work and spotting entry errors.

Arithmetic

- When adding, look for combinations of units digits that add to 10, tens digits that add to 10, and so on.
- When multiplying or dividing by a power of ten, simply move the decimal point right or left the appropriate number of places.

Estimating

- Round each number to a convenient number (such as multiples of 2, 5, or 10) to make the mental calculation easier.
- When multiplying, round one number up and the other number down.
- When dividing, round both numbers up or both numbers down.

3. Proportional Reasoning

Rates and Proportions

- See if you can write a proportion relating the unknown quantity to three known quantities. Then, solve for the unknown quantity.
- Often, you can solve a question by multiplying or dividing by a rate.
- Divide to find a unit rate.

Percent

- To change a percent to a decimal, divide the percent by 100.
- To change a fraction to a percent, divide the numerator by the denominator and multiply by 100.
- To change a decimal to a percent, multiply the decimal by 100.
- To find a percent of a number, convert the percent to a decimal, then multiply (or use the % key on your calculator).

4. Relations and Functions

If an ordered pair is part of a relation, the values in the pair will satisfy the equation for the relation.

Linear Functions

- The graph of a linear function is a straight line.
- In the equation $y = mx + b$, m is the slope of the line and b is the y-intercept.

Quadratic Functions

- The graph of a quadratic function is a parabola.
- Standard form: $y = a(x - h)^2 + k$, where (h, k) is the vertex.
- General form: $y = ax^2 + bx + c$, where c is the y-intercept.
- Factored form: $y = a(x - s)(s - t)$, where s and t are the x-intercepts (zeros).
- If $a > 0$, the parabola opens upward. If $a < 0$, the parabola opens downward.

5. Algebra

Algebra is a technique that lets you do calculations with unknown quantities as if they were known values. Letters represent the unknown quantities or variables.

Collecting Like Terms

- Add or subtract the terms that have the same variable and exponent.

Evaluating With a Given Value

- Replace the variable with the given number, then follow BEDMAS.

Solving an Equation

- Collect variable terms on one side of the equation and constant terms on the other.
- Perform the same operation on both sides of the equation to isolate the variable.

6. Tables and Graphs

Tables

- Look for a pattern among the entries, then use this pattern to solve the problem.
- If equal increments in one variable produce constant increments in the other variable, then the two variables have a linear relationship.

Graphs

- Check the axis labels to see what each axis represents and what the scale is.
- On a Cartesian graph, the value of a variable increases as you move right or up.
- To plot (x, y), move x units horizontally (left or right) and y units vertically (up or down).
- In a bar graph, a bar that extends below the horizontal axis indicates a negative value.
- On a graph of piecewise linear function, an open circle at the end of a segment means that the end point is not included in the segment. A closed circled means that the end point is included.
- On pie charts (circle graphs), the values marked in each section are usually percents.

7. Math Literacy

- Use the **Glossary** on pages 446–455 of the textbook.
- Consider the meaning of the parts of longer words. For example, in *trinomial*, *tri* means three.
- Many familiar words have special, precise meanings in mathematics, for example, *intercept*, *mean*, and *similar*.

8. Previous Section

- Check the examples and key concepts in the previous section of the textbook.
- Look for similar Practise questions in the previous section of this workbook.
- Check your notes and assignments for the topic.

For more help, see the table of key equations on pages 193–195.

Succeed on the Chapter Tests

Most students find these techniques helpful. Use the ones that work best for you.

The Basics

Start now.

- Set aside time to study every day.
- Studying as you go along makes it easier to understand the next day's lesson.

Use your classroom time.

- Listen and make notes.
- Ask questions if you do not understand a concept.

Catch up if you miss a class.

- Read the section in the textbook.
- Try the workbook questions on your own. Compare your answers to those given by the teacher.
- Getting caught up saves you time overall.

Make study notes.

- Rewrite the Key Concepts for each section in your own words.
- Read through the notes you made in class. Add any additional concepts or tips to your study notes.

Do examples.

- Review the examples in the textbook.
- Cover the solutions and work them out yourself. Then, compare your solutions to the ones in the textbook.

Target weak points in your understanding.

- Keep a list of questions you had trouble with in the Practise sections and in the Chapter Review.
- Read the textbook section for each of these questions. Then, try the questions again.
- If you still cannot answer the question, ask your teacher or a classmate for help.

Get a head start.

- Keep your study notes up-to-date.
- Choose questions to practise the night before the test.
- Prepare a "test kit" with all the items you need. Make sure you have a calculator, a pencil, an eraser, and a ruler.

More Study Methods

Make a schedule.

- Review one or two sections each day during the week before the test.
- Study at the same time each day if possible.

Study with a partner.

- One partner explains step by step how to answer the odd-numbered questions. The other partner explains the even-numbered questions.
- If both of you have trouble with a particular question, work on it together.

Make your own practice test.

- Write one or two questions for each section. Include communication and application questions. Working with a partner can make it easier to come up with ideas for questions.
- Prepare an answer key for your practice test.
- Try a practice test written by someone else in your class. Note topics that are difficult for you. Review these topics before the real test!

Make study cards.

- Copy several typical problems for each section onto index cards or small pieces of paper. Choose problems from the textbook, the workbook, or assignments from your teacher. Write the question and the section number on the front of the card. Write the complete solution on the back of the card. Here is an example.

Front

Section 6.2

What is the width of the canyon between points A and B?

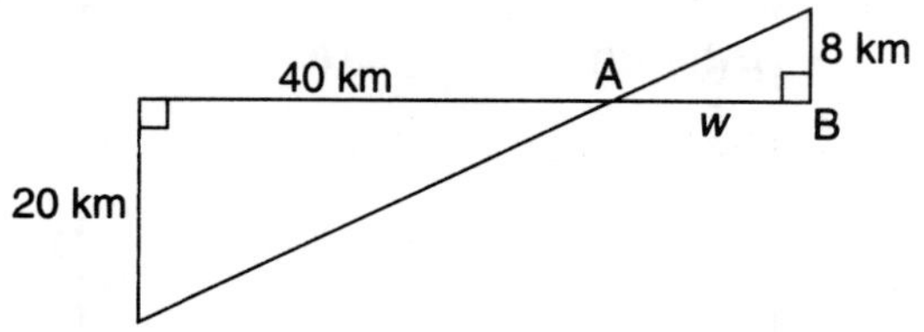

Back

The two triangles formed are similar.
Let w represent the width of the canyon.

$$\frac{w}{40} = \frac{8}{20}$$

$$w = 40 \times \frac{8}{20}$$

$$w = 16$$

Therefore, the canyon is 16 km wide.

- Shuffle your cards. Deal out two or three, and answer the questions on them. Compare your answers to those on the back of the cards.
- You can also use cards made by a classmate.
- If you have difficulty with a problem, review the solution, then answer one or two similar questions.

Evaluate yourself.

- If your teacher provides a self-evaluation chart, use it to find the skills that you need to practise more.

Make a Concept Map

- Your teacher may give you a concept map to complete, or you could work with a group to make one of your own.
- The map should show how the major concepts in a chapter are related.
- Add notes in the boxes to summarize the key concepts.

Here is a sample outline of a concept map for Chapter 9.

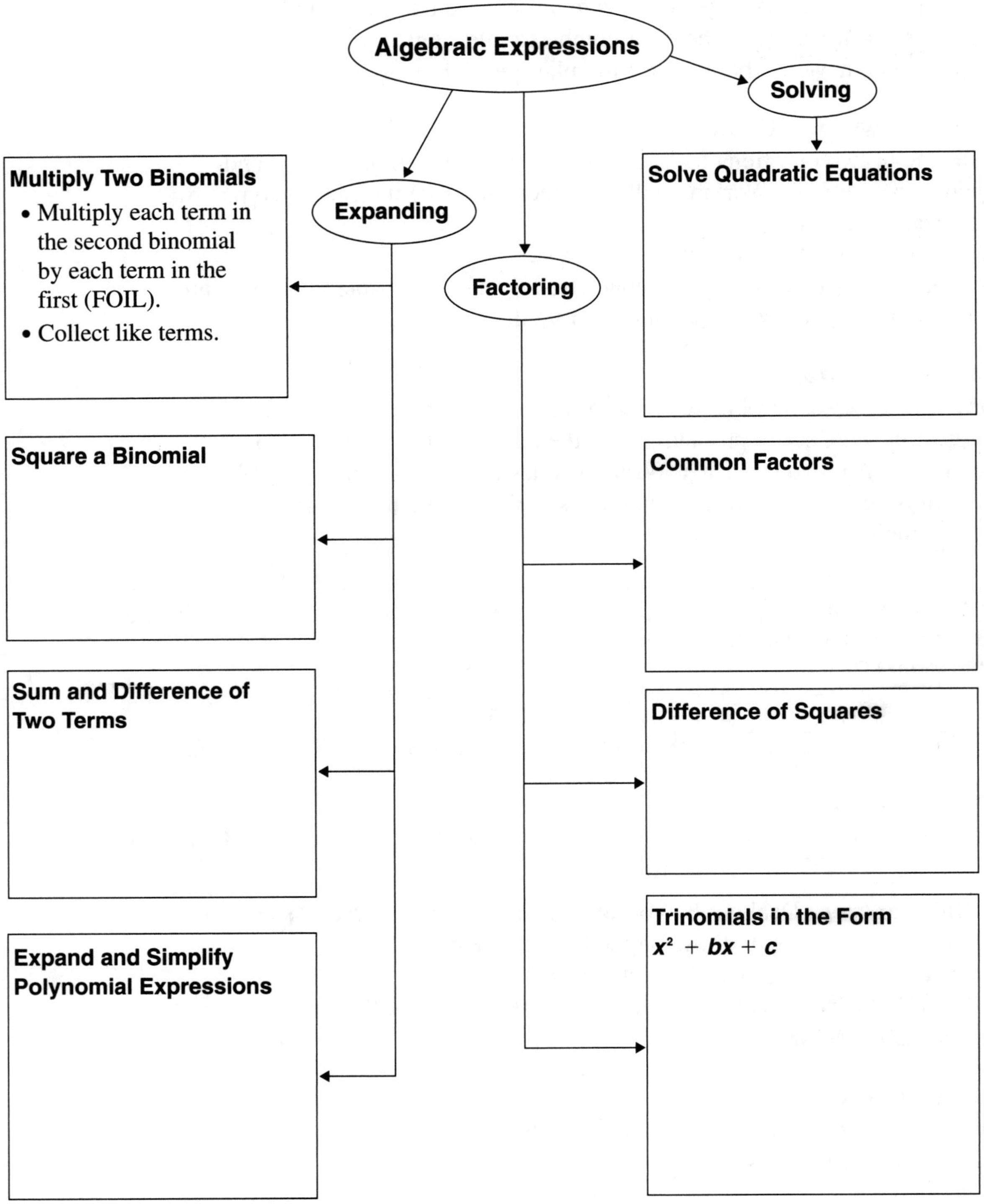

Name: ______________________ Date: ______________

CHAPTER 1 Proportional Reasoning

Get Set

Answer these questions to check your understanding of the Get Ready Concepts on pages 2–3 of the *Mathematics: Applying the Concepts 10* textbook.

Simplifying Expressions

1. Write each fraction in lowest terms.

a) $\frac{2}{16} =$ **b)** $\frac{15}{20} =$ **c)** $\frac{11}{55} =$ **d)** $-\frac{3}{21} =$

2. Write each ratio in lowest terms.

a) 12:3 = **b)** 17:34 = **c)** 25:15 = **d)** $\frac{1}{3}:\frac{1}{6} =$

Fractions, Decimals, and Percent

3. Complete this table. The first column is done for you.

Fraction	$\frac{1}{2}$	$\frac{1}{4}$	0.1			$\frac{4}{5}$	$\frac{5}{4}$	
Decimal	0.5				0.35			
Percent	50%			90%				250%

Converting Units

4. Complete each equation.

a) 1 m = ______ cm **b)** 1 km = ______ m **c)** 1 km = ______ cm

d) 4 kg = ______ g **e)** 0.03 kg = ______ g **f)** 3.400 kW = ______ W

Ranking Numbers

5. List these numbers in order from least to greatest.

0.1 0.751 $\frac{1}{4}$ $\frac{1}{2}$ $\frac{3}{4}$ 0.01 0.34

_____ _____ _____ _____ _____ _____ _____

Solving Equations

6. Solve each equation.

a) $4x = 16$ **b)** $11y = 66$ **c)** $7p = 8$

d) $0.5z = 17$ **e)** $5b = \frac{1}{3}$ **f)** $\frac{a}{12} = 3$

Name: ______________________ Date: ____________

1.1 Ratios and Proportions

Textbook pp. 4–8

Warm Up

1. Number Sense

Express the shaded portion of this bar as a fraction and as a decimal number.

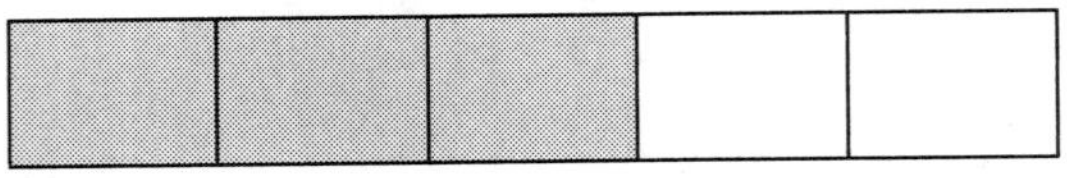

Fraction:

Decimal:

2. Mental Math/Estimating

Add the following mentally. Add the tens digits first, then add the units digits one at a time. Look for combinations that add to 10.

$24 + 54 + 33 + 16 =$

3. Proportional Reasoning

Rhys scored 22 marks out of 25 on his first math quiz. Express his score as a percent.

4. Relations and Functions

Complete this table for a car travelling at 80 km/h.

Time (min)	6	12	18	
Distance (km)	8	16		32

5. Algebra

Solve for *x*.

$3x + 7 = 40$

$3x =$

$x =$

6. Graphs and Tables

This table shows the population of two of Canada's northern territories, by age groups.

	All Ages	**0–14**	**15–64**	**65+**
Yukon	31 100	6 000	23 000	2 100
Nunavut	29 400	10 400	18 300	700

Which of these territories is likely to have the higher average age?

7. Math Literacy

In the word *percent*, *per* means ______________ and *cent* refers to the number ______________.

8. Previous Section

A floppy disk that is 60% full contains ______ times as much data as a disk that is 20% full.

Name: ______________________________ Date: ______________

Practise: Ratios and Proportions

Section 1.1

A ratio is the comparison of quantities with the __________ units.

Two-Term Ratios

1. Indicate whether the ratios in each pair are equal by filling in the blanks with either = or ≠.

a) 20:1 ___ 40:2 **b)** 6:3 ___ 18:6 **c)** 1:5 ___ 3:10 **d)** 5:2 ___ 20:3

2. Complete each proportion.

a) 24:6 = ___:1

24 is ___ times 6.
So, the missing number is ___ times 1.

b) 15:3 = ____:2

c) 10:___ = 20:6 **d)** ___:5 = 3:15 **e)** 50:4 = 25:___

3. One brand of chain saw requires a gasoline to oil mixture of 32:1.

a) The fuel tank on this chain saw holds 1000 mL. How much gasoline and how much oil do you need to fill this tank?

Total number of parts in the mixture: 32 + ___ = ____

Amount of gasoline needed: $\frac{32}{\square}$ × ________ = ______

Amount of oil needed: $\frac{\square}{\square}$ × ________ = ______

It will take _______ mL of gasoline and _______ mL of oil to fill the chainsaw.

b) What quantities of gasoline and oil do you need to make 20 L of fuel for the chain saw?

Hint
Remember to write a concluding statement.

4. One can of orange juice concentrate is mixed with three cans of water.

a) State the ratio of concentrate to water. _____:_____

b) How much orange juice can you make with one 250-mL can of concentrate?

c) How many 250-mL cans of concentrate are needed to make 5 L of juice?

continued ....

Name: ______________________________ Date: ______________

Section 1.1

Three-Term Ratios

5. The key nutrients in fertilizer are nitrogen, phosphorous, and potassium. A lawn fertilizer labelled 20:5:10 has 20% nitrogen, 5% phosphorous, and 10% potassium.

a) Calculate the amount of each of the three elements in a 1-kg bag of fertilizer.

Nitrogen | **Phosphorous** | **Potassium**

1 kg = ______ g

______ × 20% = ______

The 1-kg bag of fertilizer contains ______ g of nitrogen, ______ g of phosphorous, and ______ g of potassium.

b) Calculate the amount of each of the three elements in a 5-kg bag of the fertilizer.

c) If 1 kg of fertilizer covers 80 m^2 of lawn, how much fertilizer do you need for a lawn that is 100 m long and 60 m wide?

Area of the lawn = ________ × ________

= ________

Let *f* be the amount of fertilizer in kilograms.

Then, f:1 = ________:______

Solve for *f*:

Hint
The area of a rectangle is the length multiplied by the width.

6. The Academy Theatre has a total of 330 seats. The ratio of number of seats on the main floor (orchestra level) to the numbers on the first and second balconies is 3:2:1. How many seats are on each level?

Orchestra | **First Balcony** | **Second Balcony**

Name: ______________________ Date: ______________

1.2 Rates

Textbook pp. 9–13

Warm Up

1. Number Sense

At bedtime, the outside temperature is 4°C. Overnight, the temperature drops by 11°C. What is the outside temperature in the morning?

2. Mental Math/Estimating

Multiply mentally.

$5.23 \times 1\ 000 =$ ______________

$0.71 \times 10\ 000 =$ ______________

$2006 \times 10 =$ ______________

3. Proportional Reasoning

A recipe calls for one-half cup of flour. If you triple this recipe, how much flour will you need?

4. Relations and Functions

This table shows the relation between the age of an office photocopier and its value. Fill in the missing numbers.

Age (years)	Value ($)
0	6 000
2	3 000
	1 500
6	
8	375

5. Algebra

Isolate x.

$3x = 12 + 6y$

6. Graphs and Tables

The pictograph shows the number of hours three airline pilots have flown. How many hours has Harry flown?

Each ✈ represents 500 h.

7. Math Literacy

A fraction is in lowest terms when all common factors have been divided out of the ______________ (top) and the ______________ (bottom).

8. Previous Section

To set 1 L of car-body filler, you need 200 mL of hardener. How many litres of this filler can you set with a 1-L bottle of hardener? (Hint: 1 L = 1000 mL)

Name: ______________________ Date: ______________

Practise: Rates

Section 1.2

A rate is the comparison of quantities with ______________ units.

Unit Rates

1. Express each of the following as a unit rate. Round answers to two decimal places, if necessary, and state the units for each answer.

   a) 30 mm of rain in 3 h ______________

   b) $4.99 for 24 cans of pop ______________

   c) $50 for 4 h of work ______________

   d) 14 laps in 4 min ______________

   e) 30 mm of rain in half an hour ______________

2. Determine the better buy for each of these school supplies. Show your calculations.

   a) A box of 10 pens for $1.99 or a box of 12 pens for $2.29

   b) 250 sheets of paper for $0.79 or 500 sheets for $1.49

   c) A box of 10 floppy disks for $2.49 or a box of 25 disks for $5.99

Problem Solving With Rates

3. In Windsor, Ontario, a portable stereo sells in an electronics store for a total cost of $284, including taxes. In Detroit, Michigan, the same stereo sells for US$187, including the state sales tax. Which is the cheaper price if US$1 = CDN$1.4106 ?

continued ....

Section 1.2

4. a) Complete this time sheet for an employee earning $8.25 per hour. Round your calculations to the nearest cent.

b) A new contract gives the employee time-and-a-half pay (1.5 times the regular hourly rate) for working on Sundays. Find the hourly rate and the gross pay for working 5 h on a Sunday.

Time-and-a-half rate:

Gross pay for 5 h on a Sunday:

Day	Hours Worked	Gross Pay
Monday	8.0	
Tuesday	7.5	
Wednesday	7.0	
Thursday	8.0	
Friday	8.5	
Sunday	5.0	
Totals		

5. Dylan just returned from a 4500-km return trip to Florida. On this trip, he used 265 L of gasoline, which cost him the equivalent of CDN$206.

a) On average, how far did Dylan's car travel per litre of gasoline? Round your answer to the nearest tenth of a kilometre.

b) Calculate the fuel efficiency of Dylan's car in litres per 100 km. Round your answer to one decimal place.

c) Calculate his average cost for a litre of gasoline, to the nearest tenth of a cent.

d) When Dylan filled the fuel tank for the first time in the U.S.A., his car needed 14.78 US gallons of gasoline. A US gallon equals approximately 3.785 L. How much gasoline did he buy, to the nearest litre?

e) Dylan estimates that he spent a total of 60 h "behind the wheel" on his trip. What was his average driving speed?

Name: ______________________ Date: ______________

1.3 One Number as a Percent of Another

Textbook pp. 14–18

Warm Up

1. Number Sense

A student says that the shaded area of the circle is 90% of the circle because it forms a right angle. Do you agree? Explain.

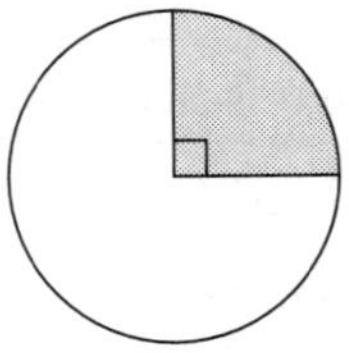

2. Mental Math/Estimating

Divide mentally.

$5.23 \div 1\,000 =$ ______________

$0.71 \div 10\,000 =$ ______________

$2006 \div 10 =$ ______________

$100 \div 5 =$ ______________

3. Proportional Reasoning

A baseball player hits 5 home runs during the first 27 games of the season. At this pace, how many home runs would he hit in a season of 162 games?

4. Relations and Functions

A cable company uses the formula $C = 7n + 14$, where C is the monthly cost in dollars and n is the number of satellite television options. What is the monthly cost for eight options?

5. Algebra

Rearrange this formula to isolate r.

$I = Prt$

6. Graphs and Tables

This graph shows an overall __________ for the year.

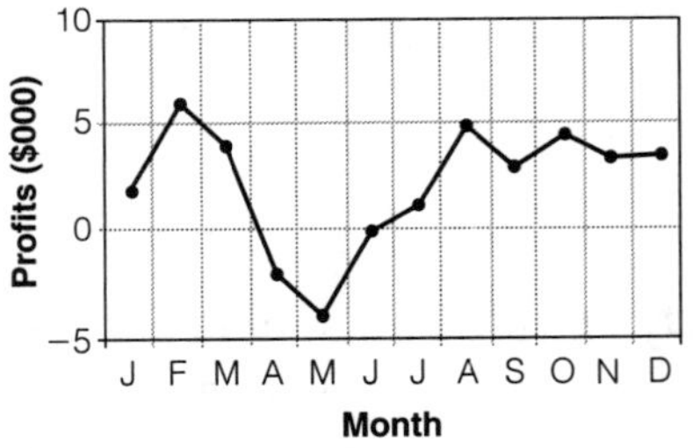

7. Math Literacy

What does BEDMAS stand for?

B ______________

E ______________

D ______________

M ______________

A ______________

S ______________

8. Previous Section

One weekend, 6 students shovelled snow from 15 roofs. Find the unit rate (roofs/student).

Name: ______________________________ Date: ______________

Practise: One Number as a Percent of Another

Section 1.3

1. Express each of the following as a percent.
   a) 3 out of 4 **b)** 18 out of 20 **c)** one quarter

   d) $\frac{1}{20}$ **e)** $\frac{125}{120}$ **f)** 50:80

2. A students' council buys soft drinks at a unit price of 35¢ a can and sells them for $1 each at basketball games. Calculate the markup and the percent markup.

   Markup =

   Percent markup =

Hint
Markup is the difference between the cost price and the selling price.

3. Over the past year, a shrub grew from a height of 40 cm to 56 cm.
   a) Calculate the percent increase in height.

   b) Express the shrub's height now as a percent of its height last year.

4. In 1970, the population of Mississauga was 52 186. By 2000, the population had grown to 610 700. Express this population growth as a percent. Round your answer to the nearest percent.

continued ....

Name: ______________________ Date: ____________

Section 1.3

5. A long-distance provider cut the price of calling anywhere in Canada from 7¢ per minute to 5¢ per minute. Express this decrease as a percent. Round your answer to one decimal place.

6. In 2002, the final game for the Grey Cup trophy had a television audience of 4 400 000 viewers, a record for Canadian football. The 2003 Grey Cup game had a television audience of 3.8 million viewers.

   a) How many fewer people watched the 2003 Grey Cup game?

   b) Express the drop in viewers from 2002 to 2003 as a percent of the 2002 total, rounded to one decimal place.

7. Express the drop in sales at Glenda's Great Gadgets as a percent of the sales in 2002. Round your answer to one decimal place.

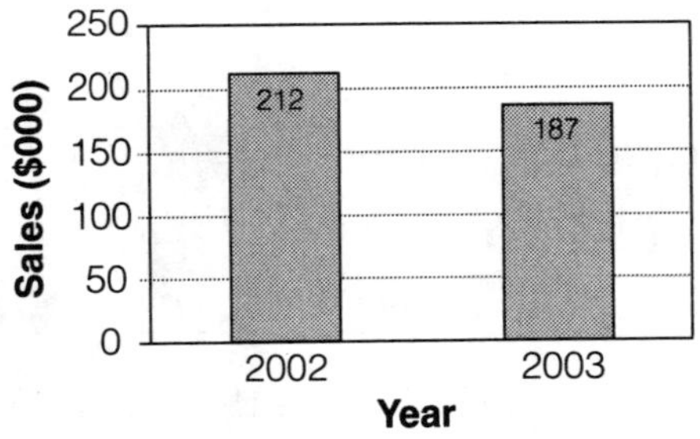

8. An advertisement for a used-car dealer states that prices on all vehicles are reduced by *at least* 20%. A car that was priced at $12 999 is now on sale for $10 599. Is the advertising claim correct? Show the calculations to support your answer.

Name: ______________________________ Date: ______________

1.4 Percents of Numbers

Textbook pp. 19–23

Warm Up

1. Number Sense

Using a protractor, a classmate reads the measure of $\angle C$ as 150°. The actual measure of $\angle C$ is likely ______.

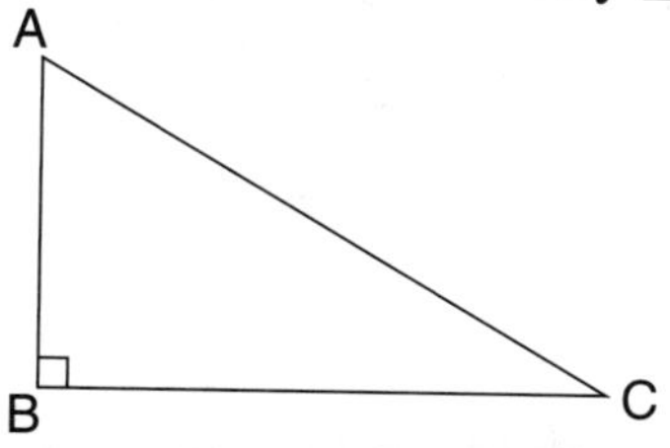

2. Mental Math/Estimating

At a rate of 9¢/min, the cost of a 32-min long-distance call is about

A 32¢
B \$3.00
C \$3.20
D \$30

3. Proportional Reasoning

Complete this table of values given that y is proportional to x.

x	0	1	2	3	4
y	0	3	6		

4. Relations and Functions

This graph shows that the air pressure is 90 kPa at an altitude of about ______ m.

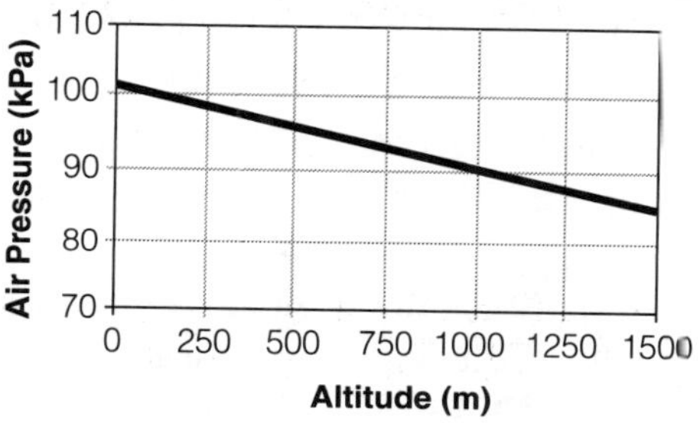

5. Algebra

Solve for y.

$\frac{1}{4}y = 9$

$y =$

$y =$

6. Graphs and Tables

The graph in question 4 shows that an increase of 1000 m in altitude corresponds to a ____________ in air pressure of about __________ kPa.

7. Math Literacy

A ____________ is a comparison of quantities with different units.

8. Previous Section

In 2003, the exchange rate for the US dollar dropped from CDN\$1.57 to CDN\$1.29. Express this decrease as a percent.

Name: ______________________________ Date: ______________

Practise: Percents of Numbers

Section 1.4

Calculating Commissions

1. A salesperson at a local car dealership earns a 6% commission on sales.
   a) Calculate the commission on the sale of a $24 000 car using each of the three methods below.

Method 1	Method 2	Method 3
24 000 × 6%	24 000 × 0.06	24 000 × 6 ÷ 100
=	=	=

   b) Explain why the three methods give the same answer.

Hint
A commission is a payment based on a percent of the sales made.

2. Each salesperson at an electronics store earns commissions that vary with the amount he or she sells. At this store, the commission rates are
   - 4% on the first $10 000 in sales each month
   - 5% on the next $20 000 in sales that month
   - 7% on any further sales during the month

   a) Complete this table of the sales staff's earnings. Show your calculations.

Employee	Sales This Month	Commission on First $10 000	Commission on Next $20 000	Commission on Sales over $30 000	Total Earnings
Tran	$48 567	4% × ______ = $	5% × ______ = $	7% × ______ = $	
Sandi	$63 813				
Bryan	$29 450				

   b) Explain why an employer would pay salespeople using this method.

continued ....

Name: ______________________________ Date: ______________

Section 1.4

Calculating Taxes and Discounts

3. In Ontario, the PST rate is ______.

   Throughout Canada, the GST rate is ______.

4. A coffee maker sells for $39.99. Calculate each tax and the total amount that you would pay for the coffee maker.

   PST: $39.99 × __________ = $ __________

   GST: $39.99 × __________ = $ __________

   Total cost: ________ + _______ + ______ = ___________

   So, the cost of the coffee maker with both taxes is _____________.

5. At both the sporting goods stores in a local shopping mall, a pair of hockey skates normally sells for $119.99 plus PST and GST.
   - Today, MuchSports is selling the skates for 15% off the regular price.
   - Sportathon is offering a "no taxes" special. (More accurately, the price already includes the taxes.)

   a) Your friend says that these two stores are actually charging the same price for the skates. Do you think your friend is right?

   b) Find the total cost for a pair of skates purchased from each store. Show your calculations.

   MuchSports **Sportathon**

   c) Explain any difference between the total costs at the two stores.

Name: ______________________ Date: ______________

1.5 Interpret Scale Diagrams

Textbook pp. 24–28

Warm Up

1. Number Sense

Complete these conversions.

30 cm = _______ m

_______ mm = 4.5 cm

240 ms = _______ s

_______ g = 1.674 kg

2. Mental Math/Estimating

Calculate mentally.

10% of $275 is ______________.

50% of 30 people is ______________.

75% of 200 cars is ______________.

3. Proportional Reasoning

Rice and water are added to a rice cooker in a 1:1 ratio. How much water needs to be added to 4 cups of rice?

4. Relations and Functions

The formula relating the area, A, of a circle to the radius, r, is $A = \pi r^2$. Determine the surface area of the water in a round wading pool with radius 15 m.

5. Algebra

Find the perimeter of a field with length 100 m and width 65 m.

$P = 2\,(l + w)$

$= 2\,(\qquad + \qquad)$

$= 2\,(\qquad)$

$=$

The perimeter is ______________.

6. Graphs and Tables

About ________% of the animals at this shelter are cats.

Shelter Animals

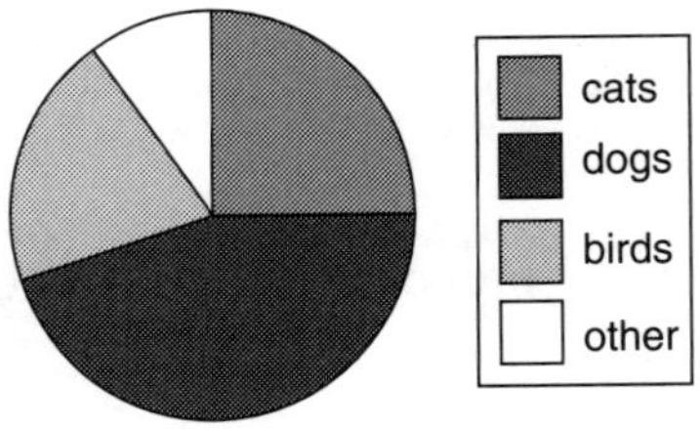

7. Math Literacy

A ratio is a comparison of quantities with the ____________ units.

8. Previous Section

A school bus costs $52 000. Determine the total cost with GST and PST added.

Name: ______________________________ Date: ______________

Practise: Interpreting Scale Diagrams

Section 1.5

This floor plan shows part of the ground floor of a cottage.

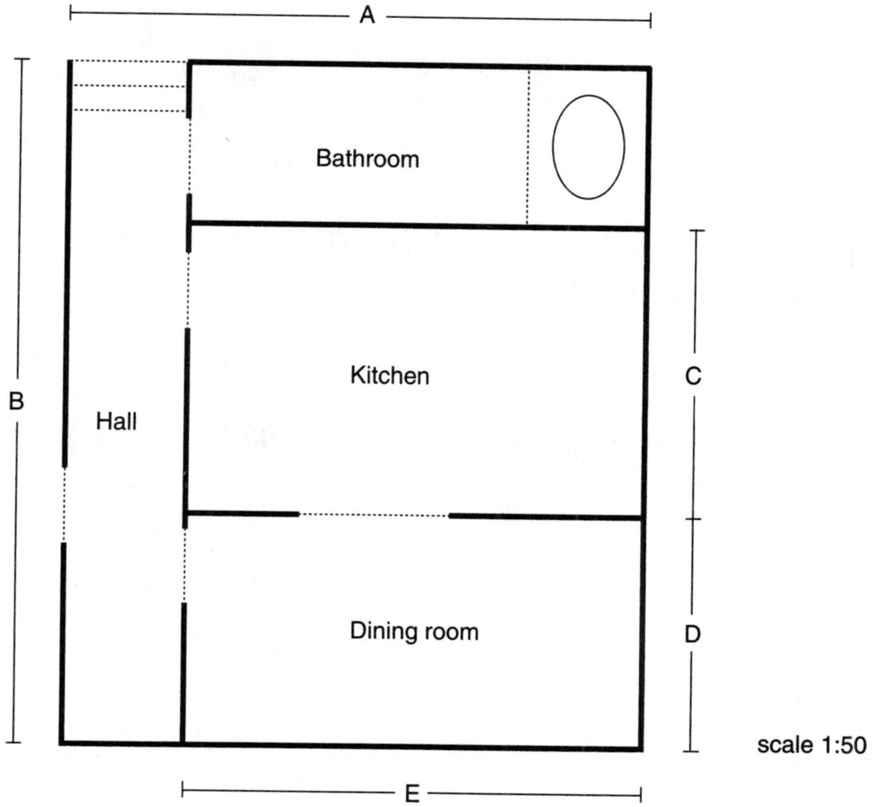

1. a) Use the floor plan to complete this table. Measure to the centre of the lines. Round your measurements to the closest millimetre.
   b) Label the actual dimensions in the appropriate places on the floor plan.

Dimension	Measurement (cm)	Actual Dimension (m)
A		
B		
C		
D		
E		

2. How many tiles will you need to cover the kitchen floor if you use tiles with an area of 400 cm^2 each?

   Area of kitchen: __________ × __________ = ____________

   Number of tiles:

continued ....

Section 1.5

3. You want to add a decorative moulding all around the edge of the dining room ceiling. How much moulding should you buy?

Hint
You need to measure the perimeter.

4. You are also considering putting a fireplace in the dining room. This fireplace will be 140 cm wide and 30 cm deep. Draw the fireplace to scale on one of the dining room walls.

Other Scale Diagrams

5. A stop sign has an actual width of 60 cm. Determine the scale of the diagram below.

Scale ______________

6. The Canadian flag has a width to height ratio of 2:1. On a 1:40 scale drawing of a flag, its width is 4.5 cm. What is the actual size of this flag?

Actual height = ______________ Actual width = ______________

Name: ______________________ Date: ____________

1.6 Draw Scale Diagrams

Textbook pp. 29–33

Warm Up

1. Number Sense

List these numbers in order from least to greatest.

4.12 4.112 4.2 0.42 4.01

_____ _____ _____ _____ _____

2. Mental Math/Estimating

Estimate by rounding.

$252.37 + $491.09 − $111.86

3. Proportional Reasoning

Calculate the total tax payable on the following purchases in Ontario.

Jeans	$89.99
T-shirt	24.99
Sweater	69.99

Total before taxes:

Total taxes = $ ________ × ________%

= $ ________

4. Relations and Functions

Tina's weekly earnings, E, are calculated using the formula $E = 0.15s + 250$, where s is her sales. All amounts are in dollars. How much does Tina earn in a week when she makes no sales?

5. Algebra

Simplify the following expression by collecting like terms.

$3a + 4b - 8c - a + 3b + 5c$

$=$

6. Graphs and Tables

The Great Lake that has about a third of its area in Canada is Lake ___________.

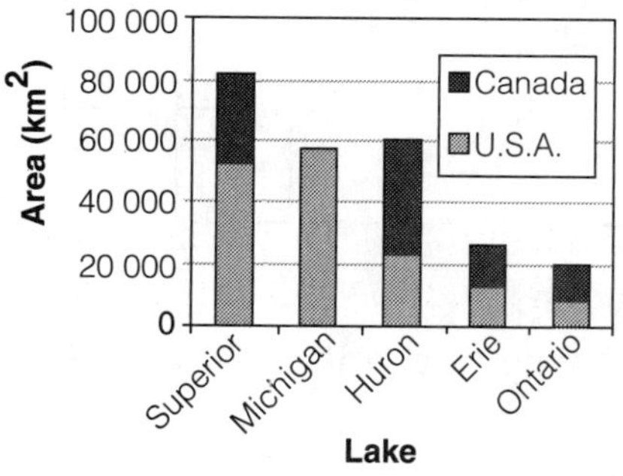

7. Math Literacy

Label the indicated parts of a circle.

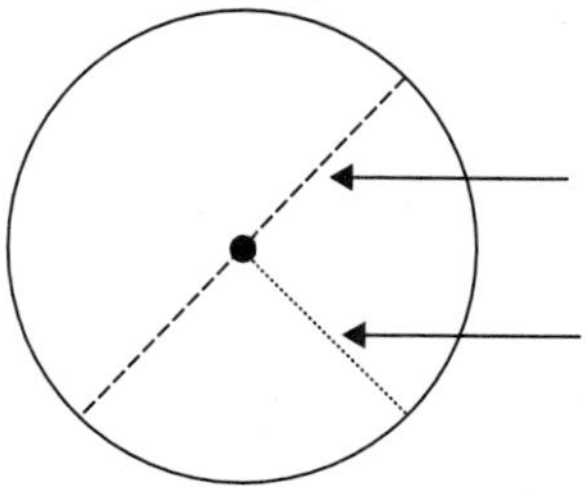

____

____

8. Previous Section

Guelph Airport is 49 km from Hamilton Airport. How far apart are they on a map with a scale of 1:200 000?
(Hint: 1 km = 100 000 cm)

Name: ______________________________ Date: ______________

Practise: Drawing Scale Diagrams

Section 1.6

1. Using a scale of 1 square equals 3 cm, draw a scale diagram that shows the length and width of the back cover of this workbook. Also show the size and position of the three holes.

2. This drawing of a golf tee has a 1:2 scale. Make an actual-size drawing of the golf tee.

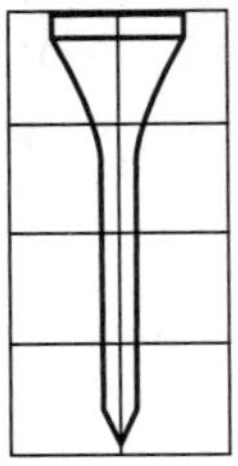

Name: ______________________________ Date: ______________

1.7 Valid and Invalid Proportional Reasoning

Textbook pp. 34–38

Warm Up

1. Number Sense

Explain how to find 10% of a number without using a calculator.

2. Mental Math/Estimating

Evaluate mentally.

$1 - 2 + (-3) - (-4) + 5 =$

3. Proportional Reasoning

A local store has a hit rap CD on sale for \$19.99. The same CD is available from a website for US\$14.99. Which is the cheaper price if US\$1 = CDN\$1.4293? Show your calculations.

4. Relations and Functions

This scatter plot shows that

A mass decreases with age
B age decreases with mass
C mass increases with age
D age and mass are not related

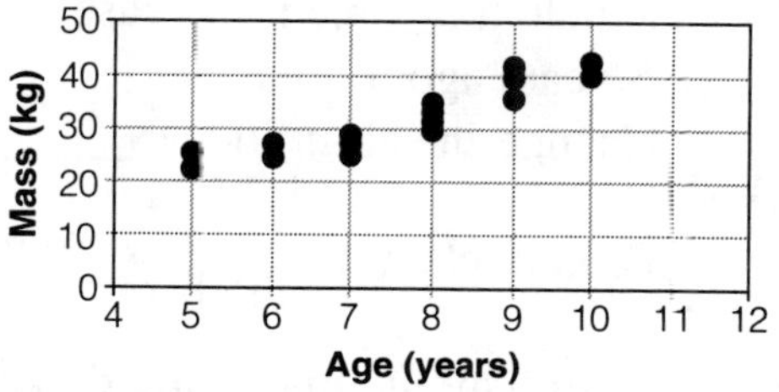

5. Algebra

Find the value of x when $y = 0$.
$2x + 5y = 20$

6. Graphs and Tables

This graph could be misleading because much of the ______________ axis is not shown.

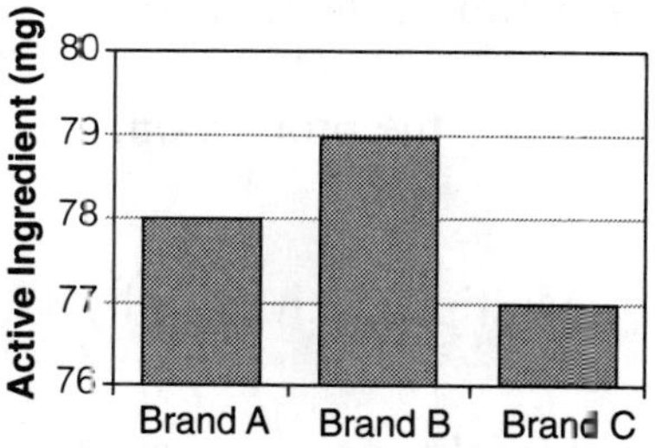

7. Math Literacy

90° angles are often called ________ angles.

8. Previous Section

Is a 5:1 scale suitable for a drawing of a 180-cm by 120-cm bookcase on 28-cm by 22-cm sheet of paper? Explain.

Name: ______________________ Date: ____________

Practise: Proportional Reasoning

Section 1.7

1. "Cookie sales are skyrocketing," says the marketing department. Here is the graph they use to support this claim.

a) Use this graph to complete the table of annual sales.

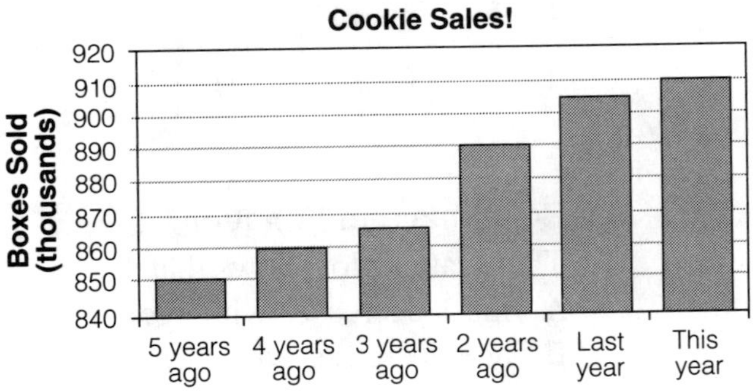

Year	Boxes Sold (thousands)
5 years ago	850
4 years ago	860
3 years ago	
2 years ago	
Last year	
This year	

b) Calculate the percent increase in sales (to 0.1%) from

i) 5 years ago to this year

Change in sales: 860 − _____ = _____

Percent change: $\frac{\square}{850} \times 100\% =$ ______

ii) last year to this year

c) Explain why the marketing department's graph might be considered misleading.

2. Palmerston High School has 1200 students. Of the 24 students in the grade 9 mathematics class, 3 are left-handed.

a) Estimate the number of left-handed students at this school, n.

Write the proportion: $\frac{n}{1200} = \frac{\square}{\square}$

Multiply both sides by 1200: $\frac{n}{1200} \times 1200 = \frac{\square}{\square} \times 1200$

Simplify: $n =$ ________

b) A new student transfers to the class. What does your estimate of the number of left-handed students at the school become if the new student is

i) left-handed

ii) right-handed

Hint
The class now has 25 students.

c) What can you conclude about estimates based on small samples?

Name: ______________________________ Date: ______________

Chapter 1 Review

Chapter 1 Review

The date of the Chapter 1 test is: ____________________.
Use these questions to check whether you are ready for this test.
For help preparing for the chapter test, see the study tips on pages x–xii.

1.1 Ratios and Proportions, textbook pages 4–8

1. Determine the unit price of a cola that costs \$3.99 for a pack of 12 cans.

2. A newborn child normally triples its birth weight in a year. If a baby weighed 4.30 kg at birth, what is it likely to weigh on its first birthday?

1.2 Rates, textbook pages 9–13

3. A leaky faucet drips 0.6 mL of water per second. How many litres of water does this faucet waste in 1 day?

4. The price for crude oil is usually given in US dollars per barrel. Find the cost in Canadian dollars for a barrel of crude oil selling at US\$24.32 when the exchange rate is US\$1 = CDN\$1.2975.

1.3 One Number As a Percent of Another, textbook pages 14–18

5. On a test, a student scored 43 marks out of 73. On an examination, the same student scored 107 out of 160. Express both scores as percents. Then, circle the higher score.

Test score **Examination score**

1.4 Percents of Numbers, textbook pages 19–23

6. A knitting pattern for a child's sweater calls for 28 rows in the body. An adult sweater in the same pattern is 150% bigger than the child's sweater. How many rows are in the body of the adult sweater?

continued ....

Name: ______________________ Date: ______________

Chapter 1 Review

1.5 Interpret Scale Diagrams, textbook pages 24–28

7. The wheelbase of a car is the distance between the front and back axles. Determine the actual wheelbase of the car in this scale drawing.

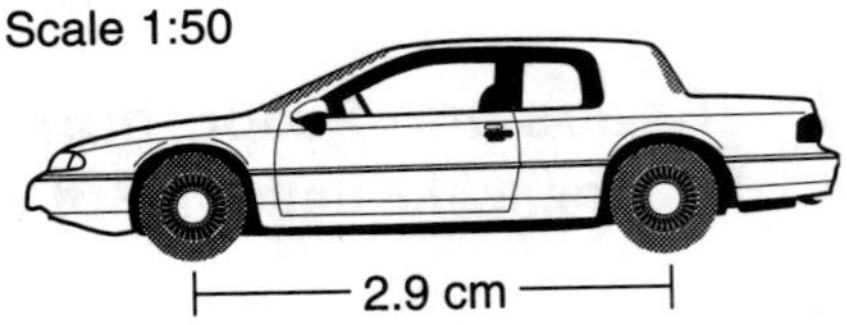

1.6 Draw Scale Diagrams, textbook pages 29–33

8. A Canadian football field is 110 yards long and 65 yards wide. Often, the end zones extend another 20 yards beyond the goal posts at each end of the field. Draw a scale diagram of this playing field and the end zones using a scale of 1 square = 20 yards.

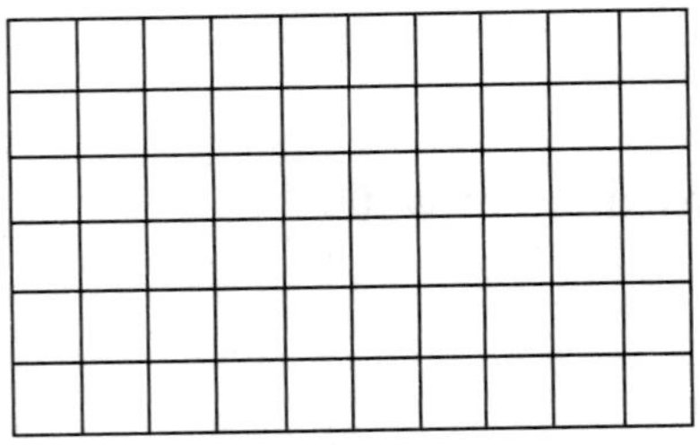

1.7 Valid And Invalid Proportional Reasoning, textbook pages 34–38

9. Here are two graphs of average house prices in a Hamilton neighbourhood during the last year. Which graph may be considered misleading? Explain why.

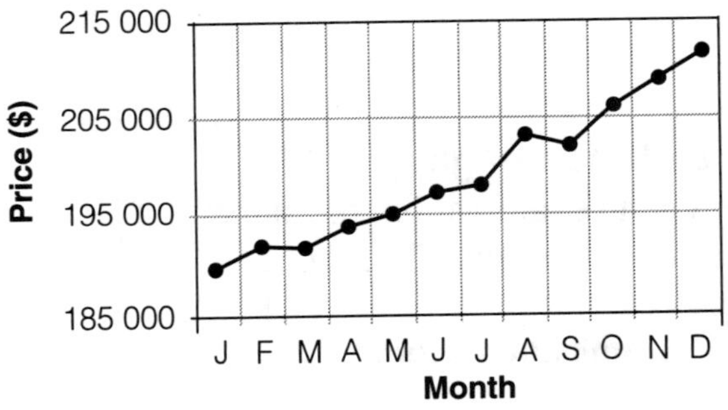

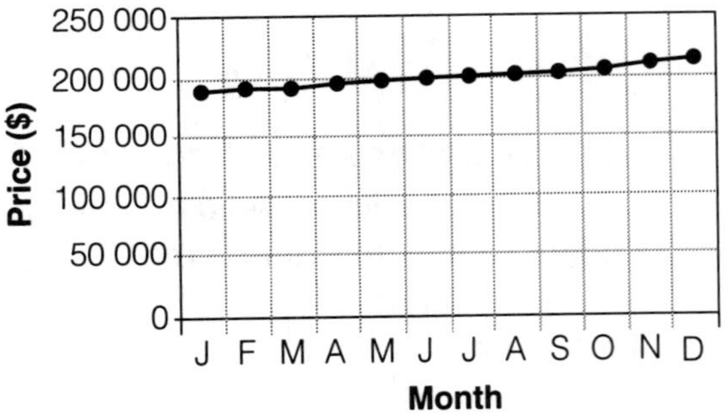

10. A poll of 800 residents of a city found that 540 support the new mayor. The city has about 1 720 000 residents. Estimate how many support the mayor.

Name: ______________________________ Date: ______________

Rich Problem: Road Map

Chapter 1
Rich Problem

1. The official road map of Ontario has a scale of 1:700 000. Explain what this ratio means.

2. How many kilometres does 1 cm on the map represent?

3. Calculate the actual distances represented on the official Ontario road map by
   a) 3 cm **b)** 5 cm **c)** 2.5 cm **d)** 0.8 cm

4. Use this map to complete the table of driving distances.

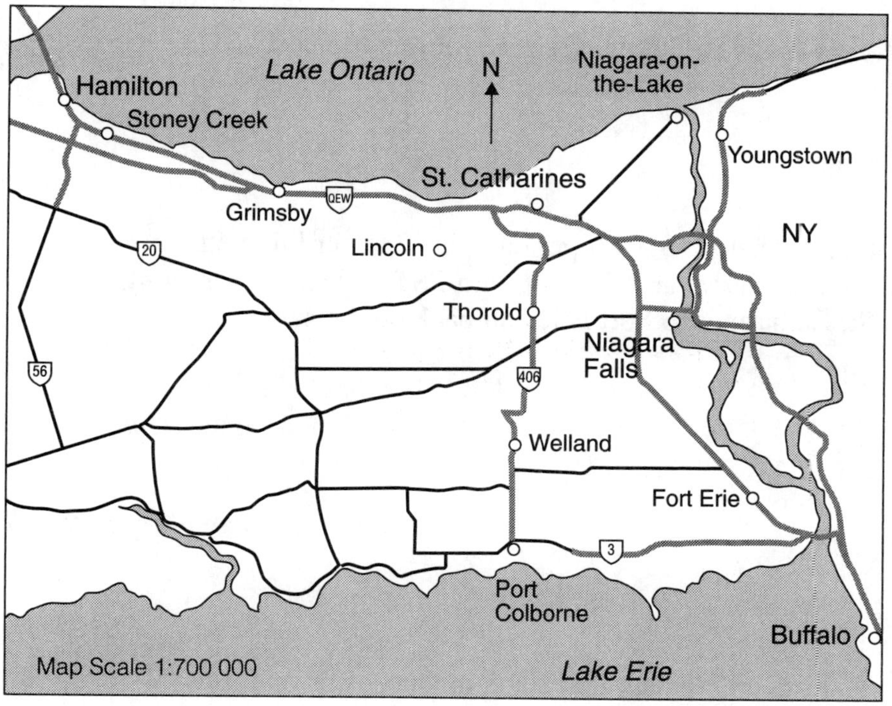

Hint
A piece of string is a handy tool for measuring distances on the map when the roads are not straight.

Trip	Distance on Map (nearest 0.1 cm)	Actual Driving Distance (nearest km)
St. Catharines to Fort Erie		
Niagara-on-the-Lake to Welland		
Thorold to Youngstown, NY		
Port Colborne to Grimsby		

continued ....

Name: ______________________________ Date: ______________

Chapter 1 Rich Problem

5. How long would it take to drive from Niagara-on-the-Lake to Welland at an average speed of 60 km/h?

6 a) If a car's fuel-efficiency rating is 9 L/100 km, how much gasoline would the car use on a drive from Thorold to Youngstown and back? Round your answer to one decimal place.

b) At 76.9¢ per litre, how much would the gasoline for this trip cost?

7. A local car-rental company charges $19.99 per day plus 23¢ per kilometre driven. Determine the rental charge and the cost with PST and GST for renting a car for a trip from St. Catharines to Fort Erie and back on the same day.

Total distance travelled:

Rental charge:

Sales taxes:

Total cost:

8. The Bruce Trail is a 800-km hiking path that starts in Queenston and runs through both St. Catharines and Grimsby. The maps in the guidebook for the Bruce Trail have a scale of 1:50 000.

a) What distance does 1 cm represent on one of these maps?

b) Why would the Bruce Trail maps have a scale with a much smaller ratio than the one for the official Ontario road map?

Name: ______________________________ Date: ______________

CHAPTER 2 Equations and Formulas

Get Set

Answer these questions to check your understanding of the Get Ready Concepts on pages 46–47 of the *Mathematics: Applying the Concepts 10* textbook.

Evaluating Expressions

1. Evaluate without using a calculator.

a) $6 - 13 =$ ______ **b)** $\frac{42}{6} =$ ______ **c)** $-4(-5 + 7) =$ ______

d) $6^2 =$ ______ **e)** $2^6 =$ ______ **f)** $-10 + 4 - 9 =$ ______

2. Evaluate each expression.

a) 15% of $180 **b)** 7% of (500)(4) **c)** 12×5^2

Simplifying Expressions

3. Simplify each expression by collecting like terms.

a) $2b + 4b - b =$ ________ **b)** $t - 3t - t + 7t + 2t =$ ________

c) $-6h + 4d - 3d + 4h + 8d =$ ________ **d)** $3v - v + 6v - 4 =$ ________

4. Expand each expression.

a) $3(x + 4) =$ **b)** $-2(3r - 1) =$

c) $\frac{1}{2}(4t - 12) =$ **d)** $4(3m - 2n) =$

Working With Fractions

5. Find the least common denominator for each set of fractions.

a) $\frac{2}{3}, \frac{3}{4}$ **b)** $\frac{5}{6}, \frac{13}{12}$ **c)** $\frac{3}{10}, \frac{7}{15}$ **d)** $\frac{7}{12}, \frac{4}{3}, \frac{3}{8}$

6. Evaluate.

a) $\frac{1}{4} + \frac{3}{8}$ **b)** $\frac{3}{5} - \frac{1}{3}$ **c)** $\frac{7}{9} \times \frac{-9}{7}$ **d)** $\frac{-7}{3} \div \frac{5}{6}$

Name: ______________________________ Date: ______________

2.1 One-Step Equations and Formulas

Textbook pp. 48-53

Warm Up

1. Number Sense

How many seconds are in one day?

2. Mental Math/Estimating

If numbers to be added cluster about a particular value, you can estimate their sum by multiplying. Estimate this sum.

$28.67 + 24.12 + 26.45 + 25.90$

$\doteq 4 \times$ ________

$=$ ________

3. Proportional Reasoning

A runner measures her heart rate and counts 19 beats in 10 s. Convert this rate to beats per minute.

4. Relations and Functions

For a speed of 90 km/h, $t = \frac{d}{90}$, where t is the time in hours it takes to travel a distance of d kilometres. How long does it take to travel 270 km at this speed?

5. Algebra

Solve for each variable.

$3a = 3$ $b + 3 = 0$ $\frac{c}{100} = 0$

6. Graphs and Tables

This table shows a ______________ relationship between wind speed and wind chill for all the temperatures.

		Temperature (°C)				
		0	−5	−10	−15	−20
Wind Speed (km/h)	16	−8	−14	−20	−26	−32
	24	−11	−18	−25	−32	−38
	32	−14	−21	−28	−36	−42
	40	−16	−23	−31	−38	−46
	48	−17	−25	−33	−41	−48

7. Math Literacy

For the expression $3x^2 + 7$, identify each of the following.

Variable ____________

Coefficient ____________

Exponent ____________

Constant ____________

8. Previous Section

James sprinted 100 m in 12.9 s. Explain why the proportion $\frac{100}{12.9} = \frac{1000}{t}$ might not give an accurate estimate of the time he would take to run a kilometre.

Name: ______________________________ Date: ______________

Practise: One-Step Equations and Formulas

Section 2.1

1. Solve each equation.

a) $t + 5 = 14$

$t + 5 - \_\_\_ = 14 - \_\_\_$

$t = \_\_\_\_$

b) $u - 5 = -14$

c) $-5 = v - 14$

d) $7x = 14$

$\dfrac{x}{\square} = \dfrac{14}{\square}$

$x = \_\_\_\_\_\_$

e) $-7 = -14y$

f) $\dfrac{z}{7} = -14$

2. A manufacturer of computer chips tests each chip as it comes off the production line. The number of chips that pass the quality-control tests is $p = rn$, where r is the pass rate and n is the number of chips in the batch. The manufacturer has an order for 15 000 chips of a type that has a pass rate of 0.97. How many chips does the manufacturer have to make to fill this order?

Identify the known quantities: ____ = 15 000 and ____ = 0.97

Method 1: Substitute First

Substitute in the known values:

$p = rn$

$\_\_\_\_\_\_\_\_ = \_\_\_\_\_\_\_\_\_ \times n$

Solve for the unknown value:

$\dfrac{\square}{\square} = \dfrac{\_\_ \times n}{\square}$

$\_\_\_\_\_\_\_\_\_ = n$

Method 2: Solve First

Solve for the unknown value:

$p = rn$

$\dfrac{\square}{\square} = \dfrac{rn}{\square}$

$\dfrac{\square}{\square} = \dfrac{n}{\square}$

Substitute in the known values:

$\dfrac{\square}{\square} = n$

$\_\_\_\_\_\_\_\_ = n$

Hint
Check your work by comparing the answers for the two methods.

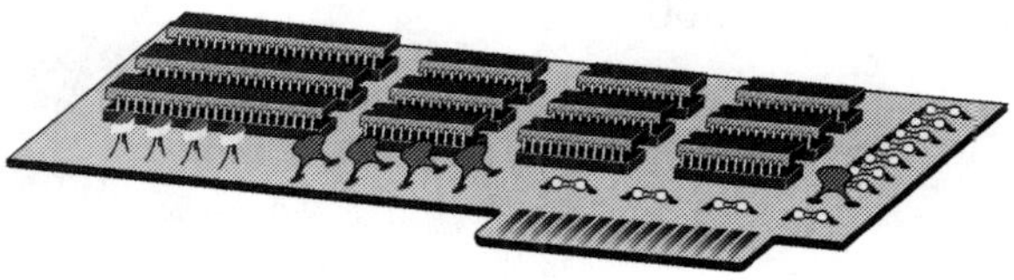

Name: ______________________ Date: ______________

2.2 Two-Step Equations and Formulas

Textbook pp. 54-59

Warm Up

1. Number Sense

When asked to add 341 + 670 + 522, a student answers 1535. However, another student says the answer cannot end with 5. Explain the second student's reasoning.

2. Mental Math/Estimating

Estimate this product by rounding the numbers to convenient whole numbers. Round one number up and the other number down.

$47.267 \times 11.2 \doteq$ ______ $\times$ ______

$=$ ______

3. Proportional Reasoning

Jogging 4 km each day for one week gives a total distance of ________ ______.

4. Relations and Functions

Write a formula for the time, t, in hours, that it will take to travel a distance of d kilometres at a speed of 80 km/h.

5. Algebra

Solve for x.

$$6 = \frac{30}{x}$$

6. Graphs and Tables

A long-distance telephone company charges according to the following graph.

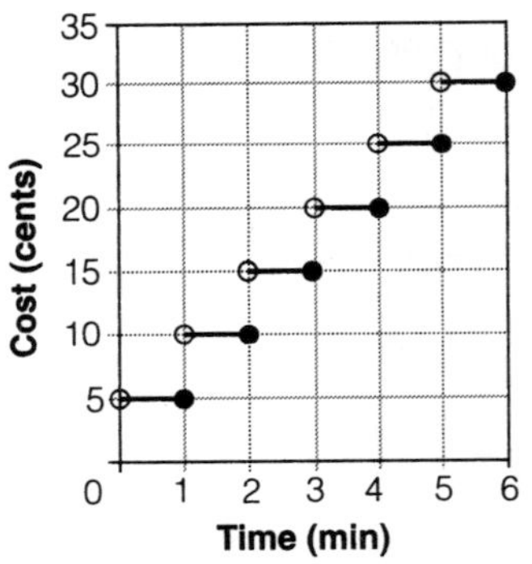

The cost of a 5-min call is __________.

7. Math Literacy

Draw a line to join each metric prefix to its value.

kilo	1 000 000 000
mega	1 000
giga	1 000 000

8. Previous Section

Find the width of a poster that has a length of 90 cm and an area of 5400 cm^2.

$A = lw$

______ $=$ ______ $\times$ ______

Name: ______________________ Date: ____________

Practise: Two-Step Equations and Formulas

Section 2.2

1. Circle the error in the incorrect solution below. Then, insert an extra step to correct the error and find the actual value of n.

Incorrect Solution

$5n - 4 = 10$

$5n = 10 - 4$

$5n = 6$

$\frac{5n}{5} = \frac{6}{5}$

$n = 1.2$

Corrected Solution

$5n - 4 = 10$

2. Solve each equation.

a) $3m + 1 = 10$ **b)** $2h + 7 = 15$ **c)** $4 - 2d = -2$

d) $5y - 3 = 14$ **e)** $6 + 4w = 9$ **f)** $2.5p + 7 = 13.4$

g) $\frac{3}{4}v = 21$ **h)** $-\frac{2}{5}f = 6$ **i)** $-\frac{15}{19}b = 0$

3. Check your answers for parts a) and h) of question 2 by substituting into the equations.

For $3m + 1 = 10$,

L.S. = **R.S.** =

For $-\frac{2}{5}f = 6$,

L.S. = **R.S.** =

continued ....

Name: ______________________________ Date: ______________

Section 2.2

4. **a)** One formula for the slope of a line is $m = \frac{\text{rise}}{\text{run}}$. Rearrange this formula to find a formula for the run.

b) Find the run for a rise of 4 in a line with a slope of $-\frac{1}{2}$.

5. The formula for the area of a circle is $A = \pi r^2$. Find the radius of a circle with an area of 113 cm^2. Round your answer to two decimal places.

Hint
On a scientific calculator you can use the $\boxed{\pi}$ key to enter the value of π and the $\boxed{\sqrt{\ }}$ key to find a square root.

6. A taxi company uses the formula $C = 1.50d + 4.50$, where C is the total charge and d is the distance travelled, in kilometres. Find the distance travelled if a customer is charged $29.00. Round your answer to the nearest 0.1 km.

Name: ______________________________ Date: ______________

2.3 Equations and Formulas With More Than One Variable Term

Textbook pp. 60-64

Warm Up

1. Number Sense

Continue the pattern.

1, 4, 7, 10, _____, _____, _____

Describe the pattern.

2. Mental Math/Estimating

Estimate the value of these expressions.

$9.9^2 \doteq$

$7.8^2 \doteq$

$6.1^2 \doteq$

3. Proportional Reasoning

If there are 13 steps between floors in an apartment building, how many steps are between the ground floor and the roof if the building has 21 floors?

4. Relations and Functions

List the two values of y that correspond to $x = 2$ in this graph.

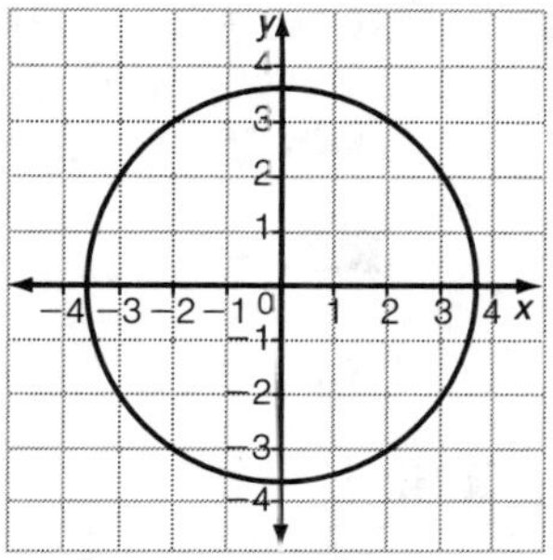

5. Algebra

Expand and simplify.

$4(2x - 3) - 3(x - 6)$

6. Graphs and Tables

A long-distance telephone company charges according to the following graph.

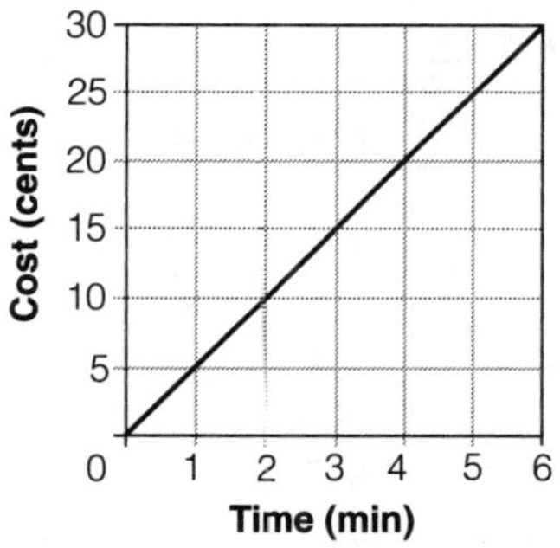

The cost of a 5-min call is __________.

7. Math Literacy

Draw a line to join each metric prefix to its value.

deci	$\frac{1}{1000}$
centi	$\frac{1}{100}$
milli	$\frac{1}{10}$

8. Previous Section

Solve for h.

$15 + 3h = 6$

Name: ______________________________ Date: ______________

Practise: Equations With Multiple Terms

Section 2.3

1. Solve each equation. Then, check your answer by substituting it into the equation.

a) $4 - t = 2t + 10$

$4 - t - \_\_t = 2t + 10 - \_\_t$

$4 - \_\_t = \_\_$

$4 - \_\_t - \_\_ = \_\_ - \_\_$

$\_\_t = \_\_$

$t = \_\_$

L.S. $= 4 - t$ **R.S.** $= 2t + 10$

L.S. $= 4 - \_\_$ **R.S.** $= 2(\_\_) + 10$

L.S. $= \_\_$ **R.S.** $= \_\_ + 10$

R.S. $= \_\_$

L.S. ____ **R.S.**

b) $z - 9 = 2z + 1 + 4z$

c) $4(k - 1) = 2(k + 1)$

$\_\_k - \_\_ = \_\_k + \_\_$

$4k - \_\_ - \_\_k = 2k + \_\_ - \_\_k$

$\_\_k - 4 = \_\_$

$\_\_k - 4 + \_\_ = \_\_ + \_\_$

$\_\_k = \_\_$

$k = \_\_$

L.S. $= 4(k - 1)$ **R.S.** $= 2(k + 1)$

L.S. $= 4(\_\_ - 1)$ **R.S.** $= 2(\_\_ + 1)$

L.S. $= 4(\_\_)$ **R.S.** $= 2(\_\_)$

L.S. $= \_\_$ **R.S.** $= \_\_$

L.S. ____ **R.S.**

d) $5(x - 3) = \frac{1}{2}(x - 6) + \frac{1}{2}(x + 8)$

continued ....

Name: ______________________________ Date: ______________

Section 2.3

Calculating Taxes and Commissions

2. In Kenora, Ontario, stores must charge 7% GST and 8% PST on most purchases. Across the border, stores in Winnipeg, Manitoba, also have to charge the 7% GST, but the provincial tax rate is only 7%.

a) The equation for the total cost, C, of a taxable item purchased in Kenora is $C = p + 0.08p + 0.07p$, where p is the price before taxes. Simplify this equation.

$C =$

b) Find the total cost of a $30 pair of sunglasses purchased in Kenora.

c) Write and simplify an equation for the total cost of a taxable item purchased in Winnipeg.

d) Find the total cost of a $30 pair of sunglasses purchased in Winnipeg.

3. Kim and Monica are both paid a weekly salary plus a commission for each snowboard they sell. The formula for Kim's weekly pay is $p = 40n + 260$, where p is the pay in dollars and n is the number of snowboards she sold during the week. The formula for Monica's pay is $p = 60n + 100$.

a) What is the value of n when $40n + 260 = 60n + 100$?

b) What is the significance of this value of n?

c) Why might Monica prefer her pay formula over the one Kim has?

Name: ______________________________ Date: ______________

2.4 Multi-Step Equations and Formulas

Textbook pp. 65–71

Warm Up

1. Number Sense

Reduce each fraction to lowest terms.

$\frac{75}{100} =$ $\frac{24}{36} =$

2. Mental Math/Estimating

Estimate.

$\sqrt{102} \doteq$ $\sqrt{79} \doteq$

3. Proportional Reasoning

How long does it take to earn $275 if you are paid $11 per hour?

4. Relations and Functions

If $y = t^2$, what are the two values of t for which $y = 36$?

5. Algebra

Solve for p.

$9 - 2p = 17$

6. Graphs and Tables

This graph shows the monthly cost for calls with a long-distance package. How much does 5 h of long-distance calls cost?

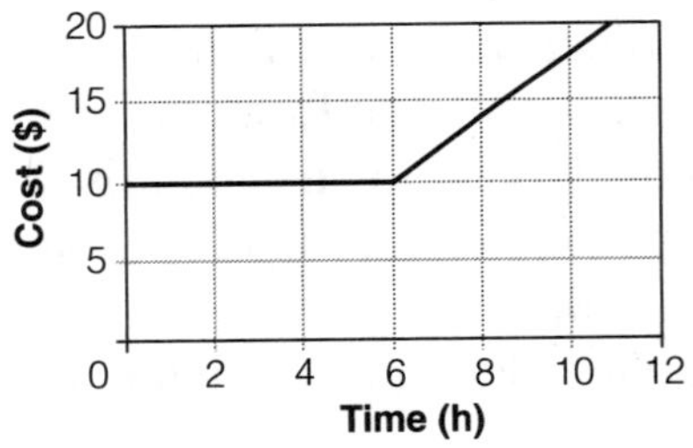

7. Math Literacy

Name the two parts of this power.

2^5 ← ______________ (5)
← ______________ (2)

8. Previous Section

Solve.

$5(n - 1) = 6(n + 2)$

Name: ____________________ Date: ____________

Practise: Multi-Step Equations and Formulas

Section 2.4

1. Solve each equation. Divide first if division will give integers on both sides of the equation. Otherwise, expand the brackets first.
   a) $3(c + 4) = 36$ b) $6(2h - 3) = 10$ c) $17 = -1.7(x - 5)$

Hint
For two or more fractions, you need the least common denominator.

2. Write the lowest number that you could multiply each equation by to eliminate the fractions.
   a) $\frac{1}{2}b + 2 = -3b$ ☐ b) $j - 1 = \frac{3}{5}j + 6$ ☐
   c) $\frac{2}{3}(5n - 1) = \frac{3}{4}(7 - 3n)$ ☐ d) $\frac{3}{8}(5 + r) = \frac{11r + 7}{12}$ ☐
   e) $\frac{-g-1}{10} + \frac{3}{5} = \frac{1}{4}(g + 3)$ ☐ f) $\frac{2}{7}d - \frac{3}{8}(2d + 1) = \frac{5d}{9}$ ☐

3. Solve each equation by clearing the fraction first. Then, check your answer by substituting it into the equation.
   a) $\frac{3}{4}(w - 9) = w$ b) $\frac{-1}{2}(k - 7) = k - 7$

$\frac{3}{4}(w - 9) \times$ ____ $= w \times$ ____

____ $(w - 9) =$ ____ w

____ $w - 27 =$ ____ w

____ $w - 27 -$ ____ $w = 4w -$ ____ w

____ $w - 27 =$ ____

____ $w - 27 +$ ____ $= 0 +$ ____

____ $w =$ ____

$w =$ ____

L.S. $= \frac{3}{4}($____ $- 9)$ **R.S.** $=$ ____

L.S. $= \frac{3}{4}($____$)$

L.S. $=$ ____

L.S. ____ **R.S.**

continued ....

Name: ______________________________ Date: ____________

Section 2.4

4. Solve each equation.

a) $\frac{4}{5}(3p - 1) = \frac{10p - 3}{4}$

b) $\frac{4y + 9}{4} = \frac{5(2y - 1)}{8}$

5. The formula for the surface area of a rectangular prism (or box) is $A = 2lw + 2lh + 2wh$.

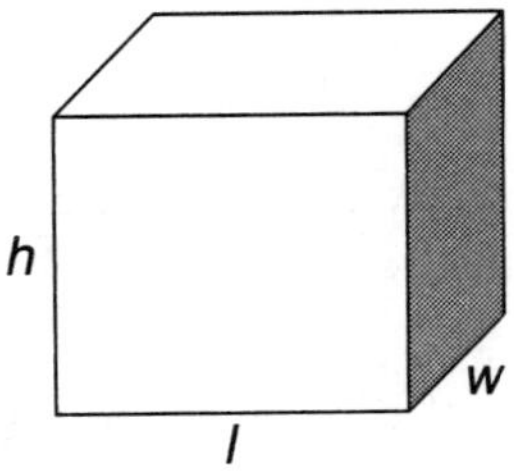

a) Rearrange this formula to isolate the variable h.

Isolate the terms with h: $A = 2lw + 2lh + 2wh$

$A -$ ____ $= 2lw + 2lh + 2wh -$ ____

$A -$ ____ $= 2lh + 2wh$

Collect the terms with h: $A -$ ____ $= h($ ____ $+$ ____ $)$

Isolate h: $\frac{A - \square}{\square + \square} = h$

b) What is the height of a rectangular prism that has a length of 12 cm, a width of 8 cm, and a surface area of 720 cm^2?

Identify the known quantities: $l =$ ______ $w =$ ______ $A =$ ______

Substitute into the formula for h: $h =$ ____________

$h =$ ____________

Name: ____________________ Date: ____________

Chapter 2 Review

The date of the Chapter 2 test is ____________________.
Use these questions to check whether you are ready for this test.
For help preparing for the chapter test, see the study tips on pages x–xii.

2.1 One-Step Equations and Formulas, textbook pages 48–53

1. Match each equation with its solution.

$3z = -9$ $\quad$ $5y = 30$ $\quad$ $x + 4 = 4$ $\quad$ $6 + w = -2$ $\quad$ $\frac{v}{2} = 40$ $\quad$ $u + 5 = -5$

-10 $\quad$ -8 $\quad$ -3 $\quad$ 0 $\quad$ 6 $\quad$ 80

2. Solve.

a) $t - 2 = 7$ **b)** $4s = -16$ **c)** $4.32 + r = 0$

d) $q + \frac{1}{4} = \frac{1}{2}$ **e)** $\frac{p}{10} = \frac{1}{2}$ **f)** $n - \frac{3}{8} = \frac{7}{8}$

2.2 Two-Step Equations and Formulas, textbook pages 54–59

3. Solve.

a) $2m - 4 = 10$ **b)** $-3 = 7 - 5l$ **c)** $-8 - 3k = 1$

d) $\frac{3}{8}x = 3$ **e)** $-\frac{4}{5}y = 20$ **f)** $\frac{3}{x} = 12$

4. The formula for expressing one quantity as a percent of another is $p = \frac{a}{b} \times 100$. Rearrange this formula to find an expression for b.

continued ....

Name: ______________________________ Date: ______________

Chapter 2 Review

2.3 Equations and Formulas With More Than One Variable Term, textbook pages 60–64

5. Solve each equation.

a) $4j - 5 = 2j + 12$ **b)** $5(t + 3) = 4t$ **c)** $3(h + 2) = 11 - 2(h - 5)$

6. Solve. Then, check your answer by substituting into the original equation.
$10(g + 2) - 4(2g - 9) = 7(g - 2) + 3(3g + 8)$

2.4 Multi-Step Equations and Formulas, textbook pages 65–71

7. Solve each equation.

a) $4(x + 7) = 16$ **b)** $3(y - 4) = 13$ **c)** $\frac{z-2}{6} - \frac{z+4}{9} = \frac{1}{2}$

8. The position of a passenger train on the eastbound track from Windsor is given by $d = 80t$, where d is the distance from Windsor in kilometres and t is the time in hours. The position of a freight train on the westbound track from Toronto is $d = 360 - 40t$. How long will it be before the trains pass each other?

Name: ______________________________ Date: ____________

Rich Problem: Building a Tennis Court

Chapter 2
Rich Problem

Volunteers are building an outdoor tennis court for a community centre near Ottawa.

- The regulation size for a doubles tennis court is 78 feet by 36 feet (23.77 m by 10.97 m).
- For safety, this tennis court will be surrounded by a high chain-link fence.
- The volunteers want the distance, d, from each edge of the court to the fence to be the same on all four sides.

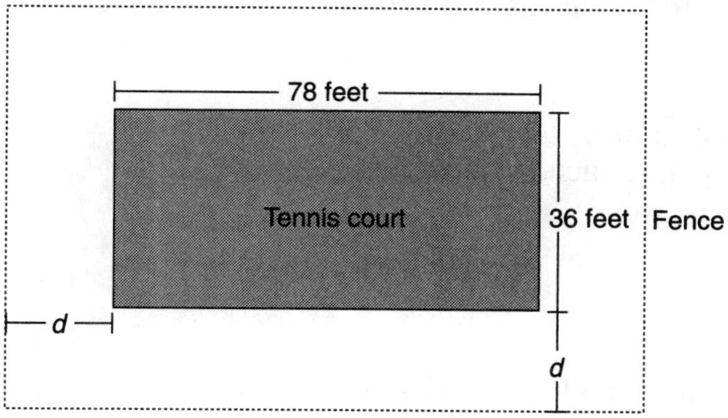

Show all calculations. Round costs to the nearest cent.

1. Write an algebraic expression for the length of one of the longer sides of the fence.

2. Write an expression for the length of one of the shorter sides of the fence.

3. Write an expression for the total length of the fence. Then, simplify this expression by expanding it and collecting like terms.

Hint
Use the formula $P = 2l + 2w$.

continued ....

Chapter 2 Rich Problem

4. The volunteers decide to build the fence 21 feet from the edges of the tennis court. Use your formula to find the total length of this fence.

5. The materials for a chain-link fence cost $6.25 per foot at an Ottawa home improvement store.

a) Find the cost of the fence materials for the tennis court before taxes are added.

b) Find the total cost of the fence materials, including PST and GST.

6. Across the river from Ottawa, a store in Hull, Quebec, sells the same fence materials for $6.15 per foot. However, Quebec has a 7.5% PST that is calculated *after* the GST has already been added!

a) How much would this store charge for the fence materials for the tennis court before taxes?

b) Write and simplify an equation for the total cost, C, of a taxable item purchased in Quebec.

c) Use your equation to find the total cost for the fence materials at the store in Hull.

7. Where are the fence materials cheaper to buy? How much will the volunteers save?

Name: ______________________________ Date: ______________

CHAPTER 3 Linear Functions

Get Set

Answer these questions to check your understanding of the Get Ready concepts on pages 78–79 of the *Mathematics: Applying the Concepts 10* textbook.

Finding Patterns

1. Fill in the missing numbers by looking for a pattern.

a) 3, 5, 7, ___, ___ **b)** 6, 2.5, −1, _____, _____ **c)** −3, 1, ___, 9, ___

d) 2, ___, 10, ___, 18 **e)** 4, ___, 0, −2, _____ **f)** $\frac{2}{3}$, $1\frac{1}{3}$, 2, ___, ___

Evaluating Expressions

2. Evaluate. Express your answers in lowest terms.

a) $\frac{9-4}{5-3}$ **b)** $\frac{6-(-2)}{8-4}$ **c)** $\frac{-7-4}{12-(-10)}$ **d)** $\frac{14-(-6)}{20-30}$

3. Complete each table of values.

a)

x	$3x - 1$
0	
1	
2	
3	
4	

b)

x	$-2x + 5$
0	
1	
2	
3	
4	

c)

x	$0.5x + 2.5$
0	
1	
2	
3	
4	

4. Which of these equations are true when $x = -2$ and $y = 4$?

a) $y = -2x$ **b)** $y = 2x + 4$ **c)** $y = 3x - 2$ **d)** $y = \frac{5}{2}x + 9$

Algebraic Expressions

5. Write an algebraic expression to represent each phrase.

a) twice the length **b)** one half of the base times the height

c) 6 units longer than the width **d)** 4 units less than a third of the radius

Name: ______________________ Date: ______________

3.1 Patterns and Ordered Pairs

Textbook pp. 80–86

Warm Up

1. Number Sense

Circle the operations that give a result larger than the original number for numbers greater than 1.

Squaring   Taking the square root

Doubling   Taking 50%

2. Mental Math/Estimating

Calculate mentally.

$17.2 \times 1000 =$

$17.2 \div 1000 =$

$17.5 + 1000 =$

3. Proportional Reasoning

If a 3-m high tree has a shadow 9 m long, how long is the shadow of a 9-m high tree?

4. Relations and Functions

The variable y is a function of x if each x-value has

A no corresponding y-value
B only one corresponding y-value
C at least one corresponding y-value
D more than one corresponding y-value

5. Algebra

Solve for x.
$4y = 2x - 8$

6. Graphs and Tables

This table shows the number of photographs that various memory cards can store at different resolutions.

Card (MB)	Resolution (megapixels) 1.0	2.0	3.0	4.0
32	91	62	40	31
64	183	125	81	62
128	367	255	162	127
256	734	510	324	254

The number of photographs a memory card can store decreases as the resolution of the photographs ____________.

7. Math Literacy

Quadruple means to increase by a factor of ____.

8. Previous Section

Solve for t.
$2t + 10 = 5(t - 1)$

Name: ______________________________ Date: ______________

Practise: Patterns and Ordered Pairs

Section 3.1

Hint
Increments in the variables are also called *first differences.*

1. Which of these sets of data have a linear relation?

a)

Increment	x	y	Increment
	0	6	
	1	8	
	2	10	
	3	12	
	5	14	
	6	16	

b)

a	b
−4	0
−2	1
0	3
2	6
4	10

The increments in x are ____________, and

the increments in y are ____________.

Therefore, the relation is ____________.

c)

p	q
−10	5
−5	3
0	1
5	−1
10	−3

d)

t	d
0	0
5	1
10	2
15	4
20	8

2. Graph each set of points to determine if they have a linear relationship.

a) (−4, 2), (0, 0), (2, −1), (4, −2)

The graph is a ____________________ line.
Therefore, these points have a
____________________ relationship.

b) (−5, −2), (−2, −1), (0, 0), (1, 5)

c) (−2, −4), (0, −2), (1, 0), (3, 4)

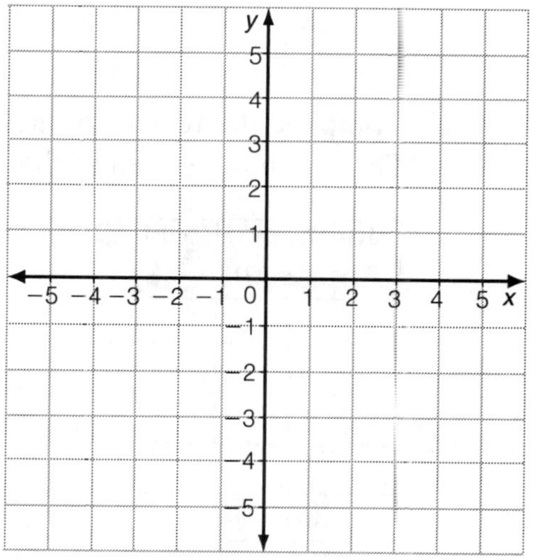

3. List the points that you plotted in each quadrant of the graph in question 2.

First quadrant:

Second quadrant:

Third quadrant:

Fourth quadrant:

continued ....

Section 3.1

4. A school cafeteria charges 50¢ each for apples.

a) Complete this table of values for n, the number of apples purchased, and C, the cost in dollars for a student who buys one apple each school day. Then, graph the data in the table of values.

Number of Apples, n	Cost, C ($)
0	
1	
2	
3	
4	
5	

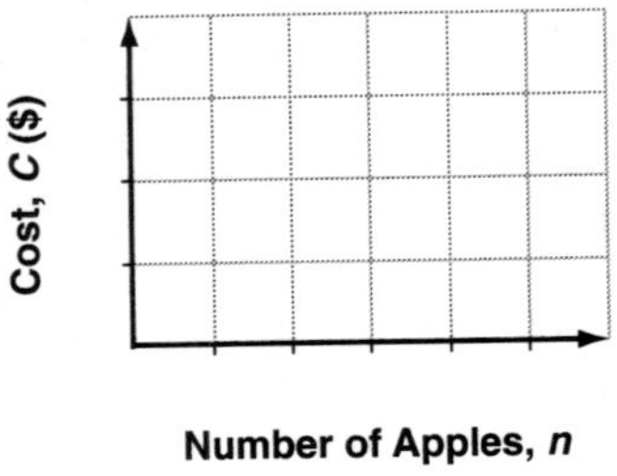

b) Complete the following table for the number of apples bought in the cafeteria each school day. Then, graph the data in the table of values.

Number of Apples, n	Cost, C ($)
0	
10	
20	
30	
40	
50	

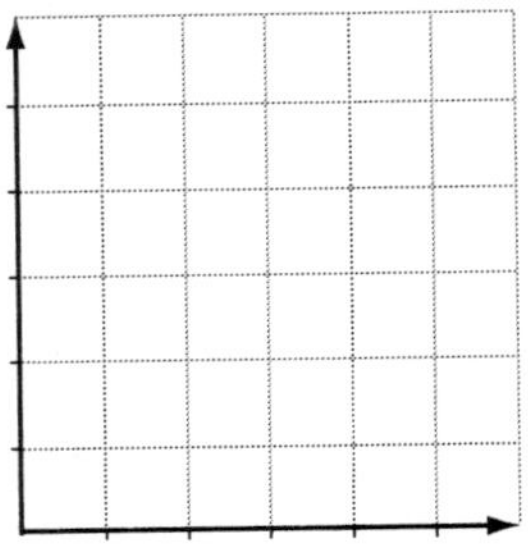

c) Complete the following table for the number of apples bought each week. Then, graph the data in the table of values.

Number of Apples, n	Cost, C ($)
0	
50	
100	
150	
200	
250	

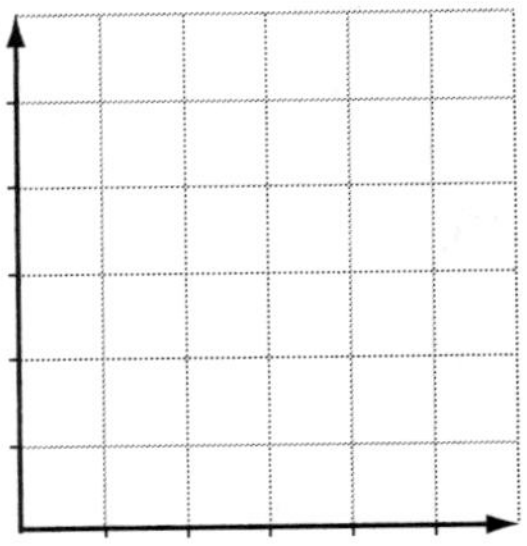

d) The graphs in parts a), b), and c) all represent the same linear function, $C = 0.5n$. List three features that these graphs have in common.

i)

ii)

iii)

Name: ______________________________ Date: ______________

3.2 Construct Tables and Sketch Graphs with Technology

Textbook pp. 87–91

Warm Up

1. Number Sense

Half of a half equals a ______________.

Half of a half of a half equals an ____________.

Half of a half of a half of a half equals a ________________.

2. Mental Math/Estimating

A CD holds about 700 megabytes (MB) of data. Recording a minute of music takes about 10 MB. Estimate how many 3.5-min songs will fit on a CD.

3. Proportional Reasoning

If one Canadian dollar is worth 8.2919 Mexican pesos, how many pesos could a Canadian traveller buy with $400?

4. Relations and Functions

The graph of the equation $y = 6x - 8$ is a __________ line that includes the point (2, ___).

5. Algebra

Use the exchange rate in question 3 to write an equation for Mexican pesos, p, in terms of Canadian dollars, d.

$p =$

6. Graphs and Tables

What does this scatter plot tell you about these two models of snowblower?

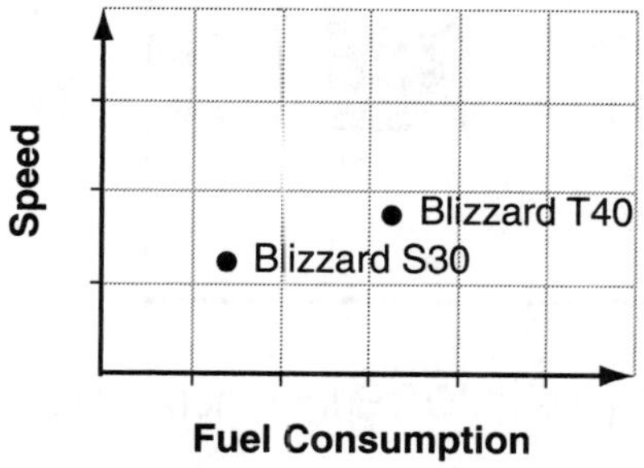

7. Math Literacy

Unscramble the two jumbled words to complete this sentence.

The graph of a _ _ _ _ _ _ (n e a r l i) function is a _ _ _ _ _ _ _ _ (t r a h g i s t) line.

8. Previous Section

How can you tell that this table represents a linear relation?

x	−2	0	2	4	6	8
y	−2	4	10	16	22	28

Name: ______________________________ Date: ______________

Practise: Tables and Graphs With Technology

Section 3.2

The screens shown below are from a TI-83 Plus graphing calculator. The display and keystrokes for other types of graphing calculators may be somewhat different.

1. Fill in the window settings you need to graph this table of values for the energy used by a 10-W light bulb.

Time (min)	Energy Used (kJ)
0	0
1	6
2	12
3	18
4	24
5	30

```
WINDOW
 Xmin=
 Xmax=
 Xscl=
 Ymin=
 Ymax=
 Yscl=
 Xres=1
```

2. Fill in the table settings to have a graphing calculator display the table of values in question 1.

```
TABLE SETUP
 TblStart=
 ΔTbl=
Indpnt: Auto Ask
Depend: Auto Ask
```

3. **a)** If you press **MODE** and then select **G-T**, the calculator will display the

__________ and the ____________ ____ ____________ at the same time.

b) Enter the equation $y = 0.5x$ for **Y1**. Then, use the settings from questions 1 and 2 to display both the graph and a table of values for the equation. Sketch the screen that results when you press **GRAPH**.

Name: ______________________________ Date: ______________

3.3 Construct Tables and Sketch Graphs Without Technology

Textbook pp. 92–96

Warm Up

1. Number Sense

Continue this pattern.

1, 2, 4, 8, ____, ____, ____

Describe the pattern.

2. Mental Math/Estimating

Convert each expression to a percent.

$0.7 =$ ____% $0.952 =$ ____%

$\frac{23}{100} =$ ____% $\frac{9}{25} =$ ____%

3. Proportional Reasoning

Some food guides recommend that you eat at least five servings of fruit or vegetables a day. How many of these servings would you eat each year?

4. Relations and Functions

Complete this table of values for the relation $W = 15n + 250$.

n	0	10	20	30
W				

5. Algebra

Find the two numbers that satisfy the equation $x^2 = 9$.

6. Graphs and Tables

The gross national product (GNP) dropped 0.2% during ______________.

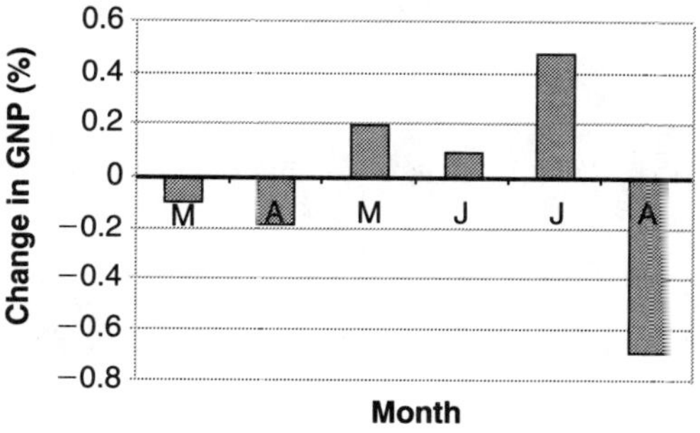

7. Math Literacy

When a graphing calculator displays the message **ERR: SYNTAX**, you have made a mistake in

A calculating the sales tax
B entering a function
C entering a number
D setting up the screen

8. Previous Section

The line in this graph meets the *x*-axis at (,).

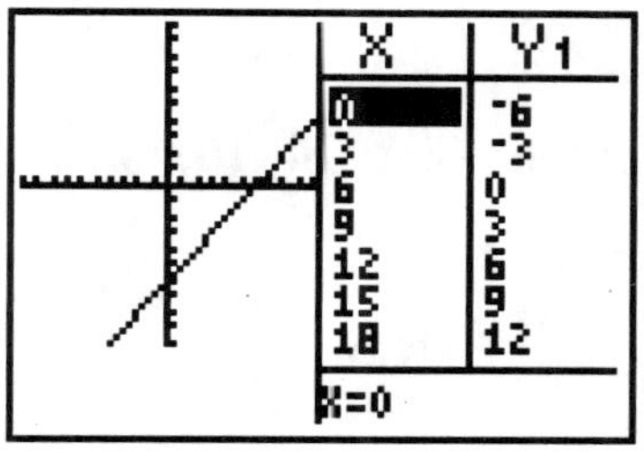

Name: ______________________________ Date: ______________

Practise: Tables and Graphs Without Technology

Section 3.3

1. Complete each table of values.

a)

x	$y = 2x - 6$	(x, y)
0	$2(0) - 6 =$	(0,)
1		
2		
3		
4		

b)

x	$y = 2x - 1$	(x, y)
−2	$-2(-3) - 1 =$	(−2,)
−1		
0		
1		
2		

2. Complete these tables of values by choosing values for *x* that will give integer values for *y*.

a)

x	$y = \frac{1}{3}x - 1$	(x, y)
0		

b)

x	$y = -\frac{3}{4}x + 2$	(x, y)
−4		

3. Plot each set of points from questions 1 and 2. Label each line.

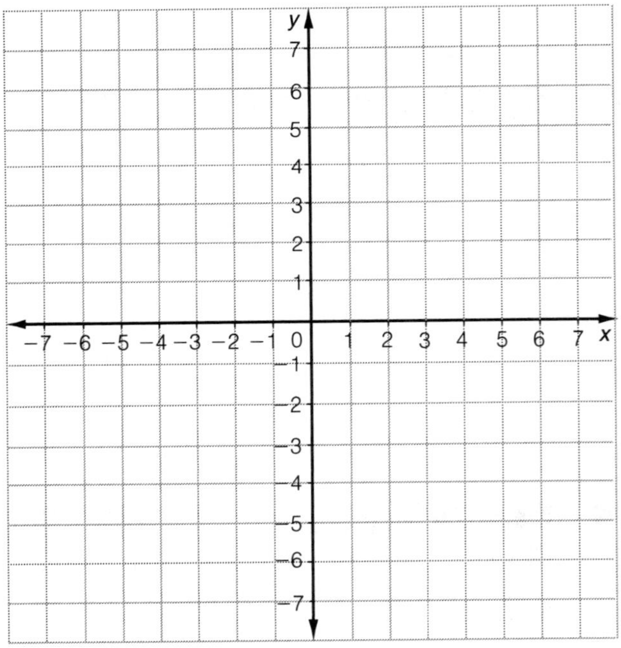

4. Determine if the point (24, 16) is on the line with the equation

a) $y = 2x - 30$

L.S. = **R.S.** =

b) $y = \frac{5}{12}x + 6$

L.S. = **R.S.** =

Name: ______________________ Date: ______________

3.4 Interpret Lines

Textbook pp. 97–103

Warm Up

1. Number Sense

Kai works after school 3 or 4 days per week for 3 or 4 h per day. If he earns $10 per hour, what are his minimum and maximum weekly earnings?

minimum: maximum:

2. Mental Math/Estimating

A couple has a mortgage loan on their house for $150 000. The annual interest rate is 5% paid at the end of the year. How much interest must they pay this year?

3. Proportional Reasoning

A tree is now 5 m high. It grows an average of 0.3 m a year. How tall will the tree be in 4 years?

4. Relations and Functions

Trace the line that represents a linear function with positive slope.

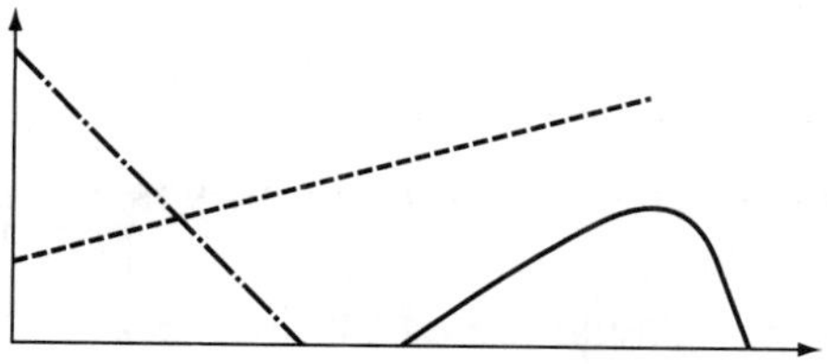

5. Algebra

Find the value of *x*, to one decimal place.
$4.6x + 5.3 = 14$

6. Graphs and Tables

A gram of fat contains 9.4 Calories.

BUTTER-FLAVOURED POPCORN PER 34-g SERVING	
Energy	200 Calories
Protein	2.8 g
Fat	11 g
Carbohydrate	17 g
Sodium	440 mg

Of the food energy in a serving of this popcorn, _______ Calories come from fat.

7. Math Literacy

Lines that never cross are

p _ _ _ _ _ _ _ _.

Lines that meet at right angles are

p _ _ _ _ _ _ _ _ _ _ _ _.

8. Previous Section

Complete this table of values of the relation $c = \frac{3}{5}h + 3$. Use three values for *h* that will give integer values for *c*.

h			
c			

Name: ______________________________ Date: ______________

Practise: Interpreting Lines

Section 3.4

1. a) For this line, the slope is +2 and the *y*-intercept is 1. Therefore, the equation of the line is

$y =$ _____ _____ _____

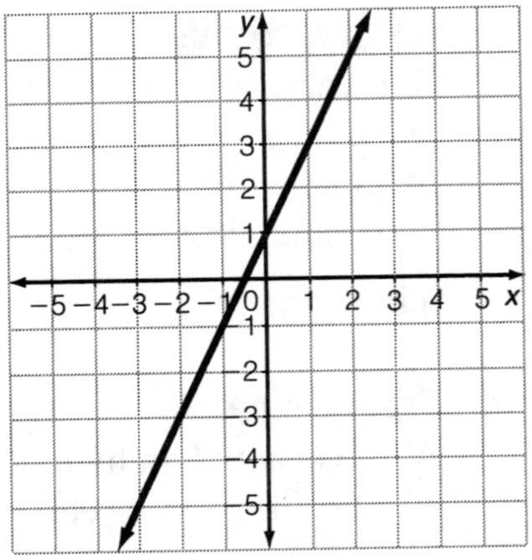

b) For this line, the change in *y* is −9 and the change in *x* is +3. The slope of the line is $\frac{\square}{\square}$ = _____.

The *y*-intercept is _____.

Therefore, the equation of the line is $y =$ ___________.

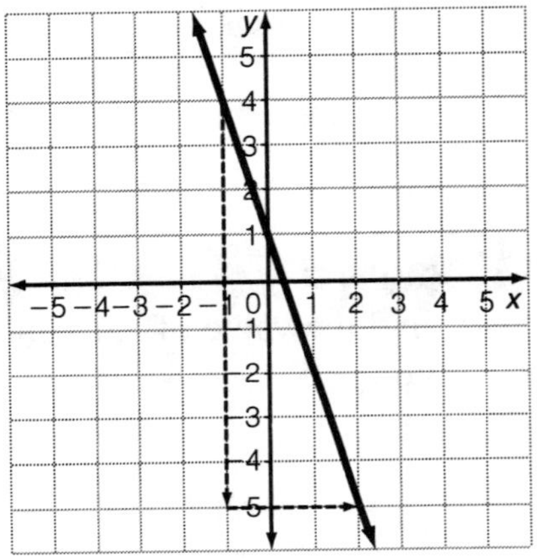

c) For this line, the change in *y* is _____ and the change in *x* is _____. The slope of the line is $\frac{\square}{\square}$ = _____.

The *y*-intercept is _____.

Therefore, the equation of the line is

$y =$ _______________.

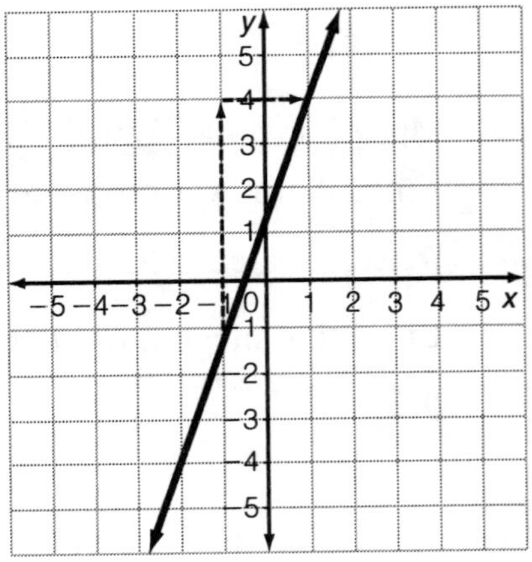

continued ....

Name: ______________________________ Date: ______________

Section 3.4

2. State the slope and y-intercept of the following lines.

a) $y = 3x - 7$

$m =$ ______

$b =$ ______

b) $y = -4x + 6$

$m =$ ______

$b =$ ______

c) $y = 2x$

$m =$ ______

$b =$ ______

d) $y = -\frac{3}{4}x + 2$

$m =$ ______

$b =$ ______

e) $y = -x$

$m =$ ______

$b =$ ________

f) $y = 5$

m = ______

b = ______

3. Plot each pair of points on the grid below, then draw a line through the two points. Find the slope, y-intercept, and equation for each line.

a) $(-2, 6)$ and $(4, 9)$

$$m = \frac{\text{difference in } y\text{-values}}{\text{difference in } x\text{-values}}$$

$m =$

$m =$

$b =$

$y =$

b) $(-1, 4)$ and $(2, -5)$

$m =$

$b =$

$y =$

c) $(-6, -8)$ and $(6, -5)$

$m =$

$b =$

$y =$

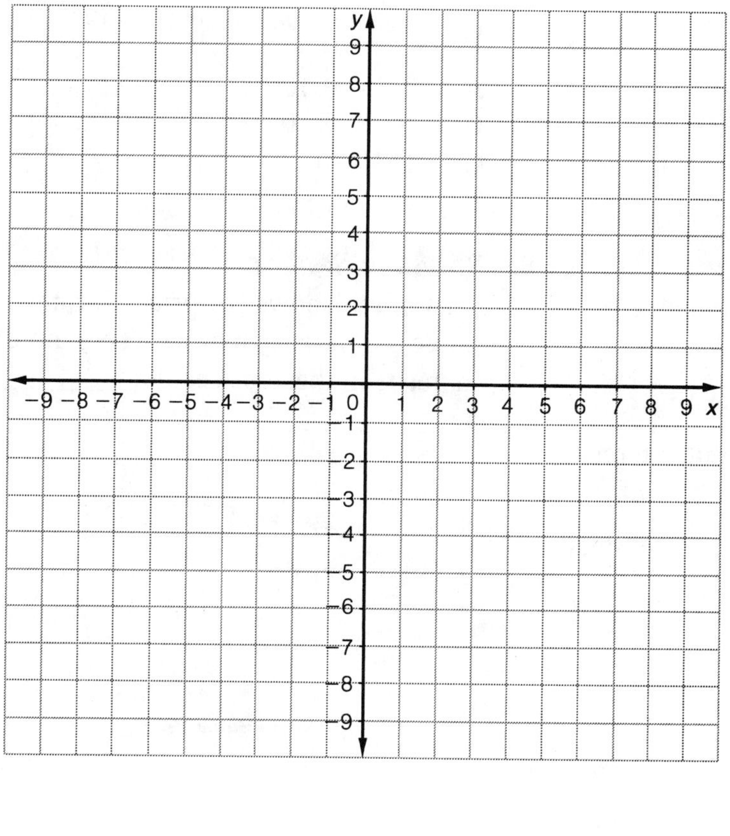

Name: ____________________ Date: ____________

3.5 Write Linear Equations by Using Tables of Values

Textbook pp. 104–109

Warm Up

1. Number Sense

If the individual digits of a number add to a total divisible by 3, the number itself is divisible by 3. Without using a calculator, circle the numbers that are divisible by 3.

134 276 318 404 580 619

2. Mental Math/Estimating

Solve.

$5a = -30$

$a =$

$5 + b = -30$

$b =$

3. Proportional Reasoning

A hardware store sells a package of two AAA batteries for $3.29 and a package of four for $5.98. Show which price is the better buy.

4. Relations and Functions

Circle the phrase that is ***not*** correct.

The slope of a linear function

A is often represented by m

B equals $\frac{\text{rise}}{\text{run}}$

C is zero for a vertical line

D is negative if the graph of the line falls to the right

5. Algebra

Use the formula $s = \frac{d}{t}$ to find the time it would take to drive 1700 km at an average speed of 85 km/h.

6. Graphs and Tables

Which function does this table represent?

x	5	10	15	20
y	48	98	148	198

A $y = 2x + 10$

B $y = 2x - 10$

C $y = 10x + 2$

D $y = 10x - 2$

7. Math Literacy

To move the image on a computer screen up or down, you adjust the

v _ _ _ _ _ _ _ _ settings.

To move the image on a computer screen left or right, you adjust the

h _ _ _ _ _ _ _ _ _ _ _ settings.

8. Previous Section

This graph shows list prices for new models of a particular car. The rate of increase in these prices is ____________ per ____________.

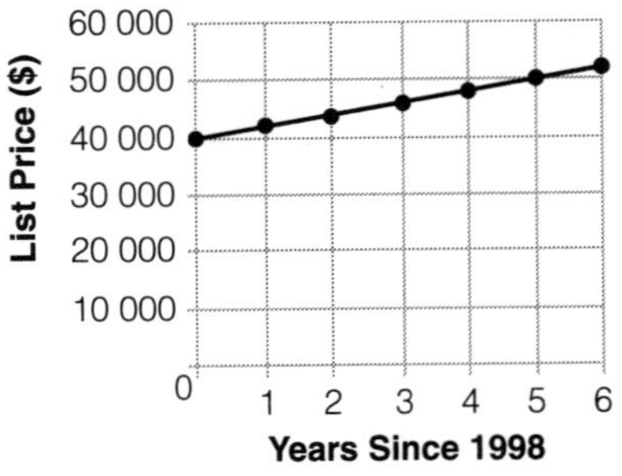

Name: ______________________ Date: ______________

Practise: Equations From Tables of Values

Section 3.5

1. Use each table of values to calculate the slope and y-intercept of the line represented by the table. Then, write the equation for each linear relation.

a)

x	y
0	2
1	5
2	8
3	11
4	14

slope: $m =$

y-intercept: $b =$

equation: $y =$

b)

x	y
1	3
2	−1
3	−5
4	−9
5	−13

slope:

y-intercept:

equation:

c)

x	y
−6	4
−5	6
−4	8
−3	10
−2	12

slope:

y-intercept:

equation:

d)

x	y
2	2
4	6
6	10
8	14
10	18

slope:

y-intercept:

equation:

2. For a service call, Sol-Ont Heating Technology charges \$75 plus \$65 per hour spent on site.

a) Complete a table of values for the cost of service calls lasting from 0 h to 6 h.

Time (h)							
Cost (\$)							

b) What are the two variables in this linear relation? What are the units for these variables?

c) Write an equation that represents the cost to customers.

d) Determine the cost of a $3\frac{1}{2}$-h service call.

Name: ______________________ Date: ____________

3.6 Write Linear Equations by Translating Written Descriptions

Textbook pp. 110–113

Warm Up

1. Number Sense

Write the fraction of an inch marked by each arrow on this enlargement of a ruler.

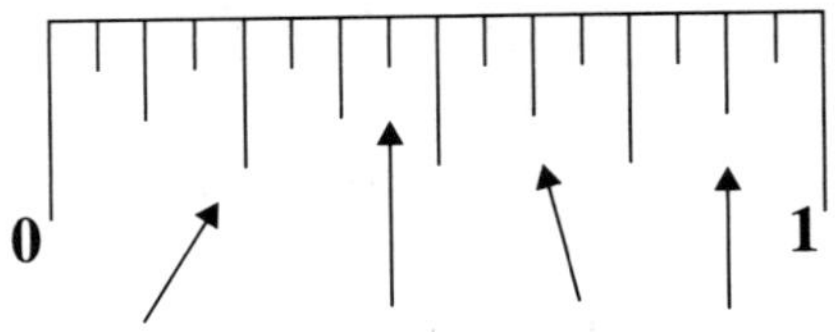

____ ____ ____ ____

2. Mental Math/Estimating

Evaluate for $c = 5$.

$75 - 2c =$

$\frac{90}{c} =$

3. Proportional Reasoning

A furniture designer wants the headboard for a bed to be 15% wider than the mattress. How wide should the headboard be if the mattress is 1.80 m across?

4. Relations and Functions

The y-intercept of a linear function

A indicates where the graph crosses the x-axis

B indicates the value of y when $x = 0$

C is always the same value as the slope of the line

D is never the same value as the slope of the line

5. Algebra

Find the measure of x.

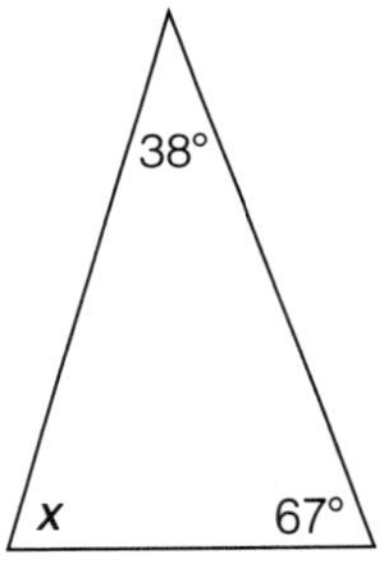

6. Graphs and Tables

A 21-inch liquid-crystal television uses about ________% less energy than the same size cathode-ray television.

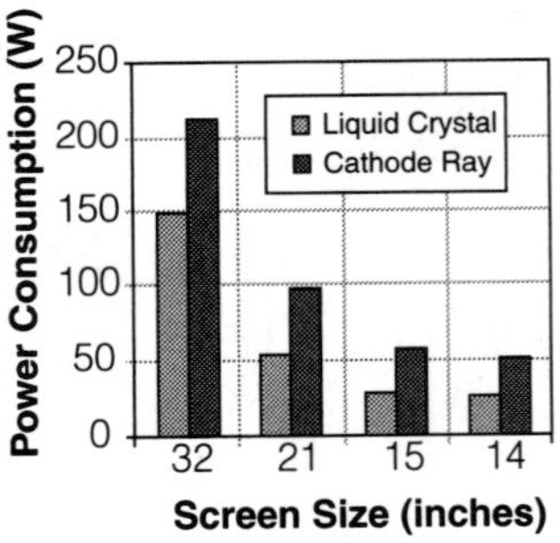

7. Math Literacy

A triangle with three unequal sides is

s __ __ __ __ __ __.

8. Previous Section

This table shows the cost for renting a small aircraft. Write an equation for c.

Time, t (h)	0	2	4	6	8
Cost, c ($)	50	200	350	500	650

$c =$

Name: ______________________________ Date: ______________

Practise: Translating to Equations

Section 3.6

1. Match each description in the left column with the corresponding equation in the right column.

Half of a number equals another number.	$x + y = 10$
An image is three times the size of the original.	$b = p + d$
The balance is the previous amount plus today's deposit.	$xy = 10$
The interest rate is the ratio of interest to principal	$0.5m = n$
The sum of two numbers is 10.	$I = 3x$
The product of two numbers is 10.	$r = \frac{I}{P}$

2. Translate each sentence into an algebraic equation. Define the variables you use.

a) Juha is nine years older than Barbara.

$j = b +$ _____, where j is _______________ ______ and b is _______________ ______.

b) The length is 5 cm greater than the width.

$l =$ _____ + _____, where l is the _______________ and _____ is the width.

c) Kevin is one-third the height of Georges.

d) The new car is twice as expensive as the used car.

e) The birch is 4 m shorter than the maple.

f) Malik's age doubled plus five equals Nalia's age.

continued ....

Name: ______________________________ Date: ______________

Section 3.6

3. Define a variable for each situation. Then, write an equation to represent the situation, and solve for the unknown.

a) Six times a number increased by 7 is 103. Find the number.

Let n represent the ______________.

_____ n + _____ = _____

b) The sum of two consecutive numbers is 87. What are the two numbers?

c) In ∠PQR, ∠P is equal to ∠Q and is twice as large as ∠R. Find the measure of ∠R.

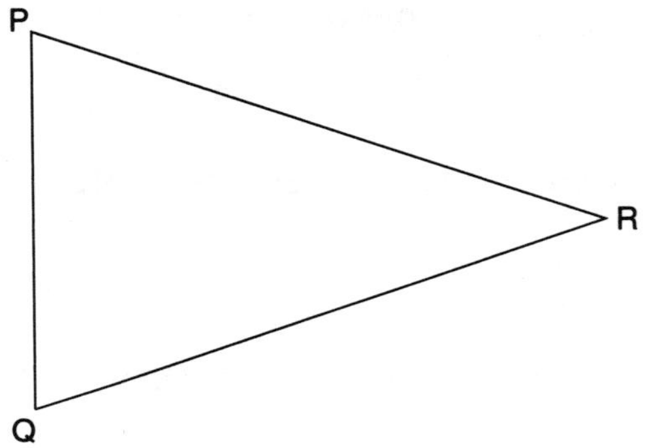

d) The width of a rectangular swimming pool is 8 m. The perimeter of the pool is 44 m. Find the length of this pool.

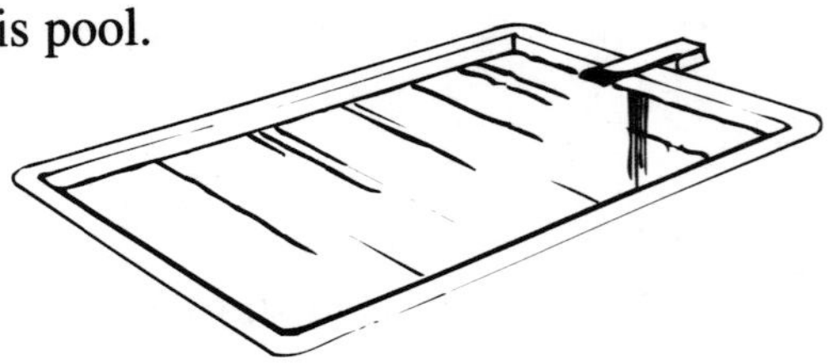

e) Rado is 10 years older than Sue. The sum of their ages is 52. How old is Rado?

Name: ______________________ Date: ______________

3.7 Rearrange Equations From One Form to Another

Textbook pp. 114–118

Warm Up

1. Number Sense

When asked to find 50% of 600, a student grabs a calculator and shouts out an answer of 30 000! What error did the student likely make?

2. Mental Math/Estimating

Use an estimate to determine the correct answer.

646.875 ÷ 75 equals

A 0.8625 **B** 8.625

C 86.25 **D** 862.5

3. Proportional Reasoning

How much interest would $100 earn in a month if the annual interest rate is 3%?

4. Relations and Functions

Trace the line that would best represent the relation between oven temperature and the baking time for a pie.

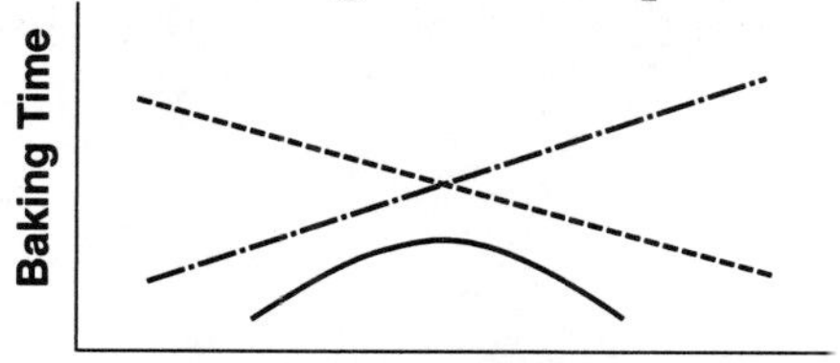

5. Algebra

Use the formula $A = 4\pi r^2$ to find the surface area of a ball with a radius of 2.5 cm. Round to the nearest square centimetre.

6. Graphs and Tables

This graph shows one of the forces acting on an airplane as it turns.

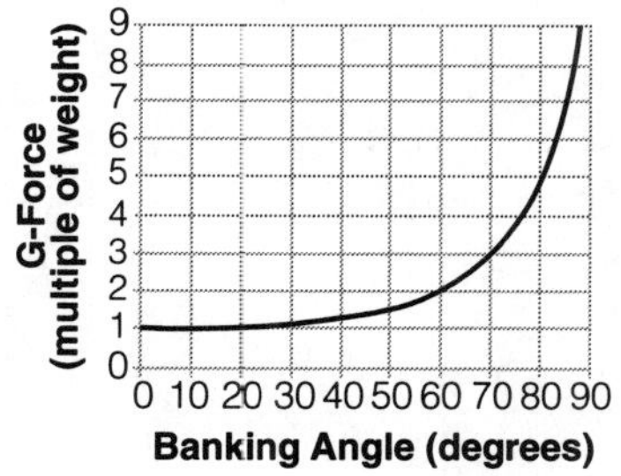

When an airplane banks at a 70° angle, the G-force is about ______.

7. Math Literacy

Name each shape.

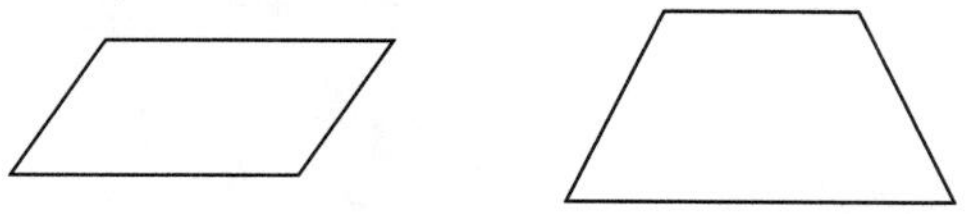

8. Previous Section

A swimming pool is being drained for repairs. Write an equation for the water level if it starts at 3.0 m and goes down 12 cm an hour.

Name: ______________________________ Date: ______________

Practise: Rearranging Equations

Section 3.7

1. Circle the equations that are in standard form.

a) $12x - 3y + 4 = 0$ **b)** $4x - 9y = 6$ **c)** $\frac{1}{2}x + 15y - 10 = 0$

d) $y = 7x - 6$ **e)** $6x - y = 0$ **f)** $4y = 7$

2. Rearrange each equation into standard form.

a) $y = 3x + 6$ **b)** $y = -2x - 12$

c) $y = x + \frac{1}{2}$ **d)** $y = -5$

3. Rearrange each equation into slope and y-intercept form.

a) $9x + y + 6 = 0$ **b)** $4x - 2y - 10 = 0$

c) $x + 2y - 8 = 0$ **d)** $y - 6 = 0$

continued ....

Name: ______________________ Date: ______________

Section 3.7

4. A computer manufacturer runs an advertisement that shows their handheld computer still working after a mountaineer accidentally drops it while climbing a cliff. You work for a consumers' organization that wants to check if this advertisement is misleading. You find a suitable spot on the Niagara Gorge and toss one of the company's handheld computers over the edge.

a) In standard form, an equation describing the motion of the computer is $98t - 10s + 50 = 0$, where t is the time, in seconds, that the computer has been falling and s is its speed, in metres per second. Rearrange the equation to get a formula for s.

b) What does the s-intercept in your formula represent?

c) The computer takes 2.4 s to reach the bottom of the gorge. How fast is the computer falling when it hits the ground?

d) How long does it take the computer to reach a speed of 50 km/h?

continued ....

Name: ______________________ Date: ______________

Chapter 3 Review

Chapter 3 Review

The date of the Chapter 3 test is ______________________.
Use these questions to check whether you are ready for this test.
For help preparing for the chapter test, see the study tips on pages x–xii.

3.1 Patterns and Ordered Pairs, textbook pages 80–86

1. a) Plot these points.
$(-6, -1)$, $(-4, 0)$, $(-2, 1)$, $(0, 2)$, $(2, -1)$, $(4, 4)$

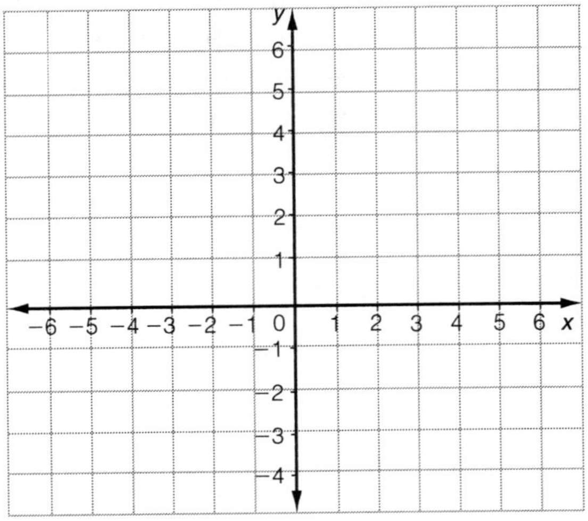

b) Which of these points is not part of a linear relation with all of the others?

c) List a point in each of the four quadrants.
Quadrant I:

Quadrant II:

Quadrant III:

Quadrant IV:

2. While training for a marathon, Michael increases his running distances every week. Complete this table of values for Michael's training schedule.

Week	1	2	3	4	5	6
Distance (km)	4	7	10			

3.2 Construct Tables and Sketch Graphs With Technology, textbook pages 87–91

3. a) Sketch how the graph of $y = -2x + 5$ will appear if you use the standard window settings on a graphing calculator.

b) What table settings would you use to generate this table of values?

TblStart = _____

ΔTbl = _____

X	Y1	
-2	9	
0	5	
2	1	
4	-3	
6	-7	
8	-11	
10	-15	

X=0

continued ....

Name: ______________________ Date: ____________

Chapter 3 Review

3.3 Construct Tables and Sketch Graphs Without Technology, textbook pages 92–96

4. a) Fill in the missing values so that the table of values represents a linear relation.

x	−4	−1	2		
y		3	1	−1	

b) Graph the data from part a).

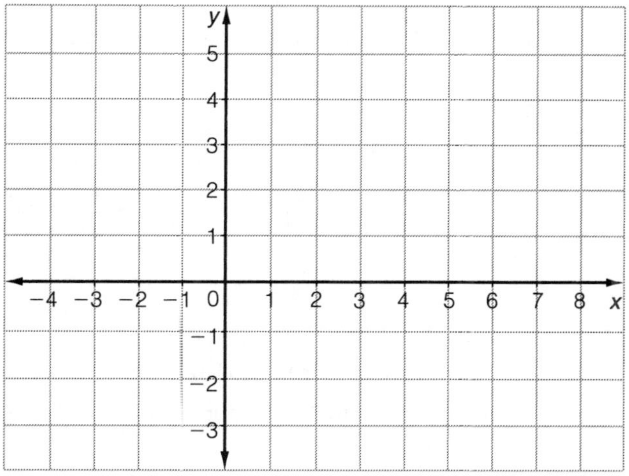

c) List two other points that lie on the graph of the linear relation.

3.4 Interpret Lines, textbook pages 97–103

5. Complete this table.

Equation	Slope	*y*-intercept
$y = 2x - 4$		
$y = -3x + 2$		
$y = x$		
$y = -x - 5$		
$y = mx + b$		

6. Find the slope of the line in question 4.

3.5 Write Linear Equations by Using Tables of Values, textbook pages 104–109

7. Find the equation for the linear relation represented by this table of values.

x	*y*
−1	3
0	6
1	9
2	12

continued ....

Name: ______________________________ Date: ______________

Chapter 3 Review

3.6 Write Linear Equations by Translating Written Descriptions, textbook pages 110–113

8. Write an algebraic equation for each sentence. Define the variables you use.

a) One number is a third of another.

b) Tina was on the Internet 2 h longer than Carmen.

c) The value of the car decreased by $4000.

9. A shipment of three cartons of jam contains 70 jars after 2 have been put on the display shelf. How many jars does a carton hold?

3.7 Rearrange Equations From One Form to Another, textbook pages 114–118

10. Write the equation $y = -\frac{5}{2}x + 7$ in the form $Ax + By + C = 0$.

11. Write the equation $5x - 3y + 9 = 0$ in the form $y = mx + b$.

Name: ______________________________ Date: ______________

Rich Problem: A Better Bulb

Chapter 3 Rich Problem

A 13-watt compact fluorescent light bulb produces about the same amount of light as an ordinary 60-watt incandescent light bulb. Each second it is on, the incandescent bulb uses 60 joules (J) of electrical energy while the compact fluorescent bulb uses only 13 J.

1. a) Calculate how much energy the 60-watt incandescent bulb uses in 1 h. Express your answer in kilojoules (kJ).

b) Calculate how much energy the 13-watt fluorescent bulb uses in 1 h.

2. Complete these tables.

60-Watt Bulb	
Time (h)	**Energy Used (MJ)**
1	
2	
3	
4	
5	
6	

13-Watt Bulb	
Time (h)	**Energy Used (MJ)**
1	
2	
3	
4	
5	
6	

Hint
A megajoule (MJ) is a million joules.

3. Write an equation for the energy used by each bulb. Define the variables.

60-Watt Incandescent | **13-Watt Fluorescent**

continued ....

Name: ____________________ Date: ____________

Chapter 3
Rich Problem

4. Use this grid to graph the data from both tables in question 2. Label the two lines.

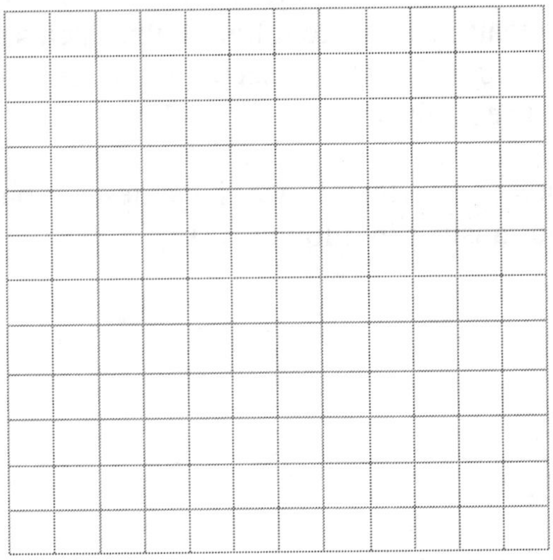

Hint
Remember to label the axes.

5. What do the slopes of the lines on the graph represent?

6. How can you tell from the graph that the incandescent bulb uses energy at a greater rate than the fluorescent bulb?

7. **a)** How much energy will you save each year if you use a 13-W fluorescent bulb to replace a 60-W incandescent bulb in a light fixture? Assume that the light is on about 3000 h a year.

b) How much money would you save each year if your local utility charges 2.1¢ per megajoule for electricity? Round to the nearest cent.

Name: ______________________________ Date: ______________

CHAPTER 4

Piecewise Linear Functions

Get Set

Answer these questions to check your understanding of the Get Ready concepts on pages 166–167 of the *Mathematics: Applying the Concepts 10* textbook.

Equations of Lines

1. Determine the slope, y-intercept, and equation of the line in each graph.

a)

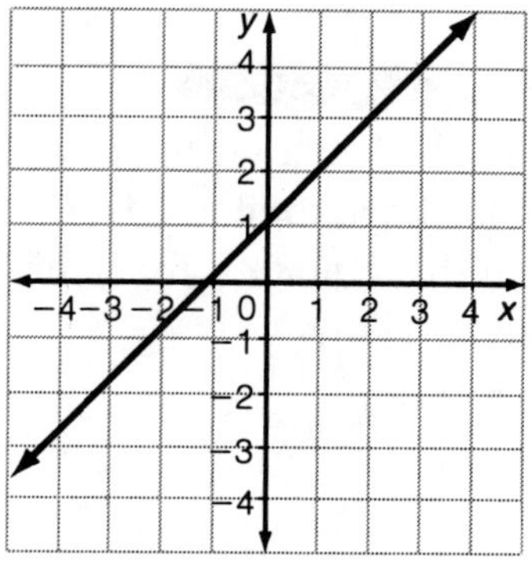

slope:

y-intercept:

equation:

b)

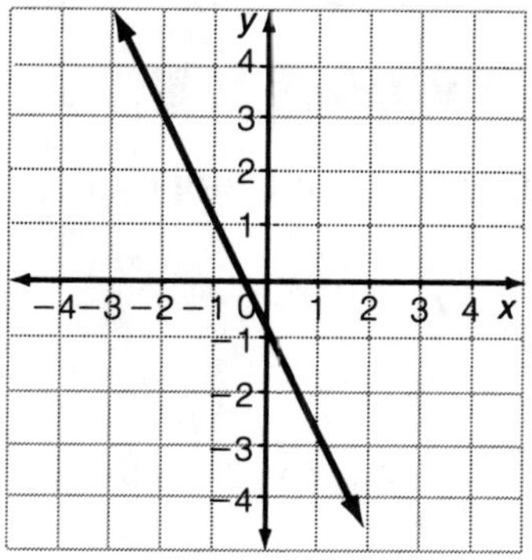

slope:

y-intercept:

equation:

Inequalities

2. Complete each statement with the appropriate inequality sign, > or <.

a) -4 ____ -10 **b)** -4 ____ 8 **c)** 0 ____ -9 **d)** -9 ____ 0

3. Match each statement with the corresponding algebraic expression.

a) the diameter is greater than the radius	$d \leq 4$
b) the paperback edition costs less than the hard-cover one	$b \geq w$
c) the distance is no greater than 4 units	$C > 6r$
d) the width is less than or equal to the length	$s \leq 2b$
e) the diameter is less than a third of the circumference	$d < \frac{1}{3}r$
f) bicycling is at least 4 times as fast as walking	$w \leq l$
g) the circumference is greater than 6 times the radius	$d > r$
h) the subway is no more than twice as fast as a bus	$p < h$

Name: ______________________ Date: ____________

4.1 Explore Piecewise Linear Functions

Textbook pp. 132-138

Warm Up

1. Number Sense

Rank these numbers from least to greatest.

$\frac{3}{4}$ $\quad 0 \quad -\frac{3}{4} \quad -0.6 \quad \frac{1}{2} \quad 0.6 \quad -\frac{1}{2}$

___ ___ ___ ___ ___ ___ ___

2. Mental Math/Estimating

In a standard-rate turn, an aircraft turns 360° in exactly 2 min. At this rate, how long does it take to turn 90°?

3. Proportional Reasoning

Draw a line segment with a slope of $\frac{1}{4}$.

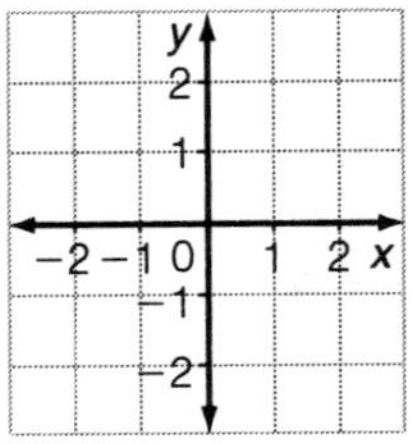

4. Relations and Functions

Sabina is paid \$150 a week plus \$10 for each bicycle she assembles. Define the variables in this equation for Sabina's weekly pay.

$p = 150 + 10n$

5. Algebra

Show that the point (2, 3) is on the line $y = 4x - 5$.

L.S. = **R.S. =**

6. Graphs and Tables

This graph shows a breakdown of the \$636 million budgeted for the Toronto police force.

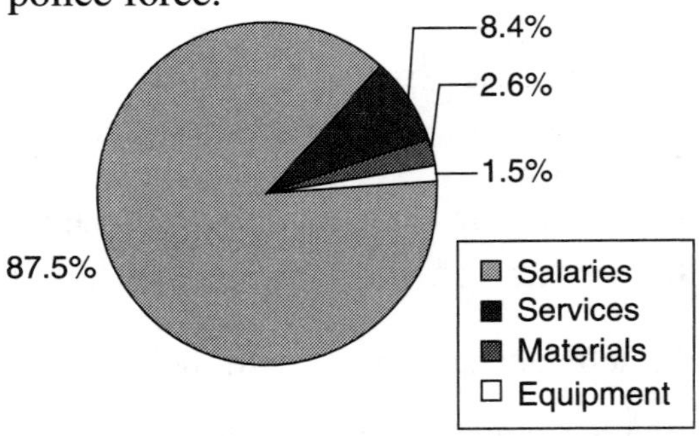

The amount the police force spends on materials is ________________.

7. Math Literacy

An annual event occurs every __________.

A semi-annual event occurs every _____ ________________.

8. Previous Section

Which linear equation is in standard form?

A $y = 4x + 6$ **B** $3x + y - 10 = 0$

C $2x + 8y = 5$ **D** $x = 5y + 9$

Name: ______________________ Date: ____________

Practise: Piecewise Linear Functions

Section 4.1

1. To save energy, most computers switch into a standby mode after 5–10 min of inactivity. This graph shows the energy used by the computer in Tina's office one afternoon.

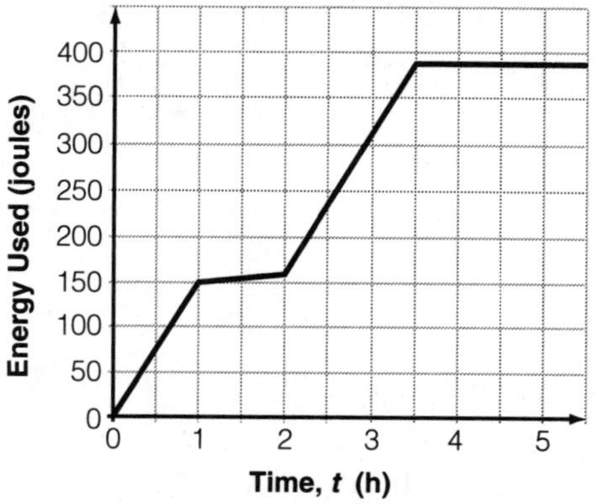

a) Write a description of the graph.

b) Explain how you can tell that the graph represents a piecewise linear function.

c) Complete this table of the time intervals for the segments of the graph.

Line Segment	Time Interval
I	0 ___ t ___ 1
II	
III	
IV	

d) When was the computer in standby mode?

e) How can you tell that the computer was turned off after $3\frac{1}{2}$ h?

continued ....

Name: ______________________ Date: ____________

Section 4.1

2. Companies that rent sound and lighting equipment for concerts and theatres usually offer large discounts for longer rentals. This graph shows the fees for renting a stage light for up to a month.

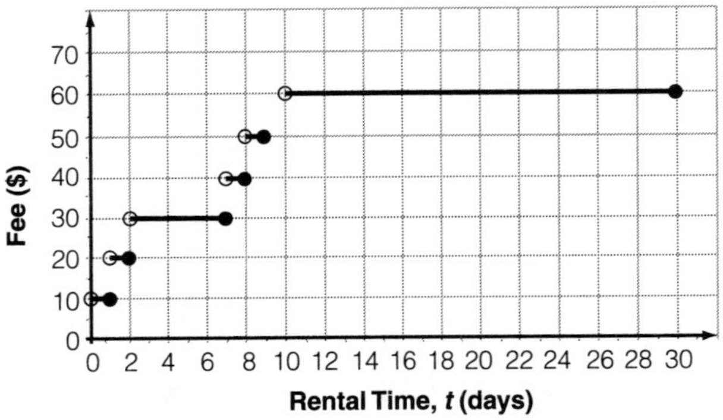

a) Does this graph show a piecewise linear function? Explain why or why not.

b) What do the breaks in the graph indicate?

c) Complete this table of values for the graph.

Rental Interval (days)	Fee ($)
$0 < t$ ___ 1	10
1 ___ t ___ 2	20

Hint
The circles at the ends of each line segment tell you whether the end points are part of the segment.

Name: ______________________________ Date: ______________

4.2 Construct Piecewise Linear Functions With Technology

Textbook pp. 139–145

Warm Up

1. Number Sense

Continue the pattern.

1, −2, −5, −8, ____, ____, ____

Describe the pattern.

2. Mental Math/Estimating

John and Azriela's new house costs \$189 500. Their down payment is 5% of the cost, or about

A \$100 **B** \$1000

C \$10 000 **D** \$100 000

3. Proportional Reasoning

On a 1:200 scale drawing, a garage is 3 cm long. What is the length of the actual garage, in metres?

4. Relations and Functions

Which point is on the graph of both $y = 6$ and $y = 3x$?

A (1, 6)

B (2, 6)

C (5, 15)

D (–1, –3)

5. Algebra

Expand and simplify.

$2(2x + 3) + 5x - 1$

6. Graphs and Tables

This graph shows the amounts a lawyer charges for small jobs.

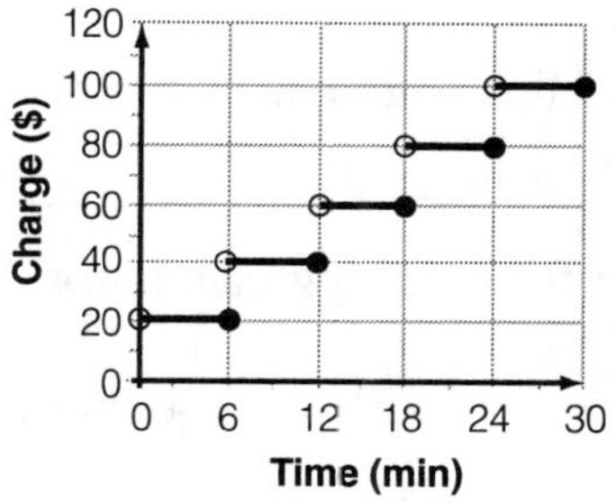

For 23 min of work, this lawyer charges \$____.

7. Math Literacy

How often does a biannual event occur?

8. Previous Section

How much does the lawyer in question 6 charge for 24 min of work?

Name: ______________________ Date: ____________

Practise: Piecewise Functions With Technology

Section 4.2

1. Find the equation for each line segment in this piecewise linear function. Write an inequality to show the interval of x-values for each segment. Then, write the expression you would enter to graph the line segment with a graphing calculator.

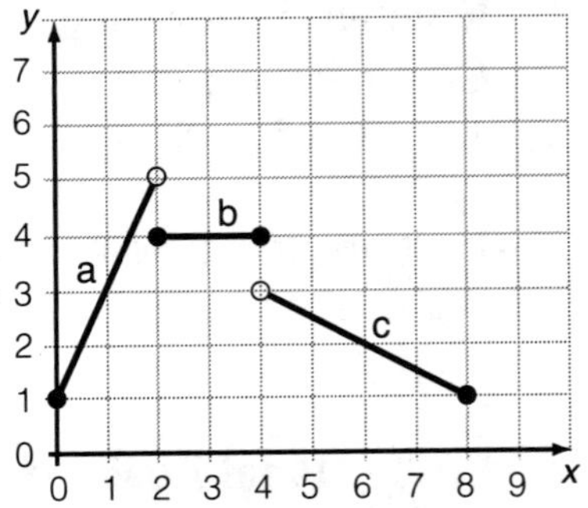

a) slope $= \frac{\text{rise}}{\text{run}}$ y-intercept =

$= \frac{\square}{\square}$

=

Therefore, the equation of the line segment is

$y =$ ______$x +$ ___.

Interval of x-values: 0 ___ x ____ 2

Expression for graphing calculator: **Y1** =

b) slope = y-intercept =

Hint
For help with expressions for graphing calculators, see pages 140–141 of the textbook.

Equation of line segment: $y =$

Interval of x-values: 2 ___ x ___ ____

Expression for graphing calculator: **Y2** =

c) slope = y-intercept =

Equation of line segment: $y =$

Interval of x-values:

Expression for graphing calculator: **Y3** =

2. Write an expression that combines the results from question 1 so that they can all be entered into **Y1**.

Y1 =

Name: ____________________ Date: ____________

4.3 Construct Piecewise Linear Functions Without Technology

Textbook pp. 146-152

Warm Up

1. Number Sense

Circle the two window settings that must be 0 if you want to show a graph of only the first quadrant.

```
WINDOW
 Xmin=
 Xmax=
 Xscl=
 Ymin=
 Ymax=
 Yscl=
 Xres=1
```

2. Mental Math/Estimating

A pack of 1000 sheets of lined paper is about 10 cm thick. The thickness of a 10-page project is about

A 0.01 cm

B 0.1 cm

C 1 cm

D 10 cm

3. Proportional Reasoning

A National Hockey League hockey puck has a diameter of 3.0 inches (about 7.6 cm). How many pucks can lie flat in a 12 inch by 12 inch box?

4. Relations and Functions

Do the points $(-3, -2)$, $(0, 1)$, and $(1, 2)$ have a linear relation?

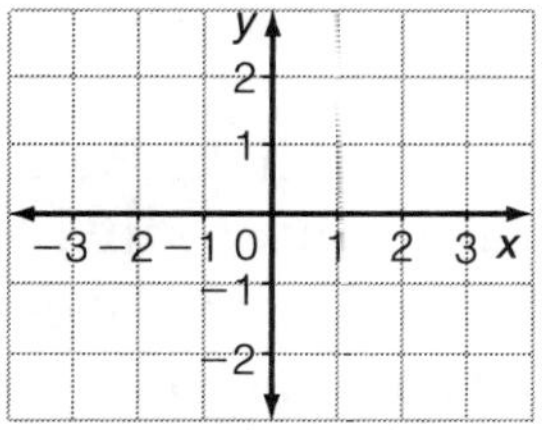

5. Algebra

Simplify.

$7x - 5 - (3x + 2)$

6. Graphs and Tables

A flyer from a lumber yard lists these costs for lengths of 2 by 4 spruce.

Length (cm)	Cost (¢/cm)
120–300	1.10
300–500	1.40

The cost, including taxes, for a 4-m length of this 2 by 4 is $_________.

7. Math Literacy

If the graph of a function consists of two or more straight lines, the function is

______________________ linear.

8. Previous Section

Complete this equation for graphing the piecewise linear function in question 6 on a graphing calculator. (Hint: You need to add eight sets of brackets.)

Y1 = 1.10X 120≤X X≤300 +
  1.40X 300<X X≤500

Name: ______________________ Date: ____________

Practise: Piecewise Functions Without Technology

Section 4.3

1. On January 12, 2004, the postage rates for sending a letter within Canada increased to

- 49¢ for letters with a mass of 30 g or less
- 80¢ for letters with a mass greater than 30 g but not more than 50 g
- 98¢ for letters with a mass greater than 50 g but not more than 100 g

Complete this table and graph for these postal rates. Use open and closed circles to show which end values are included in the line segments on the graph.

Line Mass (g)	Postage (¢)
0 ___ *x* ___ 30	
30 ___ *x* ___ 50	
50 ___ *x* ___ 100	

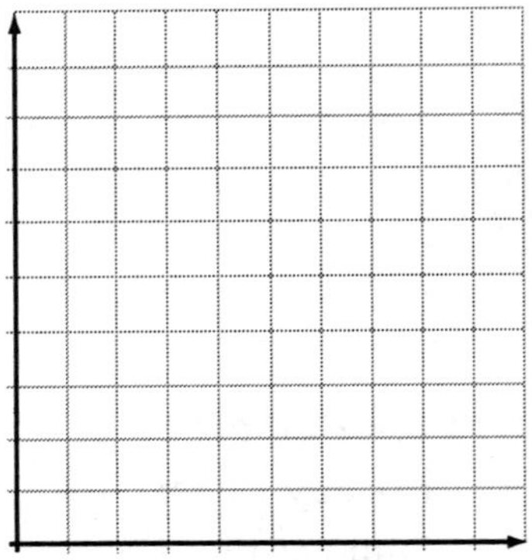

2. Leora has a summer job with the Parks and Recreation Department. She earns $8.40 per hour, and her regular shifts Monday to Friday total 40 h a week. For any overtime work, Leora earns time-and-a-half (1.5 times the regular hourly rate). The department limits overtime to a maximum of 16 h per week.

a) Write an equation relating Leora's *regular* pay (y) to the number of hours she works (x). For what values of x does this equation apply?

$y =$ for $0 \le x$ ____ 40

b) Is this relationship linear? Explain.

c) Write an equation relating Leora's *overtime* pay (y) to the number of hours she works (x). For what values of x does this equation apply?

$y =$ _____(8.4)($x -$ _____) for 40 ___ $x \le$ _____

$y =$

$y =$

d) Is this relationship linear? Explain.

continued ....

Name: ______________________________ Date: ______________

e) What is the maximum amount that Leora can earn in one week?

maximum pay = regular pay for ____ h + overtime pay for ____ h

= ________ × ________ + ________ × ________

= ________ + ________

=

Therefore, ____.

f) Complete this table of values for Leora's weekly pay.

Hours worked	0	10	20	30	40	41	50	56
Total earnings ($)								

g) You can graph the function for Leora's weekly pay without using all of the values in part f). Explain which three values are essential for the graph.

h) Make a graph of the relation between Leora's total earnings and the hours she works in a week. Select appropriate scales for the axes, and label them fully.

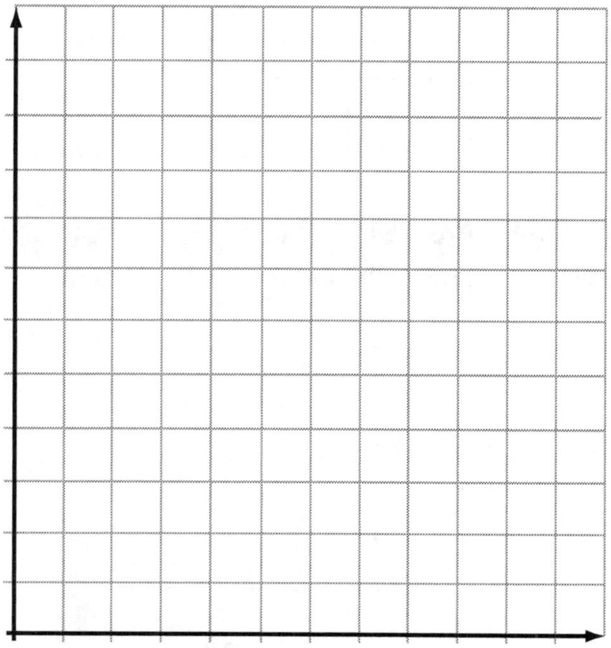

Name: ______________________ Date: ____________

4.4 Interpolation and Extrapolation

Textbook pp. 153-159

Warm Up

1. Number Sense

A restaurant chain claims "over 99 billion served." Write 99 billion as a number.

2. Mental Math/Estimating

A school hires a teacher for approximately every 23 students. If the school has 40 teachers, the number of students is about

A 80 **B** 800

C 8000 **D** 80 000

3. Proportional Reasoning

The federal income rate is 17% for taxable income of less than \$32 000. Find the federal income tax owing on a taxable income of \$27 500.

4. Relations and Functions

Rewrite the linear function $3x + y - 6 = 0$ in the form $y = mx + b$.

5. Algebra

Write an expression for the total area of this figure.

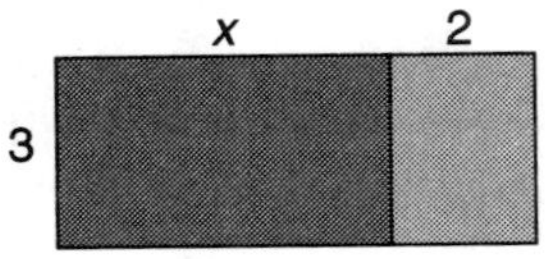

6. Graphs and Tables

Complete this table of costs for Internet service from a provider that charges 50¢ per hour with a minimum charge of \$5.00 per month.

Time (h)	Cost (\$)	Ordered Pair
2	5.00	(2, 5)
8		
10		
12		
20		

7. Math Literacy

The graph of a piecewise-linear function is made of line segments that are either

c _ _ _ _ _ _ _ _ or

s _ _ _ _ _ _ _ _.

8. Previous Section

Graph the internet costs from question 6.

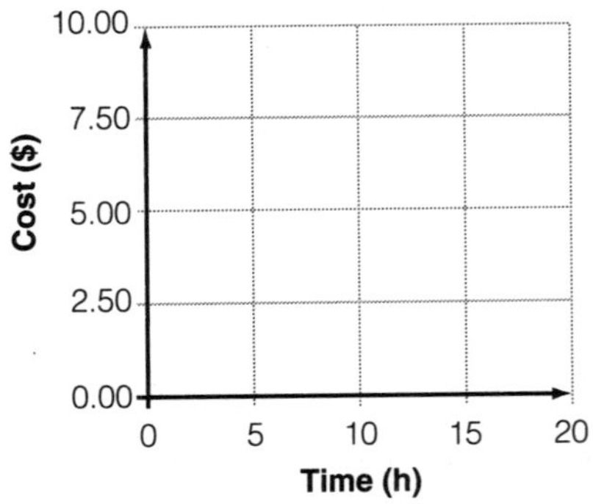

Name: ______________________________ Date: ______________

Practise: Interpolation and Extrapolation

Section 4.4

1. This graph shows the amounts Zora's Print Shop charges for photocopies.

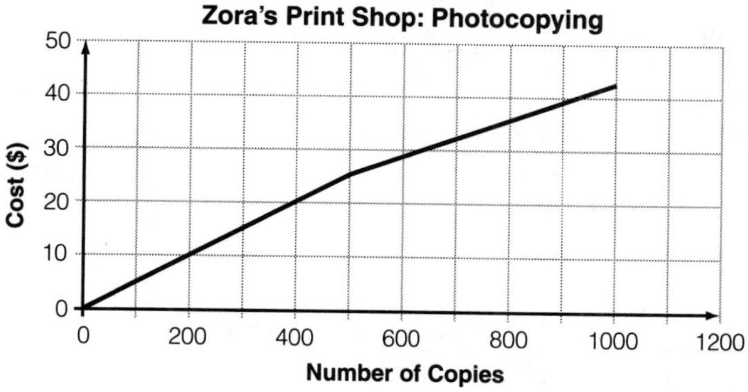

a) How can you tell from the graph that the price per photocopy decreases after the first 500 copies?

b) Use the graph to estimate the cost of

i) 400 copies ____________ **ii)** 800 copies ____________

c) In part b), you estimated values ______________ two known points. This method of estimating is called ____________________.

d) How could you estimate the cost of 1200 copies?

e) Estimate the cost of 1200 copies. ____________

f) In part e), you estimated values ____________ the given points. This method of estimating is called ____________________.

g) Estimate the cost of 1500 copies.

continued ....

Name: ______________________________ Date: ______________

2. With the wind at her back, Charmaine averaged 24 km/h for the first 90 min of a bicycle ride. After a rest, she rode home against the wind at an average speed of 18 km/h.

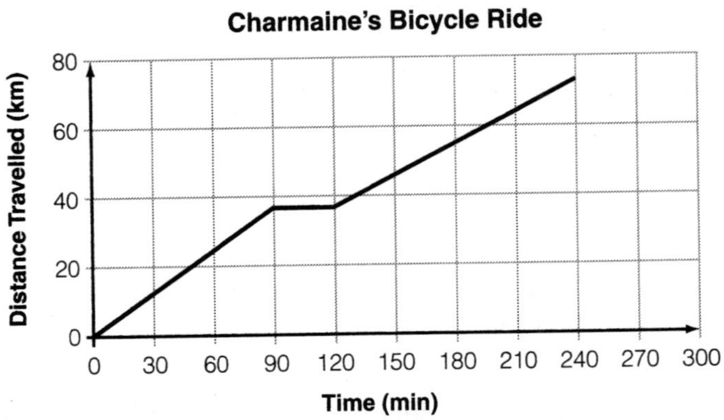

a) Estimate how long Charmaine took to ride

i) 10 km __________ **ii)** 20 km __________

b) How long did she stop to rest? __________

c) Approximately how far did she ride in 3 h? __________

d) Estimate the total distance Charmaine would have ridden after 5 h if she continues riding past her home. __________

e) This graph also shows Charmaine's bicycle ride. What variable does the y-axis represent?

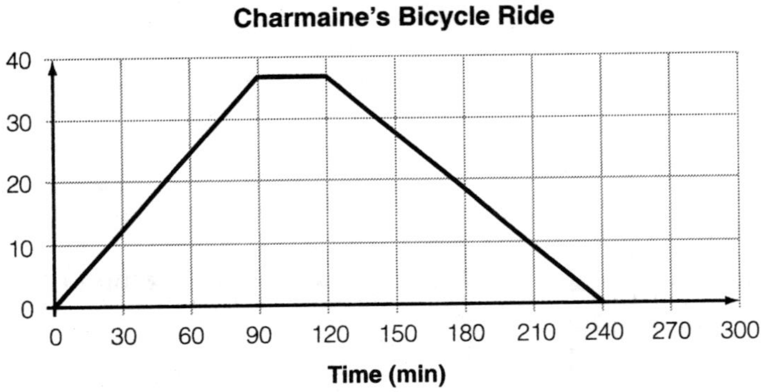

f) What does the point (240, 0) represent?

g) Sketch how you would extend this graph to show Charmaine continuing her ride past her home.

Name: ______________________________ Date: ______________

Chapter 4 Review

The date of the Chapter 4 test is ________________.
Use these questions to check whether you are ready for this test.
For help preparing for the chapter test, see the study tips on pages x–xii.

4.1 Explore Piecewise-Linear Functions, textbook pages 132–138

1. a) Does this graph represent a piecewise linear function? Explain.

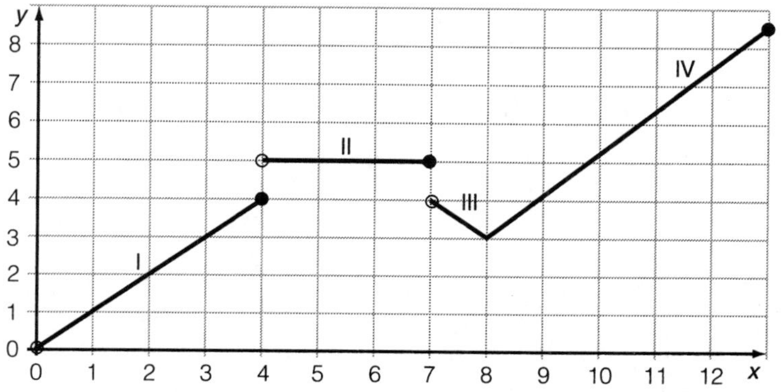

b) The open circles on the graph indicate that ______________________________ ______________________________ while the closed circles indicate that ______________________________.

c) Complete this table of the intervals of x-values for each line segment in the graph.

Line Segment	Interval of x-values
I	0 ___ x ___ 4
II	
III	
IV	

4.2 Construct Piecewise Linear Functions With Technology, textbook pages 139–145

2. Fill in the window settings needed to display the graph in question 1 on a graphing calculator.

```
WINDOW
  Xmin=
  Xmax=
  Xscl=
  Ymin=
  Ymax=
  Yscl=
  Xres=1
```

continued ....

Name: ______________________ Date: ______________

Chapter 4 Review

4.3 Construct Piecewise Linear Functions Without Technology, textbook pages 146–152

3. To train for a bicycle race, James rides laps around a track. In one training session, he maintains different speeds for 10 min each. Use this table of values to make a graph of the training session.

Time (min)	Distance (km)
0	0
10	7
20	13
30	18
40	22

4. A resort has a "stay three days, get a free day" offer. Make a graph of the cost of staying up to five days at this resort in a room with a daily rate of \$89.

4.4 Interpolation and Extrapolation, textbook pages 153–159

5. a) Use your graph in question 3 to estimate how long James took to ride 25 km. Explain your reasoning.

b) How far will James have ridden altogether if he maintains his speed for another 20 min? Explain your answer.

Name: ______________________________ Date: ______________

Rich Problem: Commission Rates

Chapter 4 Rich Problem

Kamran works in a men's clothing store. He receives a commission of

- 4% on his monthly sales up to $30 000
- 7% on his sales in excess of $30 000 per month

1. Complete this table for the commission Kamran would earn on sales up to $60 000 a month.

Monthly Sales ($)	Commission ($)
0	
10 000	10 000 × ____% = __________
20 000	________ × ____% = __________
30 000	
40 000	__________ + __________ × ____% = __________
50 000	
60 000	

2. Use the table of values to make a graph of the commissions Kamran could earn.

continued ....

Name: ______________________ Date: ______________

Chapter 4
Rich Problem

3. a) Write an equation for the commission Kamran receives on sales up to $30 000 in a month. Define the variables you use.

b) Write an equation for the total commission Kamran receives when his sales are over $30 000 in a month.

Hint
For help with expressions for graphing calculators, see pages 140–141 of the textbook.

4. a) Write the expression you would enter on a graphing calculator to graph Kamran's commission on sales up to $30 000 in a month.

Y1 =

b) Write the expression you would enter to graph enter Kamran's commission on sales of $30 000 to $60 000 in a month.

Y2 =

c) Fill in the window settings you would use for displaying the graph of **Y1** and **Y2**. Then, sketch how the graph of these two functions will appear.

```
WINDOW
  Xmin=
  Xmax=
  Xscl=
  Ymin=
  Ymax=
  Yscl=
  Xres=1
```

5. Kamran's employer offers him the option to switch to a commission of 5% on all his sales with a $200 bonus for sales of $30 000 or more in a month.

a) Complete this table for earnings with the commission plus bonus option.

Monthly Sales ($)	0	10 000	20 000	29 999	30 000	40 000	50 000	60 000
Earnings ($)								

b) Graph these earnings on the grid in question 2.

6. Describe how Kamran can decide whether to switch to the commission plus bonus option.

Name: ______________________________ Date: ______________

CHAPTER 5

Systems of Linear Equations

Get Set

Answer these questions to check your understanding of the Get Ready Concepts on pages 166–167 of the *Mathematics: Applying the Concepts 10* textbook.

Simplifying Expressions

1. Simplify each of the following expressions by collecting like terms.

a) $6m + 2 + 3m + 5 =$ ____________

b) $8y - 4 - 3y - 5 =$ ____________

c) $-3h - 2 + 4h - 1 =$ ____________

d) $-5w + 6 - 3w - 6 =$ ____________

2. Expand and simplify.

a) $3(w + 2) + 2(w + 4)$

b) $5(j - 1) + 3(2j - 4)$

Solving Equations

3. Solve by rearranging the equation and collecting like terms.

a) $3a - 4 = a + 6$

b) $4s + 2 = 2s + 10$

c) $8k - 3 = -4k + 3$

4. Find an expression for x.

a) $2x = y - 10$

b) $\frac{1}{2}x + 2y = 7$

c) $\frac{x + 2y}{3} = 0$

5. Circle the ordered pair that satisfies both equations.

a) $x + y = 3$
$2x - y = 0$
(1, 2) or (2, 1)

b) $y = 2x - 4$
$y = -x + 2$
(0, 2) or (2, 0)

Writing Equations

6. Write two equations with the variables l and w to describe a rectangular picture frame that has a length twice its width and a perimeter of 42 cm.

Name: ______________________________ Date: ____________

5.1 Solve Linear Systems With Technology

Textbook pp. 168-174

Warm Up

1. Number Sense

Continue the pattern.

1, 6, 5, 10, 9, ____, ____, ____, ____

Describe the pattern.

2. Mental Math/Estimating

Find 15% of $18.00.

10% of 18 =

5% of 18 =

Therefore, 15% of $18.00 =

3. Proportional Reasoning

Over a five-year period, a restaurant franchise grew from 1400 outlets to 2000. What was the percent increase, to the nearest percent?

4. Relations and Functions

The linear function $F = 1.8C + 32$ converts temperatures from the Celsius scale to the Fahrenheit scale. The graph of this function has a slope of _____.

5. Algebra

Find the equation of the function represented by this table of values.

x	0	1	2	3
y	5	8	11	14

6. Graphs and Tables

This tables lists the interest rates a trust company offers for guaranteed investment certificates (GICs).

Term	1-Year	2-Year	3-Year	4-Year
Rate	2.9%	3.4%	3.8%	3.95%

In its first year, a $1000 4-year GIC will pay $________ more interest than a 1-year GIC

7. Math Literacy

Explain the difference between extrapolation and interpolation.

8. Previous Section

This scatter plot shows the value of used models of one type of X-ray machine.

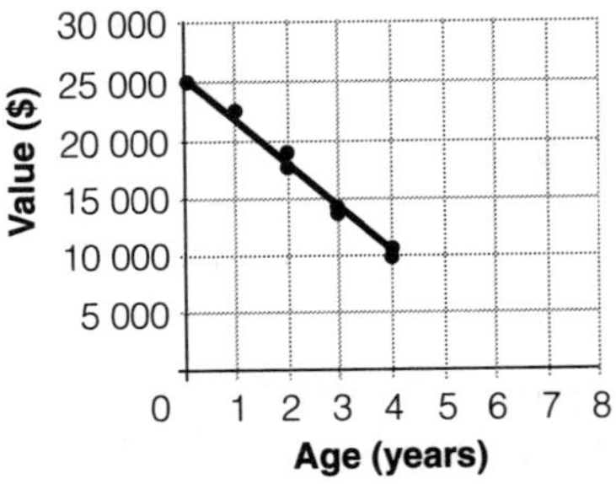

A 5-year-old machine is worth about

____________.

Name: ______________________ Date: ____________

Practise: Solve Linear Systems With Technology

Section 5.1

Larry loves playing golf but wonders whether he can afford to join either of the two local golf courses.

- The Golf and Country Club has an annual membership fee of \$1400 and charges \$55 per round of 18 holes of golf.
- Premier Links charges a \$999 annual membership fee plus \$69 per round of golf.

Larry estimates that he would play a maximum of 50 rounds of golf during the season.

1. Write an equation for the fees charged by each golf course. Define the variables.

Golf and Country Club: $y =$ ____ $x +$ _______

Premier Links: $y =$ ____ $x +$ _______

In these equations, y represents ______________________________

and x represents ______________________________.

2. a) What key opens the screen for entering equations on a graphing calculator?

b) Fill in the window settings that Larry could use to graph the cost for up to 50 rounds of golf.

```
WINDOW
 Xmin=
 Xmax=
 Xscl=10
 Ymin=0
 Ymax=4000
 Yscl=
 Xres=1
```

c) Once Larry has entered the two equations, what keys should he press to find the intersection of the two lines?

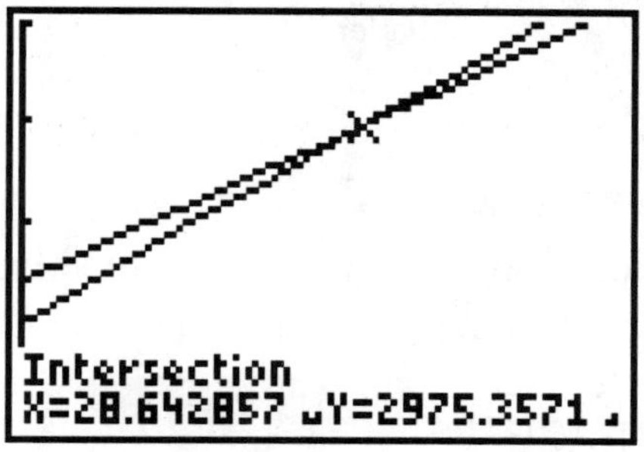

Hint
Consider which equation has the greater slope.

d) What does the graph indicate about which course will be less costly?

The Golf and Country Club will cost less if ______________________________.

Premier Links will cost less if ______________________________.

Name: ______________________________ Date: ____________

5.2 Solutions to Linear Systems

Textbook pp. 175-181

Warm Up

1. Number Sense

How many is a dozen dozen?

2. Mental Math/Estimating

Place four "+" signs in the left side of the equation to make it true.

7 6 5 4 3 2 1 = 100

3. Proportional Reasoning

A ball bounces up 60% of the height from which it was dropped. How high would this ball bounce if dropped from a height of 20 m?

4. Relations and Functions

Write an equation for the function relating the variables in this table of values.

t	1	4	7
c	7	4	1

5. Algebra

Add.

$7x + 2$
$2x + 5$
$x - 3$

6. Graphs and Tables

This graph shows a decrease in profits from the third to the fourth quarter of

$ ______________.

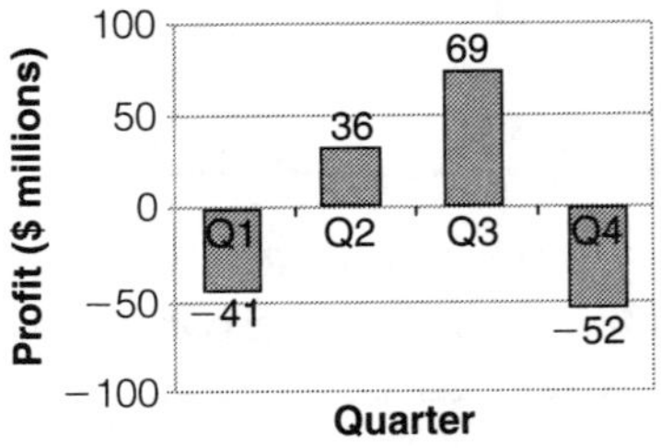

7. Math Literacy

What is a *system of equations*?

8. Previous Section

Which feature could you use to solve a linear system on a graphing calculator?

A intersect
B TRACE
C ZOOM
D All of the above

Name: ______________________________ Date: ______________

Practise: Solutions to Linear Systems

Section 5.2

Reading Graphs and Tables

1. Determine the solution to each linear system. Then, check by substituting into the equations.

a) $y = 2x + 1$ $y = -x + 4$

x	y
0	1
1	3
2	5
3	7

x	y
0	4
1	3
2	2
3	1

The two lines must intersect at (,) because ______________.

Therefore, the solution is $x =$ ____ and $y =$ ____.

Check:
For $y = 2x + 1$,

L.S. = **R.S.** =

For $y = -x + 4$,

L.S. = **R.S.** =

b) $y = \frac{1}{2}x - 3$ $y = -2x + 7$

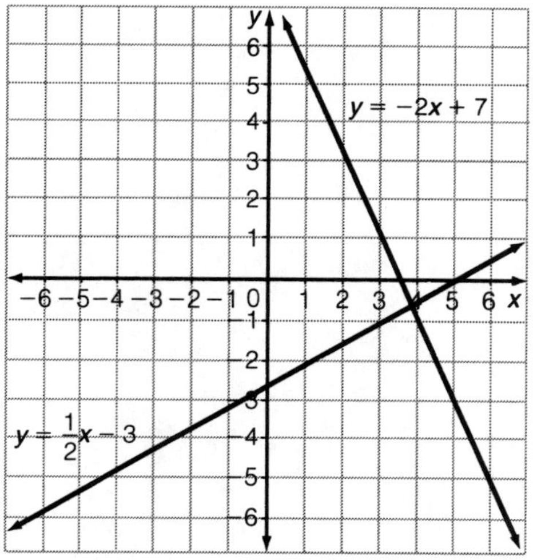

The two lines intersect at (,), so the solution is ______________.

Check:
For $y = \frac{1}{2}x - 3$,

L.S. = **R.S.** =

For $y = -2x + 7$,

L.S. = **R.S.** =

c) $y = x + 2$ and $y = -x - 4$.

Using the grid above, graph the two equations.

The point of intersection is (,).

Therefore, the solution is ______________.

Check:

Hint
Graph each line using either two points or the slope and the y-intercept. Use an extra point to check.

continued ....

Name: ____________________ Date: ____________

Section 5.2

Car Rental

2. A town has two competing car rental companies:
   - For a compact car, King Street Auto Rental charges a daily rate of \$20 plus 25¢ per kilometre driven.
   - For the same size of car, Queen Road Rentals simply charges 40¢/km with a minimum charge of \$20.

   a) Write equations for a 1-day rental from each company. Define the variables.

   King Street Auto Rental

   $C =$ ____ + _____d

   Queen Road Rentals

   $C =$ _____ for $0 < d \leq 50$ and

   $C =$ _____d for $d > 50$

   C is ____________________ and d is ____________________.

   b) Complete this table of the costs for renting a compact car for 1 day.

Distance (km)	0	50	100	150	200	250	300
Cost, King Street (\$)							
Cost, Queen Road (\$)							

   c) Graph the two functions on the same set of axes.

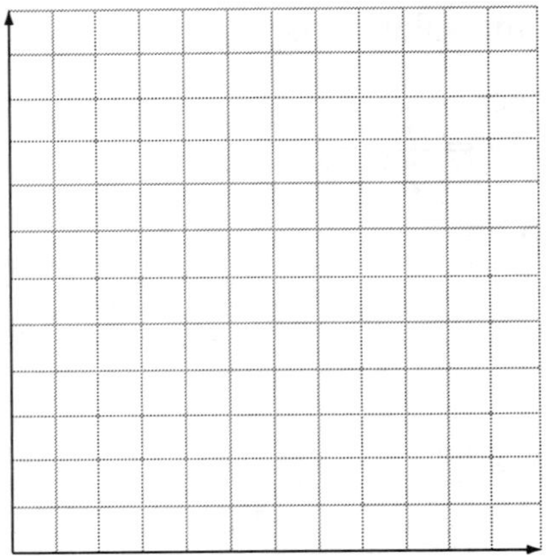

   d) For what distance do the two companies charge the same rental fee?

   e) Which company would you rent from if you expect to drive 400-km in a day?

Name: ______________________________ Date: ______________

5.3 Solve Linear Systems by Substitution

Textbook pp. 182-188

Warm Up

1. Number Sense

What is the largest number that divides evenly into both 28 and 36?

2. Mental Math/Estimating

The diagonal of this field must be between _____ m and _____ m.

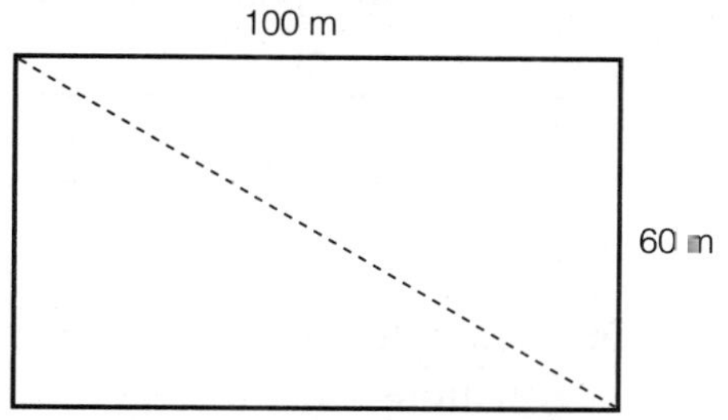

3. Proportional Reasoning

The formula for the area of a triangle is $A = \frac{1}{2}bh$. By how much does the area of a triangle increase if you double *either* the base *or* the height?

4. Relations and Functions

Find the maximum value of the function $h = -4.9x^2 + 20$.

5. Algebra

Solve for p.

$3p + 2 = 14$

6. Graphs and Tables

This train takes _____ h _____ min to travel from Cochrane to Moosonee.

Polar Bear Express		
	Distance (km)	Arrive/Depart
Cochrane	0	11:15
Fraserdale	110	12:55
Coral	154	13:40
Moosonee	298	16:20

7. Math Literacy

A "half-off" sale is the same as a "____%-off" sale.

8. Previous Section

On a graph of a system of linear equations, the _________ of ____________ of the lines represents the solution.

Name: ______________________________ Date: ______________

Practise: Solving Systems by Substitution

Section 5.3

Hint
The substitution method starts with finding an expression for one of the variables.

1. Solve each linear system by substitution.

a) $y = 4x + 14$ ① $y = -3x - 7$ ②

Step 1: Substitute the expression for y from ① into ②.

$\_\_\_\_\_\_\_\_ = -3x - 7$

Step 2: Solve for x by rearranging to get the variable terms on one side of the equation and the number terms on the other.

$\_\_\_\_\_\_\_\_ = \_\_\_\_\_\_\_\_$

$\_\_\_\_x = \_\_\_\_$

$x = \_\_\_\_$

Step 3: Substitute the value for x into one of the original equations.
Then, solve for y.
Using ①: $y = 4(\_\_\_\_) + 14$

$y = \_\_\_\_ + 14$

$y = \_\_\_\_$

Step 4: Check by substituting into the other equation.
$y = -3x - 7$ ②

L.S. = **R.S.** =

R.S. =

R.S. = Does **L.S.** = **R.S.**? ______

Therefore, the solution to the linear system is (,).

b) $y = -5x + 12$ ① $y = x + 4$ ②

Step 1:

Step 2:

Step 3:

Step 4:

Therefore, the solution to the linear system is (,).

continued ....

Name: ____ Date: ________________

Section 5.3

2. Solve this linear system by substitution.

$4x + y = 6$ ① $\qquad\qquad$ $3x - 2y = 10$ ②

Step 1: Use one equation to find an expression for y, then substitute into the other equation.

Rewrite ① in the form $y = mx + b$: $y =$ __________

Substitute this expression into ②: $3x - 2($__________$) = 10$

Step 2: Solve for x.

Step 3: Substitute $x =$ ___ into either of the original equations, then solve for y.

Using ①: $4(\quad) + y = 6$

____ $+ y =$

$y = 6$ ______

$y =$

Step 4: Check by substituting into the other equation.

$3x - 2y = 10$ ②

L.S. $= 3($___$) - 2($___$)$ $\qquad$ **R.S.** $= 10$

L.S. $=$

L.S. $=$ $\qquad$ Does **L.S.** $=$ **R.S.**? ______

Therefore, the solution to the linear system is (,).

Name: ______________________ Date: ______________

5.4 Solve Linear Systems by Elimination

Textbook pp. 189-196

Warm Up

1. Number Sense

Insert the remaining digits from 1 to 9 so that all rows, columns, and diagonals add to 15.

	1	
	5	
		2

2. Mental Math/Estimating

What is the smallest number that can be evenly divided by 1, 2, 3, 4, 5, and 6?

3. Proportional Reasoning

The formula for the area of a triangle is $A = \frac{1}{2}bh$. By how much does the area of a triangle increase if you double *both* the base and the height?

4. Relations and Functions

Draw a graph of the linear function with slope 1 and y-intercept -1.

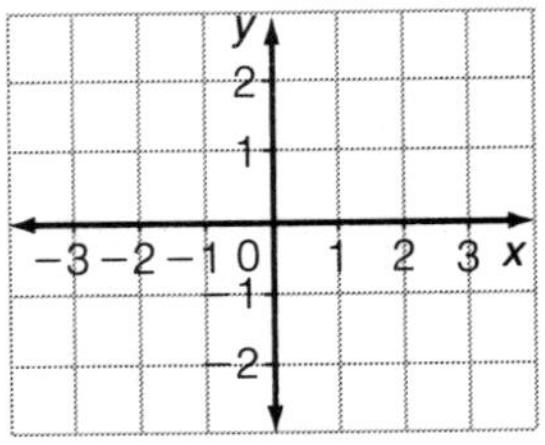

5. Algebra

Expand.

$-3(4a - 7) =$

6. Graphs and Tables

The total income of the richest 20% of Canadians first exceeded the total income of the middle 60% in ________.

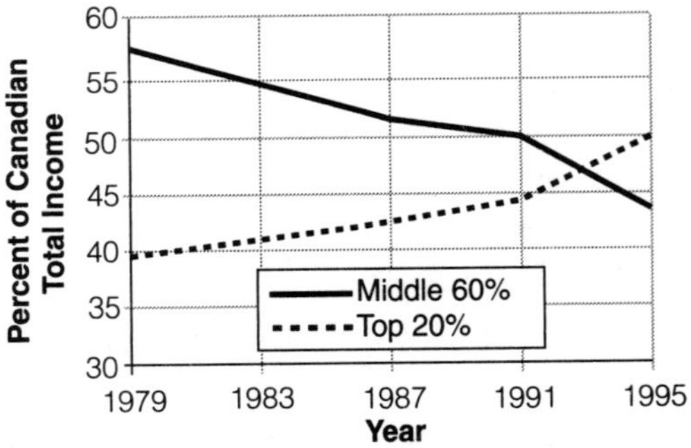

7. Math Literacy

A survey of three music stores finds the same CD selling for \$12.99, \$16.99, and \$17.99. The **m** __ __ __ price of this CD is \$15.99.

8. Previous Section

Solve by substitution.

$b = 7 - 3a$

$2a + 2b = 2$

Name: ______________________________ Date: ______________

Practise: Solving Systems by Elimination

Section 5.4

Hint
The elimination method starts by stacking two equations so that one variable can be eliminated.

1. Solve by elimination.

a) $2x + 5y = 30$ ① $4x - 5y = 0$ ②

Step 1: Check whether one of the variables can be eliminated by simply adding or subtracting the equations.

______________ the equations will eliminate the variable ___.

Step 2: Add or subtract, then solve for the remaining variable.

$2x + 5y = 30$ ①
$4x - 5y = 0$ ②

=

=

Step 3: Substitute this value for the variable into ① and solve for the other variable. Check by solving ② for this variable in the same way.

$2x + 5y = 30$ ① Check: $4x - 5y = 0$ ②

Therefore, the solution to the linear system is (,).

b) $3x + 4y = 22$ ① $3x - y = 17$ ②

Step 1: ________________ ② from ① will eliminate the variable _____.

Step 2: $3x + 4y = 22$ ①
$3x - y = 17$ ②

Step 3: Check:

Therefore, the solution to the linear system is (,).

continued ....

Name: ______________________________ Date: ______________

Section 5.4

2. Solve by elimination.

a) $6x + 5y = 32$ ① $3x + 2y = 14$ ②

Step 1: Can one of the variables be eliminated by simply adding or subtracting the equations? _______

If not, look for multiples of the equations that can be added or subtracted to eliminate one of the variables.

The *easiest* choice is to multiply ② by _______.

_______________ this multiple from ① will eliminate the variable _______.

Step 2: Add or subtract, then solve for the remaining variable.

$6x + 5y = 32$ ①

② × ____: __________

Step 3: Substitute into ① and ② and solve for the other variable.

$6x + 5y = 32$ ① Check: $3x + 2y = 14$ ②

Therefore, the solution to the linear system is (,).

b) $-2x + 3y = 13$ ① $4x + 5y = 51$ ②

Therefore, the solution to the linear system is (,).

Name: ______________________ Date: ______________

Chapter 5 Review

Chapter 5 Review

The date of the Chapter 5 test is ______________.
Use these questions to check whether you are ready for this test.
For help preparing for the chapter test, see the study tips on pages x–xii.

5.1 Solve Linear Equations with Technology, textbook pages 168–174

1. Use the standard window setting to graph each linear system with a graphing calculator. Then, use the **intersect** function to solve each system.

a) $y = 2x - 5$
$y = x + 1$
(,)

b) $y = -3x + 5$
$y = x - 7$
(,)

c) $y = 4x - 6$
$y = 2x + 1$
(,)

5.2 Solutions to Linear Systems, textbook pages 175–181

2. For each linear system, determine which ordered pair is the correct solution.

a) $2x + y = 10$
$3x - y = 10$
(2, 4) or (4, 2)

b) $x - 2y = 0$
$-x + 3y = 3$
(0, 0) or (6, 3)

3. Graph this pair of linear equations. Then, find the coordinates of the point of intersection.
$y = x - 3$
$y = -2x$

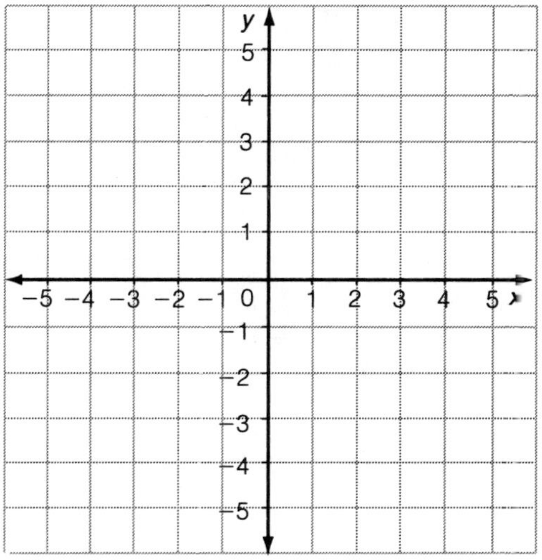

The point of intersection is (,)

continued ....

Name: ______________________________ Date: ______________

Chapter 5 Review

5.3 Solve Linear Systems by Substitution, textbook pages 182–188

4. Solve this linear system by substitution. Check your solution.

$3x - y = 40$ ① $\qquad 5x + 3y = 440$ ②

Check:

Therefore, the solution to the linear system is (,).

5.4 Solve Linear Systems by Elimination, textbook pages 189–196

5. Solve this linear system by elimination. Check your solution.

$150x + 950y = 93\,000$ ① $\qquad 300x + 800y = 87\,000$ ②

Check:

Therefore, the solution to the linear system is (,).

Name: ______________________ Date: ____________

Rich Problem: Hamburger Fundraising

Chapter 5
Rich Problem

Your high school is hosting the provincial volleyball championships. You have been asked to determine whether selling hamburgers at the games could help pay for the costs of the tournament. You find that

- the cost for renting a large gas barbecue for the three-day tournament is \$150, including fuel and taxes
- the ingredients and trimmings (beef, buns, lettuce, condiments, and so on) will cost about 50¢ per hamburger
- hamburgers priced at \$2 each sold well at other schools

1. Write an equation for the total *cost*, *C*, of providing hamburgers at the tournament Let *x* represent the number of hamburgers.

$C =$ _______ + _______

2. Write an equation for the *income*, *I*, generated by selling hamburgers for \$2 each at the tournament.

$I =$ _______

3. a) Graph the equations for the cost and income for up to 400 hamburgers. Draw the graph by hand on the grid below, or use a graphing calculator. If you use a graphing calculator, list your window settings and sketch the resulting graph.

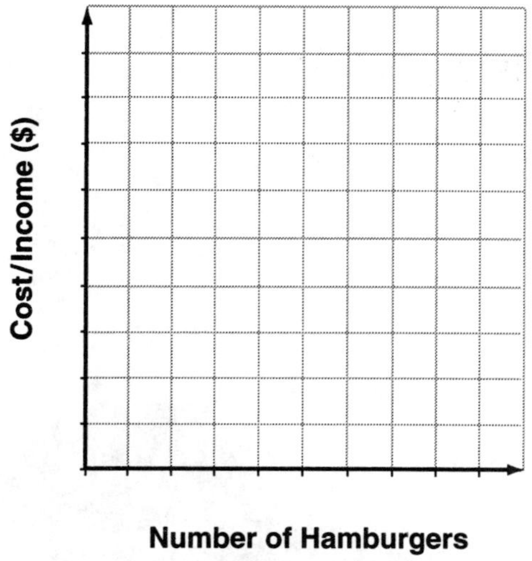


```
WINDOW
 Xmin=
 Xmax=
 Xscl=
 Ymin=
 Ymax=
 Yscl=
 Xres=1
```

Hint
To review finding the point of intersection with a graphing calculator, see page 408 of the textbook.

b) List the coordinates of the point of intersection: (,)

c) How are the cost and income related at the point of intersection?

continued ....

Name: ______________________________ Date: ______________

4. Use the substitution method to confirm the break-even point shown on your graph.

At the break-even point, $y = C =$ _______.

Therefore, _______ + _______ = _______.

Therefore, the break-even point is (,).

5. Use the elimination method to check your answer to question 4.
Stack your equations: ①
②

Solve for x:

Therefore, the break-even point is (,).

6. a) Write and simplify an equation for the profit, P, on the hamburgers.

$P = I - C$

$P =$ _______ − (_______ + _______)

$P =$

b) Explain how you could use the profit equation to find the break-even point.

Name: ______________________________ Date: ______________

CHAPTER 6 Similar Triangles

Get Set

Answer these questions to check your understanding of the Get Ready concepts on pages 204–205 of the *Mathematics: Applying the Concepts* 10 textbook.

Ratios

1. Express each ratio in lowest terms.

a) 15:45 **b)** 28:18 **c)** 9:12:15 **d)** 50:150:75

Powers and Square Roots

2. Evaluate mentally.

a) $\sqrt{64}$ **b)** 11^2 **c)** $\sqrt{144}$ **d)** 40^2 **e)** $\sqrt{3600}$

Solving Equations

3. Solve for the variable(s) in each proportion.

a) $\frac{10}{m} = \frac{2}{7}$ **b)** $\frac{x}{6} = \frac{5}{18}$ **c)** $\frac{u}{4} = \frac{10}{v} = \frac{2}{8}$

4. Solve.

a) $a^2 = 25$ **b)** $x^2 - 3 = 6$ **c)** $c^2 + 8^2 = 10^2$ **d)** $n^2 - 2^2 = 8^2$

Correspondence

5. Complete these statements about the two similar triangles.

∠L corresponds to ∠_____.

∠M corresponds to ∠_____.

∠N corresponds to ∠_____.

Side LM corresponds to side _______.

Side MN corresponds to side _______.

Side LN corresponds to side _______.

ΔLMN is similar to Δ_______.

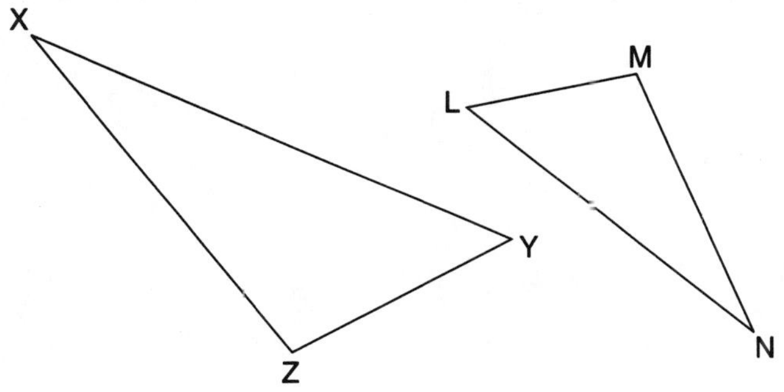

Name: ____________________ Date: ____________

6.1 Explore Similar Triangles

Textbook pp. 206–214

Warm Up

1. Number Sense

John tries to find 40% of 200. His calculator screen shows 8000. Why does this answer seem unreasonable?

2. Mental Math/Estimating

Estimate the cost, before taxes, to buy 28 pens at $1.09 each.

3. Proportional Reasoning

A clothing store finds that its sales in January usually drop about 60% from its sales in December. This store sold 1820 pairs of socks last December. Estimate the number of socks sold in January.

4. Relations and Functions

On a graph, a filled-in circle at the end of a line segment means that the segment ____________ that point.

An __________ circle indicates that the point is not part of the line segment.

5. Algebra

Solve for x.

$3x + x = 180$

6. Graphs and Tables

This table shows the time a furniture maker takes to make Muskoka chairs.

Number of Chairs	Time (h)
8	12
16	24
24	36
32	48

Making 12 chairs takes ______ h.

7. Math Literacy

The square root of n is the number that gives n when multiplied by __________.

8. Previous Section

Solve this system by elimination.

$3a + 4b = 11$

$3a + b = 5$

Name: ______________________________ Date: ______________

Practise: Similar Triangles

Section 6.1

In geometry, the word *similar* has a particular meaning. Similar triangles have the same ____________ but not necessarily the same ________.

1. Find the measure of ∠L, ∠M, and ∠T given that ΔLMN ~ ΔRST.

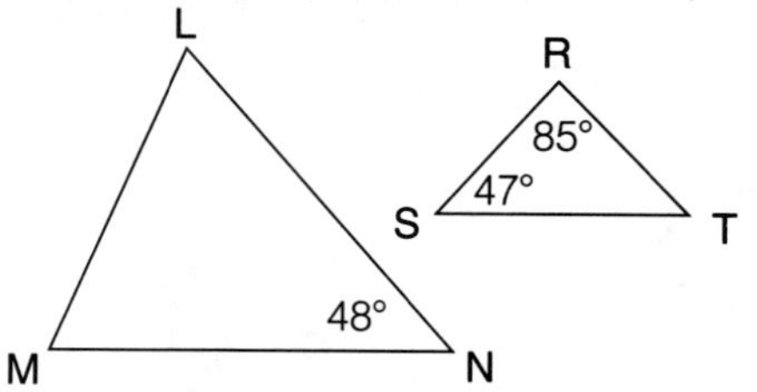

Hint
The ~ symbol means that two shapes are similar.

In similar triangles, the ________________ angles are equal.

So, ∠L = ∠_____ = _____°, ∠M = ∠_____ = _____°, and

∠T = ∠_____ = _____°.

2. These two cottage lots are similar triangles. Find the lengths of sides *y* and *f*.

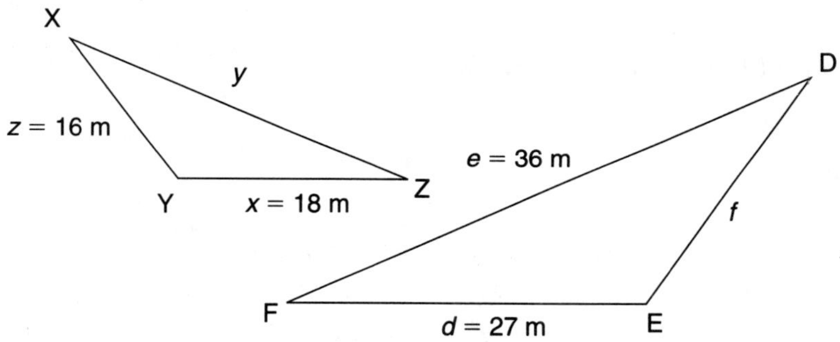

Hint
Remember that *x* represents the side opposite ∠X, *y* is opposite ∠Y, and so on.

In similar triangles, the ________________ sides are proportional.

Here, *x* corresponds to *d*, *y* corresponds to _____, and _____ corresponds to *f*.

Write the proportion: $\frac{x}{d} = \frac{y}{\square} = \frac{}{f}$

Substitute the known lengths: $\frac{18}{\square} = \frac{y}{\square} = \frac{\square}{f}$

$\frac{18}{\square} = \frac{y}{36}$ and $\frac{18}{\square} = \frac{16}{f}$

$\frac{18 \times 36}{\square} = y$ $\qquad$ ____$f = 16 \times \square$

_____ $= y$ $\qquad$ $f = \frac{16 \times \square}{\square}$

$f =$ _____

Hint
The numerators are the side lengths of one triangle, and the denominators are the side lengths of the other triangle.

Hint
Remember to give the units in your concluding statement.

continued ....

Name: ______________________ Date: ____________

Section 6.1

3. This house and garden shed were built with similar shapes.

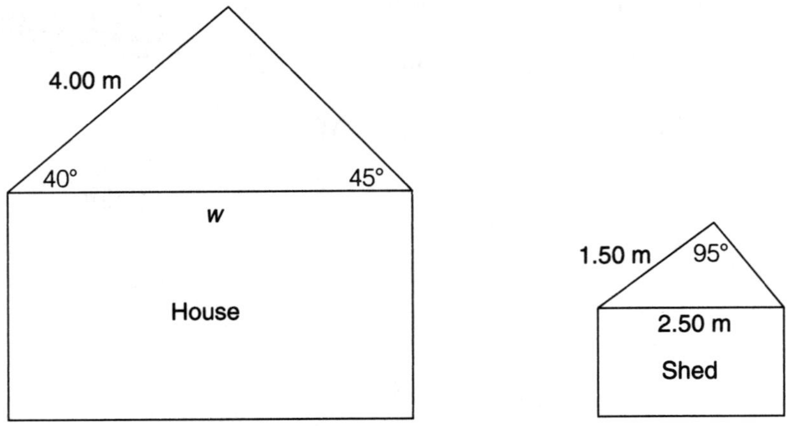

a) Find the angle at the top of the roof of the house. Explain your reasoning.

b) Describe another way to find the answer to part a).

c) How wide is the house?

4. Gerald wants to build a platform so that he has a level surface to work on while shingling the roof shown below. For the platform to be level, the profiles of the platform and the roof must be similar triangles. How high should he make the platform, to the nearest centimetre?

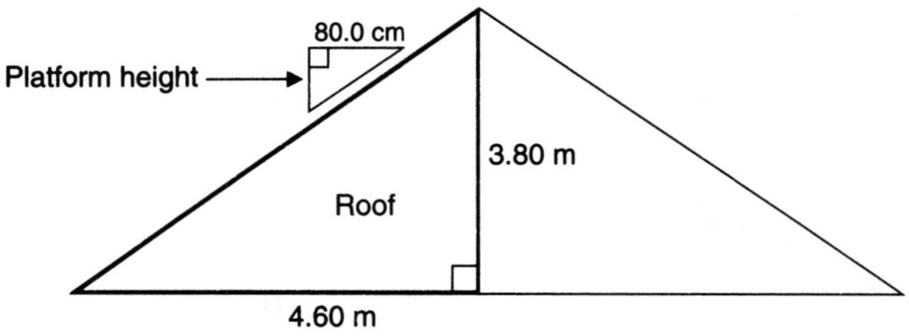

Name: ______________________ Date: ______________

6.2 Apply Similar Triangles

Textbook pp. 215–223

Warm Up

1. Number Sense

Show that -1 is not a square root of itself.

2. Mental Math/Estimating

Estimate to one decimal place.

$\sqrt{40} =$ $\sqrt{32} =$

3. Proportional Reasoning

A 1:80 scale model of a sailboat is 6.4 cm wide. How wide is the actual sailboat?

4. Relations and Functions

Determine whether the point (2, 3) is on the line defined by $y = 3x - 3$.

L.S. = **R.S.** =

5. Algebra

Write an equation to show how the three interior angles of a triangle are related.

$\angle A + \angle B + \angle C =$ ______°

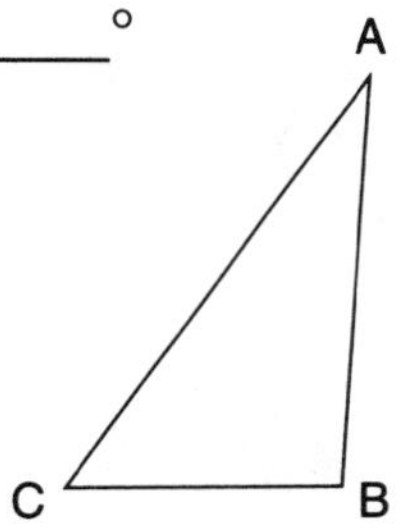

6. Graphs and Tables

This distance-time graph shows

A an increasing speed

B a decreasing speed

C a constant speed

D no information about speed

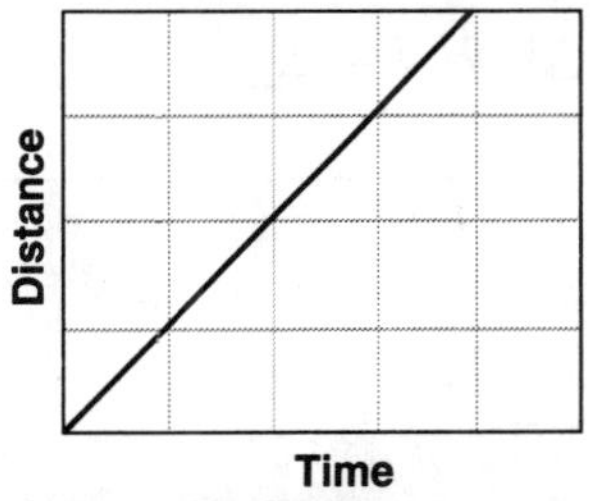

7. Math Literacy

The point on the Cartesian plane where the axes meet is the ____________.

8. Previous Section

List the angles that are equal in these two similar triangles.

$\angle X = \angle$___

$\angle Y = \angle$___

$\angle Z = \angle$___

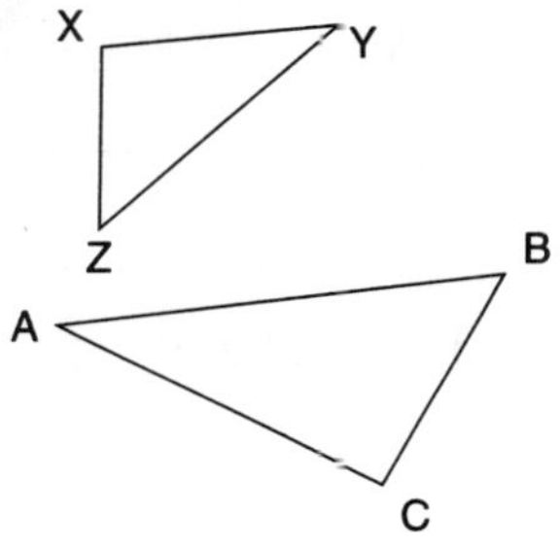

Name: ____________________ Date: ____________

Practise: Applying Similar Triangles

Section 6.2

1. a) In ΔABC, $\angle A = 25°$ and $\angle B = 75°$. Find the measure of $\angle C$.

$\angle C =$ _____° − (_____° + _____°)

= _____° − _____°

= _____°

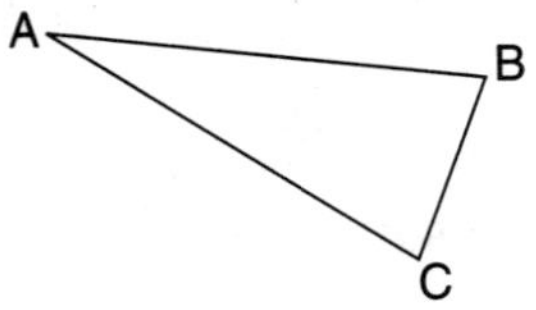

b) ΔDEF has $\angle D = 25°$ and $\angle E = 75°$. Find the measure of $\angle F$.

$\angle F =$

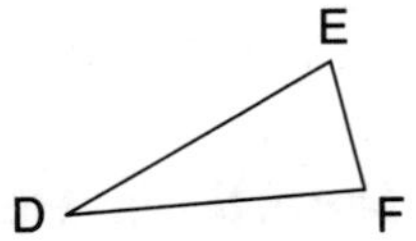

c) How is $\angle C$ related to $\angle F$? ____________________

d) How is ΔABC related to ΔDEF? ____________________

e) What can you conclude if two angles of one triangle are equal to two angles of another triangle?

2. How long is the bridge in this diagram?

The width of the bridge is represented by line segment _____.
When straight lines intersect, the opposite angles are __________. So, $\angle XWY = \angle$_____.
$\angle X =$ _____° and $\angle V =$ _____°, so $\angle X$ _____ $\angle V$.
Therefore, $\Delta UWV \sim \Delta$_______ and their corresponding sides are ____________________:

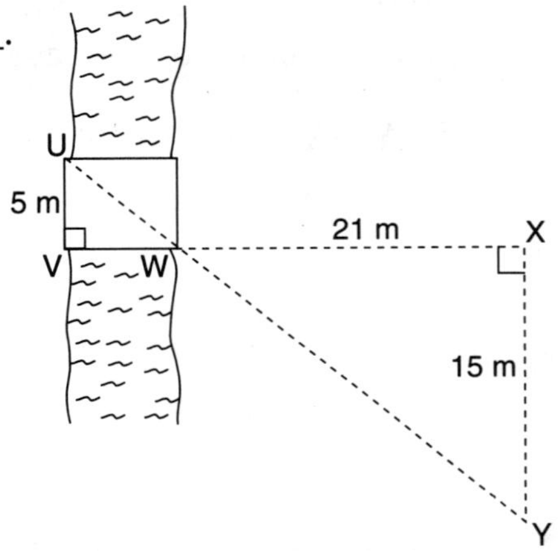

$$\frac{VW}{XW} = \frac{UV}{\square}$$

$$\frac{VW}{21} = \frac{\square}{\square}$$

$$VW = \frac{\square \times 21}{\square}$$

VW = ________

The bridge is__________ m wide.

Hint
When naming similar triangles, list the corresponding angles in the same order for both triangles.

continued ....

Name: ______________________________ Date: ____________

Section 6.2

3. Nico measured the length (RS) of the shadow of a tower (ST) while Timo measured the length (UV) of the shadow of a metre stick (VW). Use their measurements to calculate the height of the tower. (Hint: The rays from the sun are parallel.)

When a straight line crosses parallel lines, the corresponding angles (F-pattern) are ____________.

So, $\angle U = \angle$_____.

Also, $\angle WVU$ and $\angle TSR$ are both _____°,

so $\angle WVU$ ___ $\angle TSR$.

Therefore, Δ_________ ~ Δ __________.

Their ______________________ sides are proportional, so

$$\frac{ST}{\square} = \frac{\square}{\square}$$

____ (ST) = (____)(____)

ST = ____

The height of the tower is __________ ____.

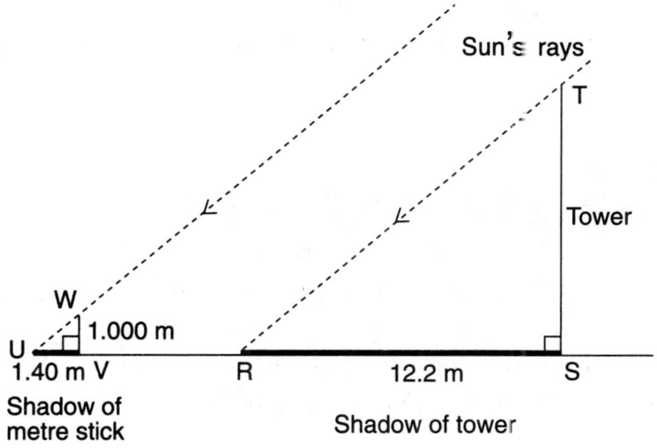

4. A triangular building lot is fenced on all three sides as shown in the diagram. A path runs through the lot, parallel to one of the sides. How long is this path?

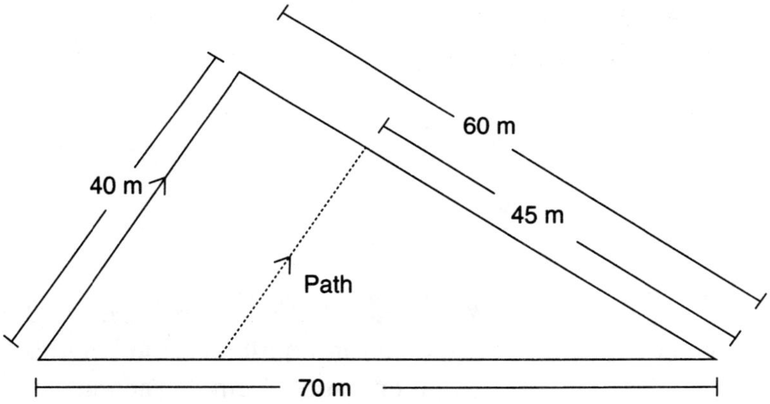

Hint
Look for a pair of similar triangles that include the same angle.

Name: ______________________ Date: ______________

6.3 The Pythagorean Relation

Textbook pp. 224-230

Warm Up

1. Number Sense

Continue the pattern.

1, 4, 9, 16, ___, ___, ___

Describe the pattern.

2. Mental Math/Estimating

Nevell worked 12.25 h at $7.75 per hour. His broken calculator gave the answer 949375 when he tried to calculate his earnings. Where should the missing decimal point be?

3. Proportional Reasoning

The sides of a triangle are 5 cm, 12 cm, and 13 cm. How long is each side if the triangle is enlarged by a factor of 3?

4. Relations and Functions

Find the slope of this line.

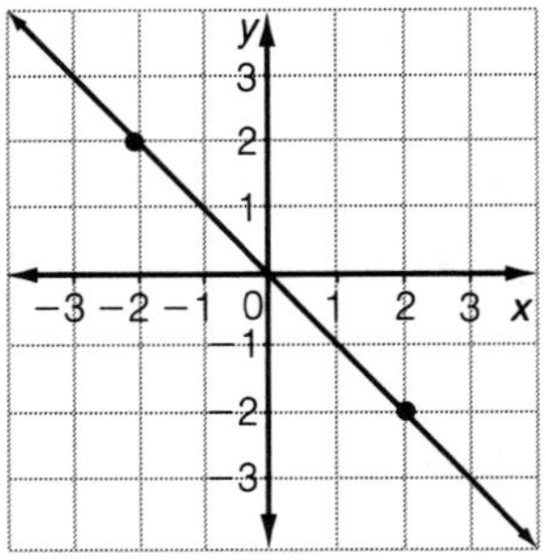

5. Algebra

Solve for d.

$2(d + 3) = 4d - (3d - 7)$

6. Graphs and Tables

Write the coordinates for the origin of the Cartesian plane.

(,)

7. Math Literacy

Explain what a small business owner means when she talks about her company's *break-even point*.

8. Previous Section

A triangle for a quilt has side lengths 4 cm, 6 cm, and 16 cm. A second triangle has side lengths 6 cm, 9 cm, and 24 cm. Show that the triangles are similar.

Name: ______________________________ Date: ______________

Practise: The Pythagorean Relation

Section 6.3

Use the word list to fill in the blanks.

The area of the ____________ placed on the ____________ side of any right triangle is equal to the ____________ of the ____________ of the squares placed on the other ____________ sides.

The Pythagorean Relation applies only to ____________ triangles.

Word List
- areas
- longest
- right
- square
- sum
- two

1. Find the length of the unknown side in each triangle. Round to the same precision as the known lengths.

a)

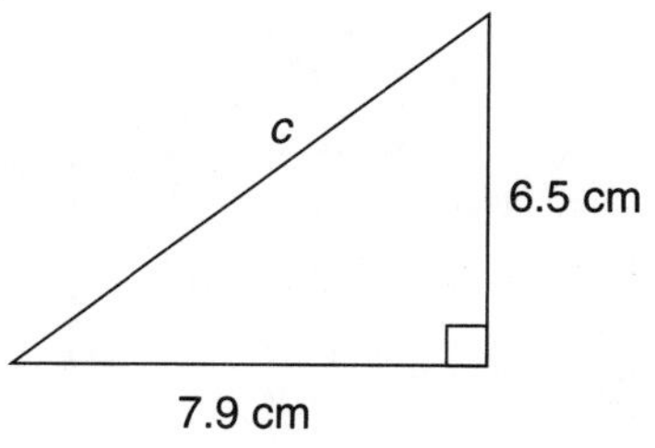

b)

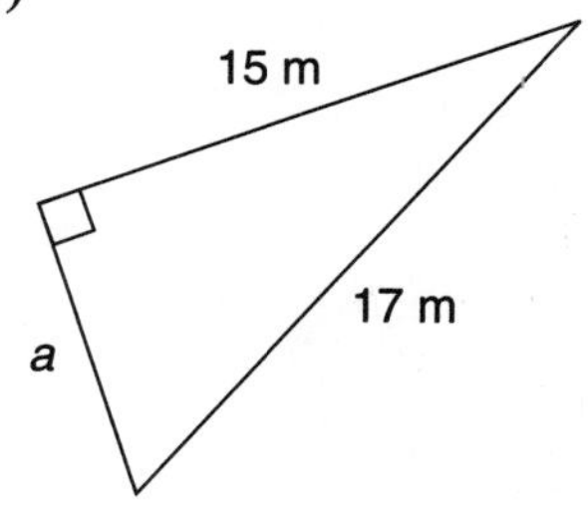

a) Identify the hypotenuse: ______

Apply the Pythagorean Relation: ______$^2 = 6.5^2 + 7.92$

Simplify: ______$^2 =$ ______ + ______

______$^2 =$ ______

Take the square root of both sides: ______ $= \pm\sqrt{\_\_\_\_\_\_}$

Round to ________ decimal place: ______ = ______

Reject the negative value since c represents a ____________.

The length of side c is _______ cm.

Hint
The hypotenuse is the longest side and is always located opposite the right angle.

b) Identify the hypotenuse: ______

Apply the Pythagorean Relation: ______$^2 = 15^2 +$ ______^{2}

Simplify: ______ = 225 + ______^{2}

Isolate the variable: ______ − ______ = 225 − ______ + ______^{2}

______ = ______^{2}

Take the square root of both sides: $\pm\sqrt{\_\_\_\_\_\_}$ = ______

Reject the negative value: ______ = ______

Therefore, the length of side a is _______ m.

continued ....

Name: ______________________ Date: ______________

Section 6.3

2. Maurits, a master carpenter, is measuring a room to check that the walls meet at right angles. He found that the room is 2.90 m wide with a diagonal of 4.32 m. How long will the room be if the corner angles are 90°? Round to the same precision as the given values.

Mark the known values on this diagram and label the unknown side.

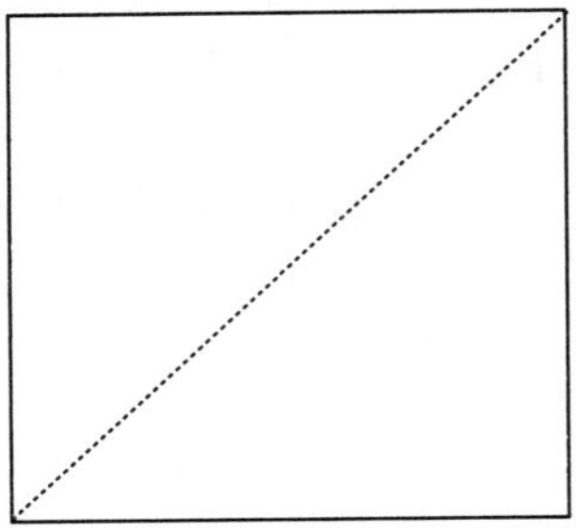

Apply the Pythagorean Relation to write an equation.

Then, solve for the unknown length.

Write a concluding sentence:

3. Jill and Micu both live in cottages on the shore of a lake. To walk to Micu's home, Jill has to travel along a straight road for 3.5 km, and then along a perpendicular road for another 2.5 km.

a) How far is it from Jill's home to Micu's by road?

Hint
Use this triangle to remember the formulas for speed, time, and distance:

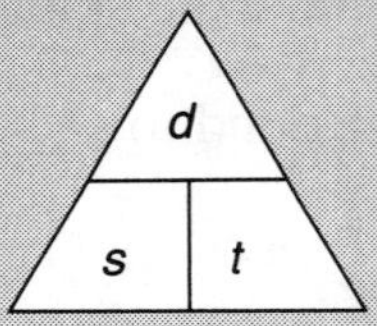

b) Jill walks about 3.0 km/h. How long does it take her to walk from her place to Micu's?

c) Jill could canoe directly to Micu's. How far is it to Micu's by water?

d) How fast does Jill have to paddle in order to reach Micu's home in less time than walking?

Name: ______________________________ Date: ______________

6.4 Similar Right Triangles: Pythagorean Triples

Textbook pp. 231-235

Warm Up

1. Number Sense

In a 5-km road race, Juan's time was 23:16 (23 min 16 s). If Juan ran at a constant pace, what was his time at the halfway point?

2. Mental Math/Estimating

Estimate how long it would take to fly 2650 km at 615 km/h.

3. Proportional Reasoning

What percent of this lot is paved?

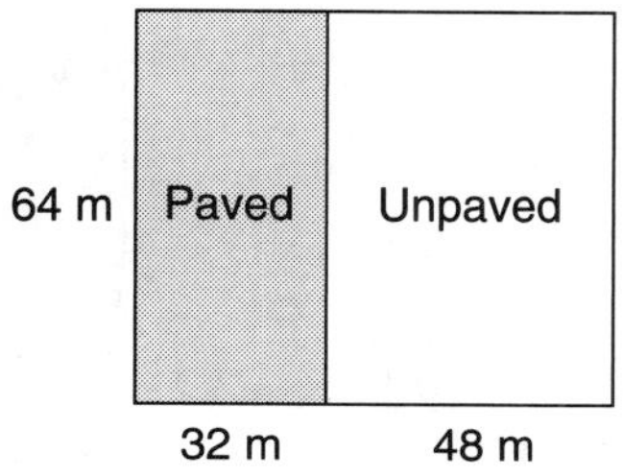

4. Relations and Functions

Do these data have a linear relation?

Speed (km/h)	Fine ($)	First Difference
80	0	
100	50	
120	150	
140	350	

5. Algebra

Find the volume of a sphere with a radius of 2.5 cm. Round to the nearest unit.

$V = \frac{4}{3}\pi r^3$

6. Graphs and Tables

Sketch a graph of the data in question 4.

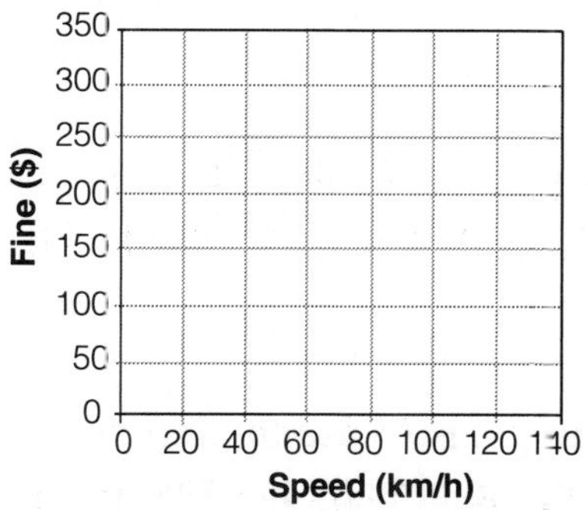

7. Math Literacy

Interpolate means

A estimate between two points on a graph
B estimate beyond the range of the data
C take a poll of a particular group
D translate from another language

8. Previous Section

Determine x.

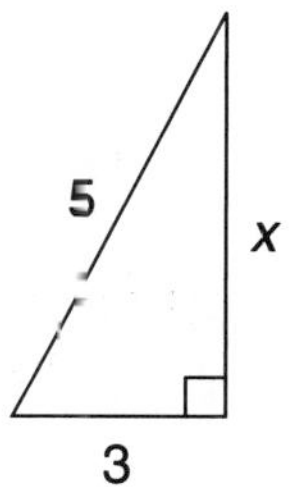

Name: ______________________ Date: ______________

Practise: Pythagorean Triples

Section 6.4

A Pythagorean Triple is a set of three ____________ numbers, $\{a, b, c\}$, that satisfy the equation $c^2 =$ _____ + _____.

1. Determine which sets of numbers are Pythagorean Triples.

a) $\{8, 15, 17\}$ **b)** $\{9, 40, 41\}$ **c)** $\{18, 80, 82\}$

$c^2 = 17^2$

$c^2 =$ _______

$a^2 + b^2 = 8^2 + 15^2$

$a^2 + b^2 =$ _______

c^2 ____ $a^2 + b^2$

Hint
You can use a shortcut for part **c)**.

2. A picture frame measures 60 cm by 80 cm. The diagonal is 100 cm. Are the corners of this frame square?

Hint
Triangles whose sides form a Pythagorean Triple always contain a right angle.

3. How far is Bailly from the crossroads?

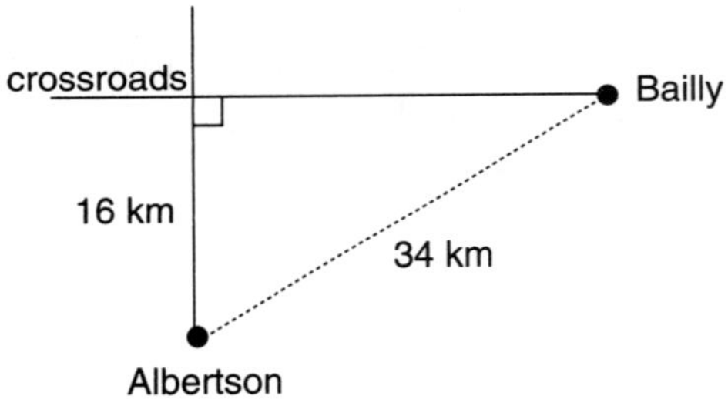

4. Liam plans to use three ropes to lay out the right angles for a beach volleyball court. He already has two ropes, one 10 m long and the other 24 m.

a) How long should the third rope be?

b) Describe how Liam can use the three ropes to draw the right angle.

Name: ____________________ Date: ____________

Chapter 6 Review

Chapter 6 Review

The date of the Chapter 6 test is ____________________.
Use these questions to check whether you are ready for this test.
For help preparing for the chapter test, see the study tips on pages x–xii.

6.1 Explore Similar Triangles, textbook pages 206–214

1. Which of these pairs of triangles is similar? Explain.

a)

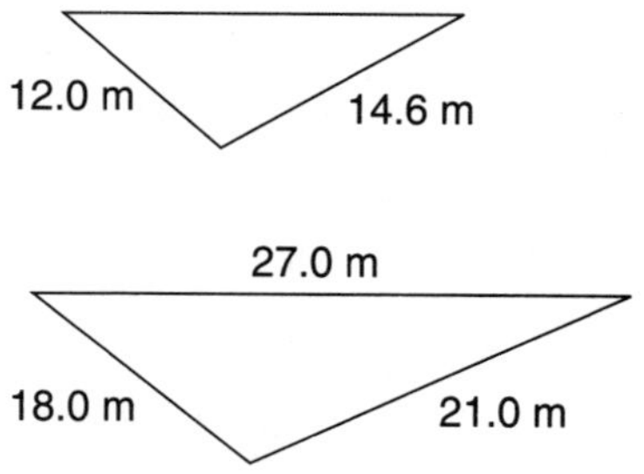

b)

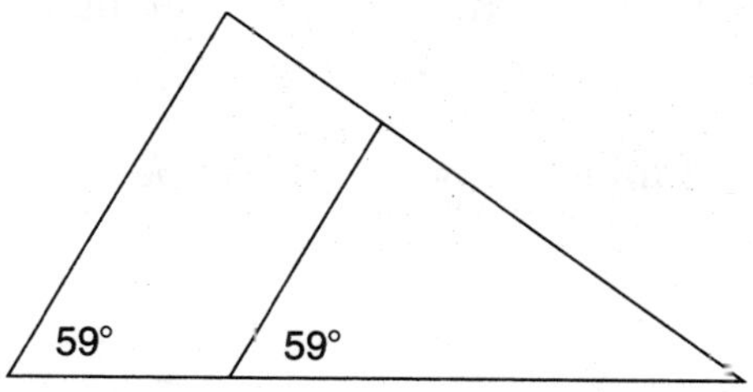

6.2 Apply Similar Triangles, textbook pages 215–223

2. Erin made an emergency landing in a grassy field. She knows that she can fly her small plane out of the field safely only if the trees at the end are less than 15 m tall. When she sits 20.0 m from the base of the trees and 2.5 m from her mechanic, she can just see the top of the trees over the mechanic's head. Her eyes are 0.40 m from the ground and her mechanic is 1.85 m tall.

a) Fill in the dimensions on this diagram.

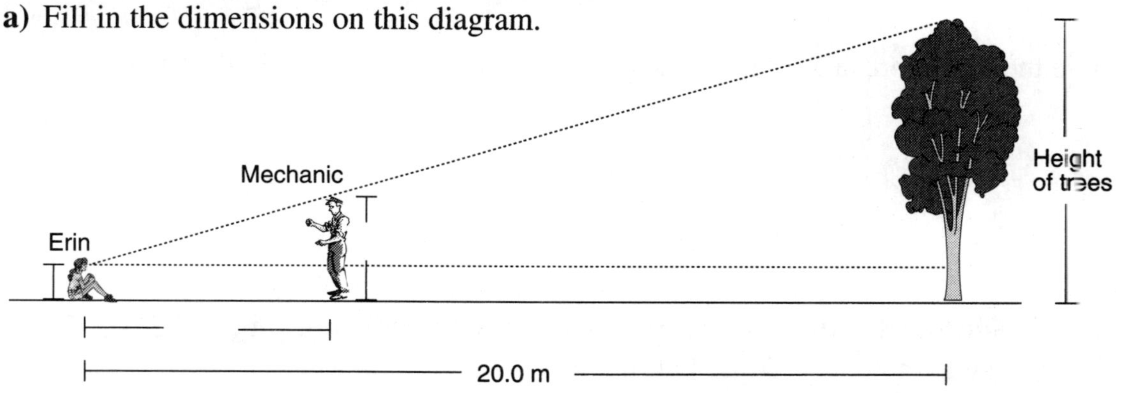

b) Should Erin try to fly out of the field? Show the calculations for your answer.

continued ....

3. A caretaker wants to replace a missing rope on a flagpole. She placed a mirror on level ground 10 m from the pole. When she stood 2.0 m further away from the flagpole she could see the reflection of the top of the pole in the mirror. The distance from the ground to her eyes is 1.7 m. (Hint: Light rays reflect from a mirror at an angle equal to the angle at which they strike it.)

a) Complete this diagram.

b) What assumption are you making about the flagpole?

c) Determine the height of the pole.

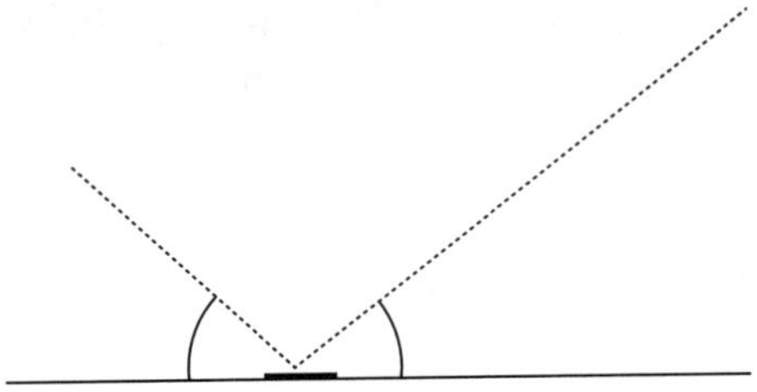

6.3 The Pythagorean Relation, textbook pages 224–230

4. The opening at the back of a delivery truck is 2.20 m high by 1.80 m wide. The height of a huge picture that needs to be moved is 288 cm.

a) Draw a diagram of the opening at the back of the truck. Show the diagonal of the opening, and label the known lengths.

b) Use the Pythagorean Relation to determine if the picture will fit in the truck.

6.4 Similar Right Triangles: Pythagorean Triples, textbook pages 231–235

5. Find c for the Pythagorean Triple $\{11, 60, c\}$.

6. What can you conclude about the corners of a tray that has dimensions 45 cm by 60 cm and diagonal 73 cm? Explain.

Name: ______________________________ Date: ______________

Rich Problem: Designing a Cable Slide

Chapter 6 Rich Problem

Northern Ontario Sporting Thrills is building a cable slide over a river. They want you to determine the length of the cable needed and its cost.

Their staff measured the height of the cliff by lowering a weighted rope over the edge. However, they had no way of directly measuring the width of the river. To solve this problem, you make the measurements shown in the aerial view.

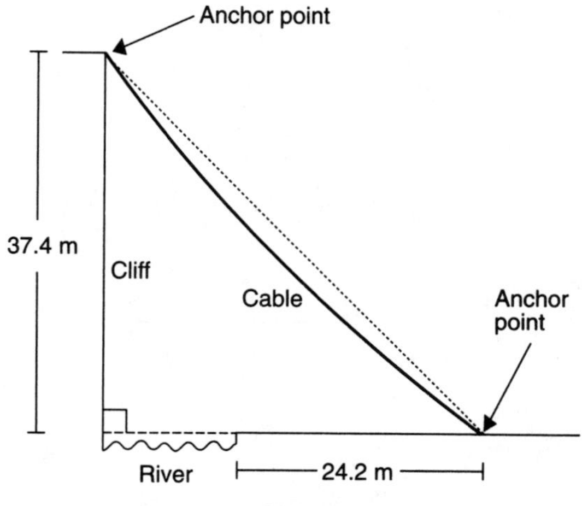

Side View

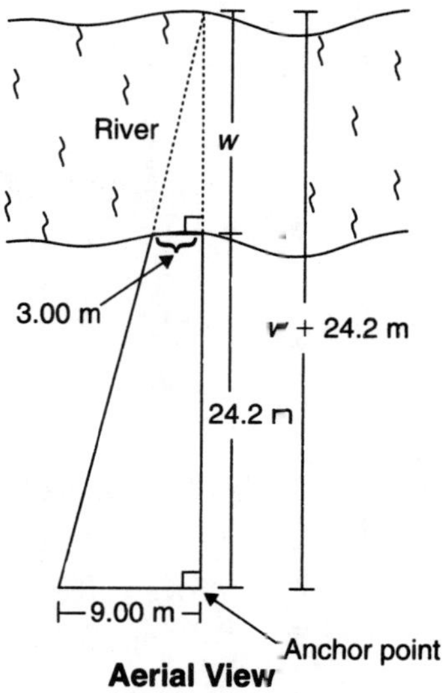

Aerial View

1. Use similar triangles to find the width of the river.

2. How far is the lower anchor point from the bottom of the cliff?

3. Find the distance, d, between the two anchor points.

continued ....

Name: ______________________ Date: ______________

Chapter 6 Rich Problem

4. The cable cannot be pulled perfectly straight. It will always sag a little. The sag will be greatest halfway between the anchor points. To make sure that you do not underestimate the length of the cable, allow for 3 m of sag. Use this diagram to estimate the length, l, of the cable. Round to the next whole metre.

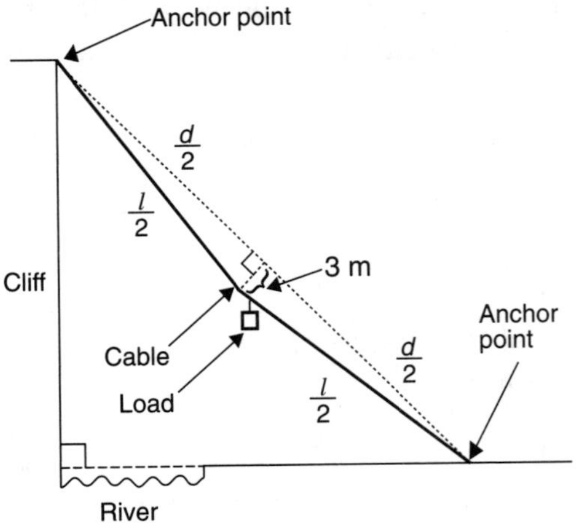

5. The cable costs $12.50 per metre including all taxes. You will need an extra metre of cable at each end to secure it safely. How much should the company budget for the cable?

Name: ____________________ Date: ____________

CHAPTER 7 Trigonometry

Get Set

Answer these questions to check your understanding of the Get Ready concepts on pages 248–249 of the *Mathematics: Applying the Concepts 10* textbook.

Evaluating Expressions

1. Evaluate, without using a calculator.

a) $6^2 =$ **b)** $0.8^2 =$ **c)** $\sqrt{49} =$ **d)** $\sqrt{1} =$

2. Evaluate, using a calculator. Round to two decimal places, if necessary.

a) $\sqrt{529} =$ **b)** $\sqrt{125} =$ **c)** $\frac{8.4}{4.8} =$ **d)** $\frac{32.0}{5.8} =$

Angle Relationships

3. Find the measure of each angle labelled with a letter.

a)

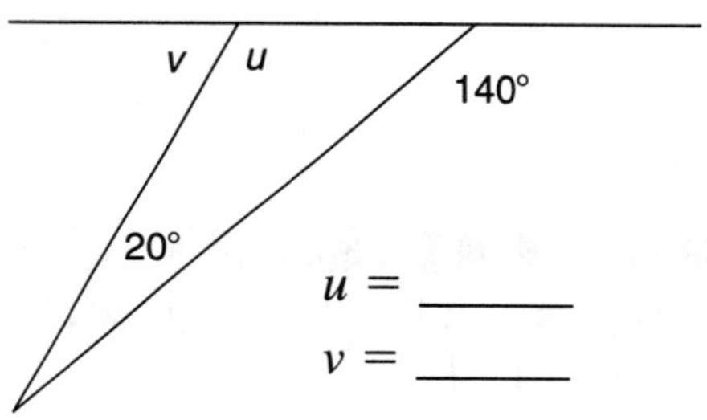

$u =$ ______

$v =$ ______

b)

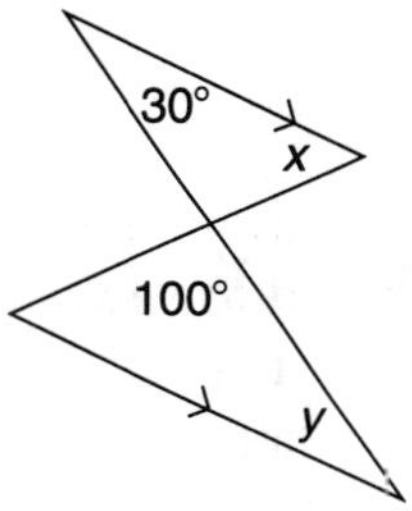

$x =$ ______

$y =$ ______

Solving Proportions

4. Solve each equation. Round to one decimal place, if necessary.

a) $\frac{a}{30} = \frac{45}{75}$ **b)** $\frac{120}{45} = \frac{210}{c}$ **c)** $\frac{12.8}{b} = \frac{9.2}{4.0}$

Pythagorean Relation

5. Find each unknown length. Round to one decimal place, if necessary.

a)

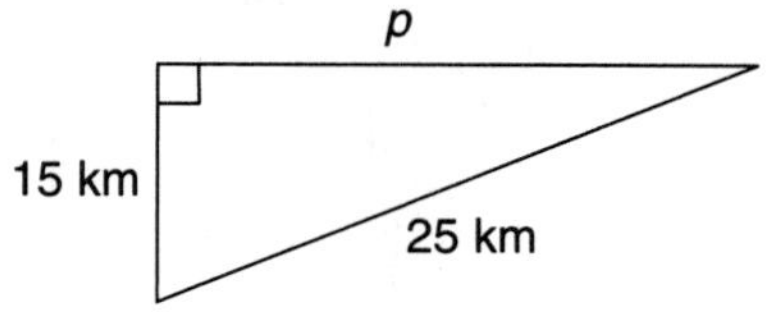

b)

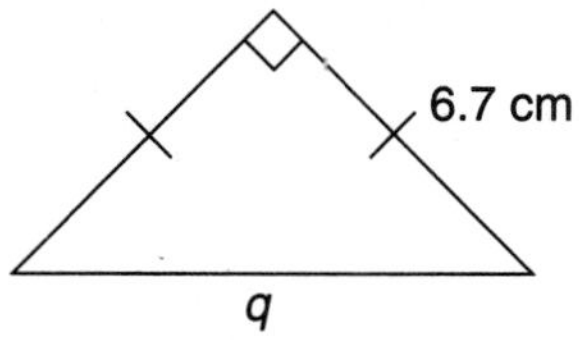

Name: ______________________ Date: ______________

7.1 Explore the Tangent Ratio

Textbook pp. 250–258

Warm Up

1. Number Sense

Without calculating the value of m, determine whether $\frac{m}{2.5} = \frac{16}{15}$ shows that

A $m < 2.5$ **B** $m = 2.5$

C $m > 2.5$ **D** $m < \frac{16}{15}$

2. Mental Math/Estimating

Estimate which whole number is closest to $\frac{181}{29}$.

3. Proportional Reasoning

Alan's keyboard speed is 45 words per minute. How many words can Alan type in an hour?

4. Relations and Functions

If $b = 6a$ when $0 \le a < 20$ and $b = 7a$ when $20 \le a \le 70$, what is the value of b when $a = 20$?

5. Algebra

The formula for simple interest is $I = Prt$. Find the value of t when $I = \$42$, $P = \$600$, and $r = 0.02$.

6. Graphs and Tables

How can you tell that Kimu walked slower after her rest?

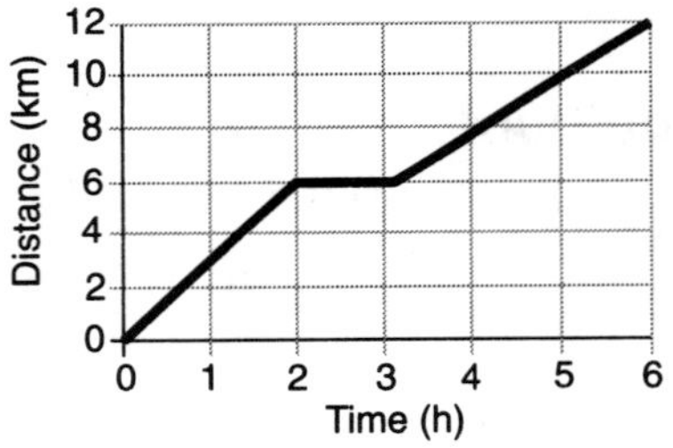

7. Math Literacy

In an ______________ triangle, each angle measures less than 90°.

8. Previous Section

Are the sides of this triangle a Pythagorean Triple?

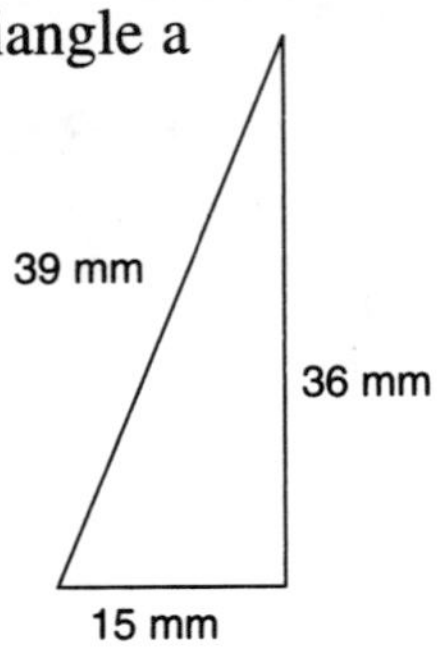

Name: ______________________ Date: ______________

Practise: The Tangent Ratio

Section 7.1

Mark the right angle symbol on ∠M. Then, label the hypotenuse of ΔLMN and the opposite and adjacent sides for ∠N.

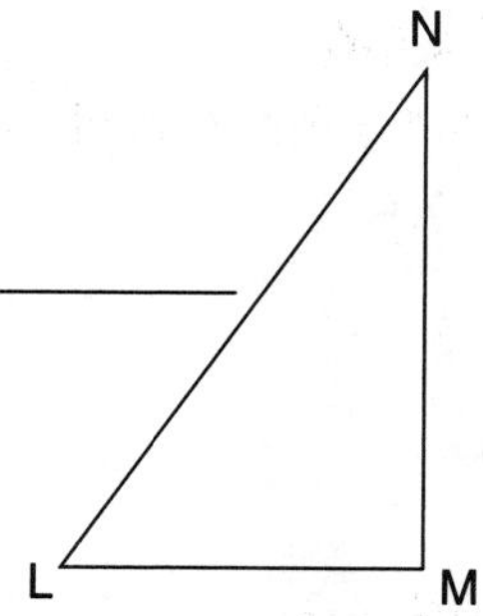

$\tan N = \dfrac{\text{opposite}}{\square}$

In ΔLMN, $\tan N = \dfrac{LM}{\square}$

Hint
Adjacent means beside.

1. a) Find the tangent of ∠A, to the nearest hundredth.

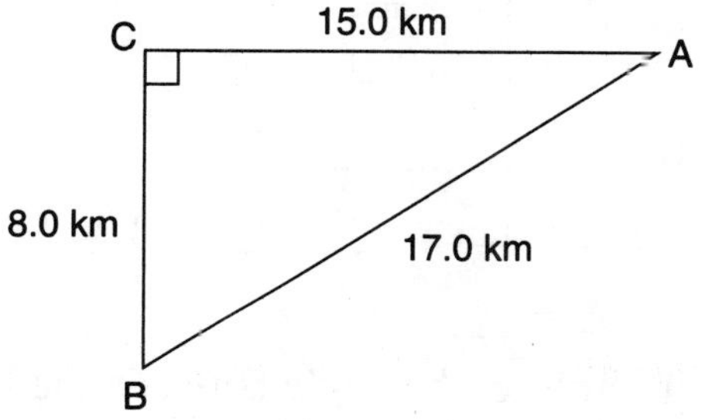

$\tan A = \dfrac{\square}{\text{adjacent}}$

For ∠A, the opposite side is ______ km long and the adjacent side is 15.0 km long.

Therefore, $\tan A = \dfrac{\square}{15.0}$

$\tan A = 0.$ _____

b) Using trigonometry, find the measure of ∠A, to the nearest degree.

∠A = tan^{-1}(________)

∠A ≐ _____°

Hint
On many calculators, you can calculate tan^{-1} by pressing 2nd or SHIFT, then the tan key. Make sure the calculator is in Degree mode.

c) Find the measure of ∠B to the nearest degree.

Method 1

$\tan B = \dfrac{\square}{\text{adjacent}}$

$\tan B = \dfrac{\square}{\square}$

tan B = _______

∠B = tan^{-1}(________)

∠B ≐ _____°

Method 2

∠A = _____° and ∠C = _____°

∠A + ∠B + ∠C = _____°

∠B = _____° − ∠___ − ∠___

∠B = _____° − _____° − _____°

∠B = _____°

continued ....

2. A helium balloon at one end of a long rope is blown by a strong wind to a position 280 m above a point on the ground 410 m from the other end of the rope.

a) Mark the known quantities on this diagram.

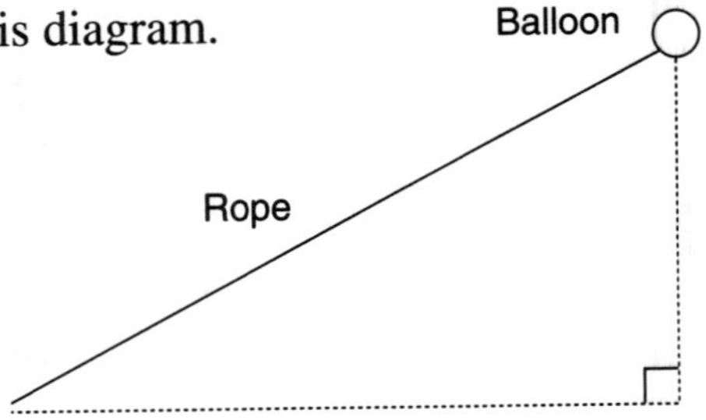

b) Find the angle between the rope and the ground, to the nearest degree.

Let ∠Z represent the angle between the rope and the ground. Label this angle on the diagram.

$\tan Z = \frac{\square}{\square}$

tan Z = __________

∠Z = $\tan^{-1}$ (__________)

∠Z ≐ ______°

Therefore, the angle between the rope and the ground measures about ______°.

c) What assumption did you have to make about the rope to solve this problem?

3. A hawk, hovering directly over a small bush, spots a mouse at an angle of 12° from the vertical. If the mouse is 8.2 m from the bush, how high is the hawk?

Let *h* represent the height of the hawk. Mark *h* on the diagram, and label the opposite and adjacent side for the 12° angle.

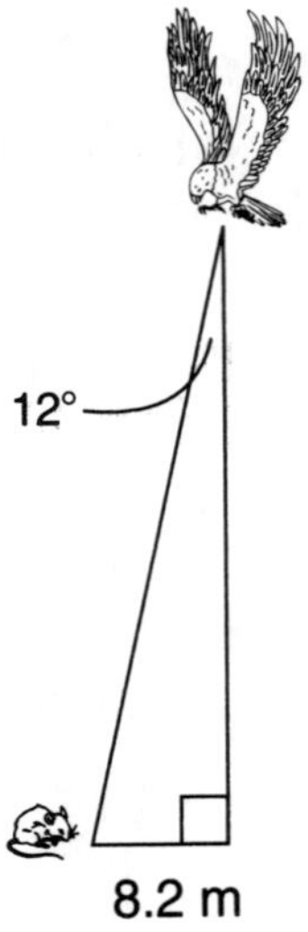

Substitute into the formula for the tangent ratio: $\tan 12° = \frac{\square}{\square}$

Solve for *h*:

Therefore, ______________________________________.

Name: ______________________ Date: ____________

7.2 Explore the Sine Ratio

Textbook pp. 259–265

Warm Up

1. Number Sense

Sketch a set of coins that total \$3.87.

2. Mental Math/Estimating

For the 2003 Ontario provincial election, 7.9 million people were eligible to vote, but only 57% of them did vote. Estimate the number of votes cast by rounding to the nearest 10% and to the nearest million.

____% of ___ million =

3. Proportional Reasoning

Solve for m. Round to two decimal places.

$\frac{m}{2.5} = \frac{16}{15}$

4. Relations and Functions

State the slope and y-intercept of the line defined by $y = 8 - 5x$.

Slope =

y-intercept =

5. Algebra

Solve the following linear system using the substitution method.

$y = 3x - 7$

$y = -2x + 8$

6. Graphs and Tables

Explain why this diagram might lead you to think that Nice'n White toothpaste outsells Everbright.

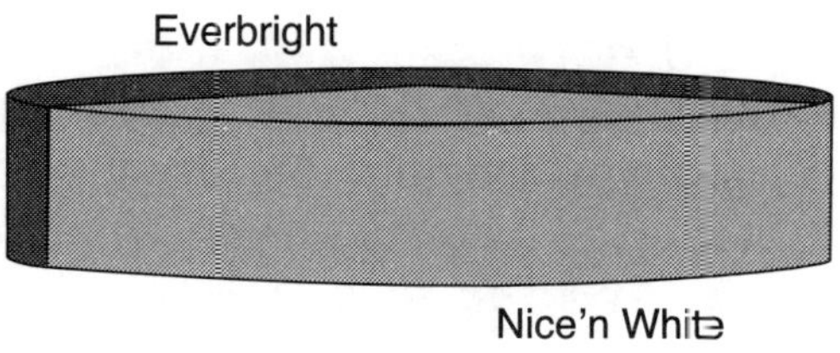

7. Math Literacy

The longest side of a right triangle is called the ______________________.

8. Previous Section

What angle has a tangent ratio of 2.2460?

Name: ______________________________ Date: ______________

Practise: The Sine Ratio

Section 7.2

The abbreviation for the tangent ratio is ______ and the abbreviation for the sine ratio is ______.

These two ratios have the same numerator, but different ______________________:

$\tan X = \dfrac{\text{opposite}}{\square}$ while $\sin X = \dfrac{\square}{\square}$

In ΔXYZ, $\tan X = \dfrac{YZ}{\square}$ and $\sin X = \dfrac{\square}{\square}$.

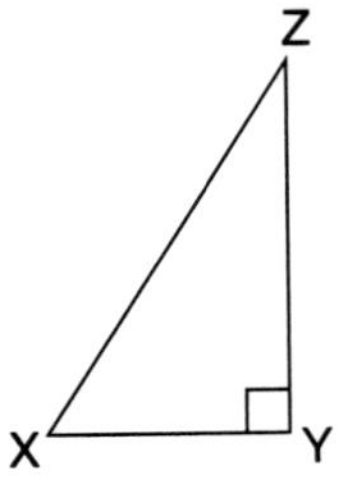

1. a) Calculate sin U, to four decimal places.

For $\angle U$, the opposite side is side ______.

In ΔUVW, the hypotenuse is side ______.

Use the Pythagorean Relation to find the length of the hypotenuse:

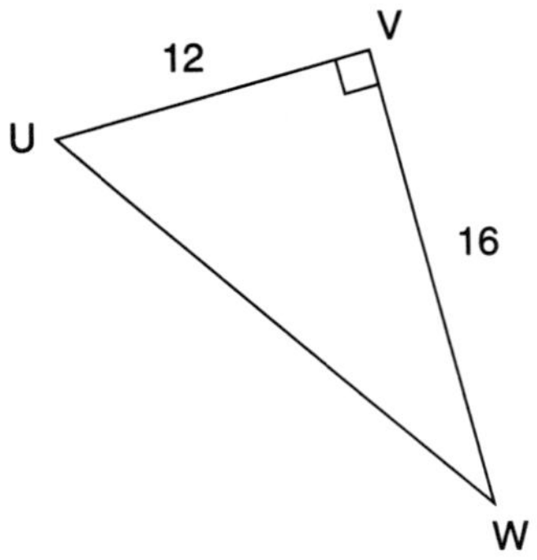

$v^2 =$ ________^{2} + ________^{2}

$v =$ ________

Substitute into the formula for the sine ratio: $\sin U = \dfrac{\square}{\square}$

b) Find the measure of $\angle U$, to the nearest degree.

$\angle U = \sin^{-1}($ __________ $)$

$\angle U =$ ________°

c) Can you determine the sine ratio for $\angle V$? Explain.

Hint
For $\angle V$, the opposite side and hypotenuse are the same side.

continued ....

Name: ______________________ Date: ____________

Section 7.2

2. When this 5.0-m long airplane is parked, its nose is 1.5 m from the ground. What angle does the body of the plane make with the ground, to the nearest degree?

3. A utility company needs to run a power cable from the southwest corner of this rectangular field to the northeast corner.

a) How long is the diagonal of the field, to the nearest metre?

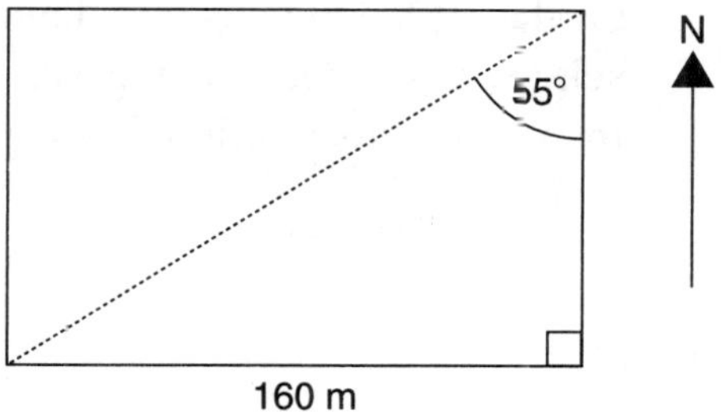

b) Use the sine ratio to find the length of the east side of the field.

Hint
The sum of the interior angles of a triangle is 180°.

c) Describe another method for finding the length of the east side of the field.

d) How much cable does the utility company save by going along the diagonal of the field instead of along the south and east sides?

Name: ____________________ Date: ____________________

7.3 Explore the Cosine Ratio

Textbook pp. 266–273

Warm Up

1. Number Sense

Adele makes nine cuts through a fallen tree with a chain saw. How many pieces has she cut the tree into?

2. Mental Math/Estimating

A pond is 52 m by 77 m and has an average depth of about 2.8 m. Estimate the volume of water in the pond.

3. Proportional Reasoning

Of the 1200 students at a downtown school, 0.5% speak Hungarian. How many students at this school speak Hungarian?

4. Relations and Functions

In some medical tests, the number of bacteria in a sample can double every 40 min. Is the growth of bacteria in these tests linear?

5. Algebra

Find the height of this triangle, to the nearest millimetre.

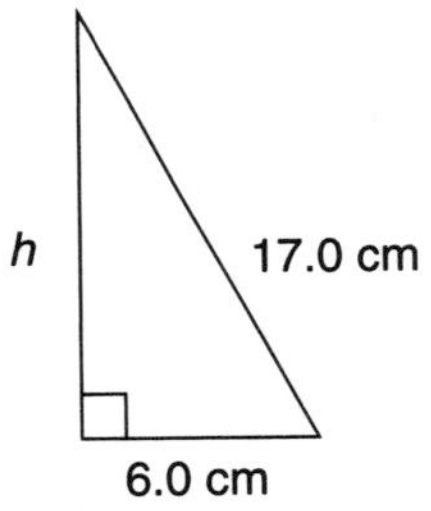

6. Graphs and Tables

Complete this graph for a person riding a Ferris wheel through two rotations.

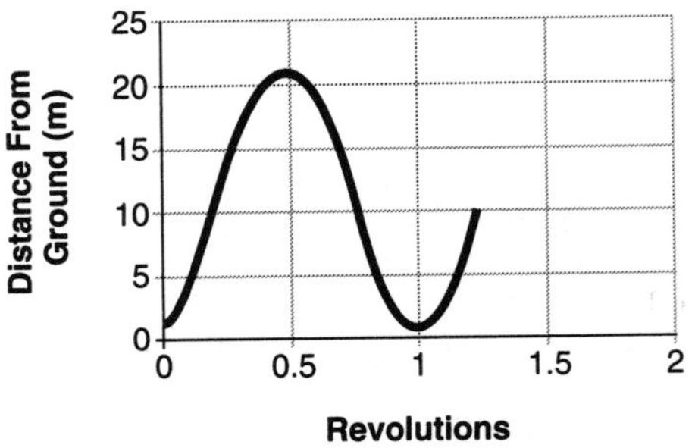

7. Math Literacy

Angles whose sum is 90° are

____________________.

8. Previous Section

The sine ratio of ∠E is

A $\frac{3}{4}$ **B** $\frac{4}{3}$

C $\frac{4}{5}$ **D** $\frac{3}{5}$

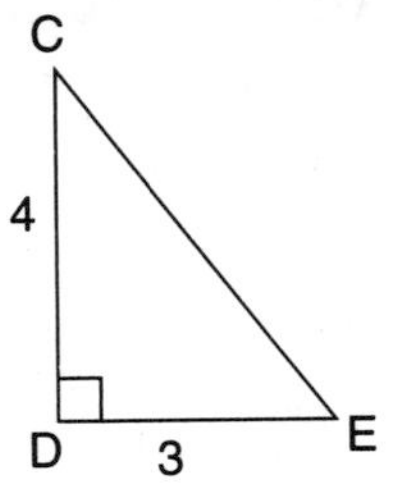

Name: ______________________________ Date: ______________

Practise: The Cosine Ratio

Section 7.3

Use the clues below to complete this crossword puzzle.

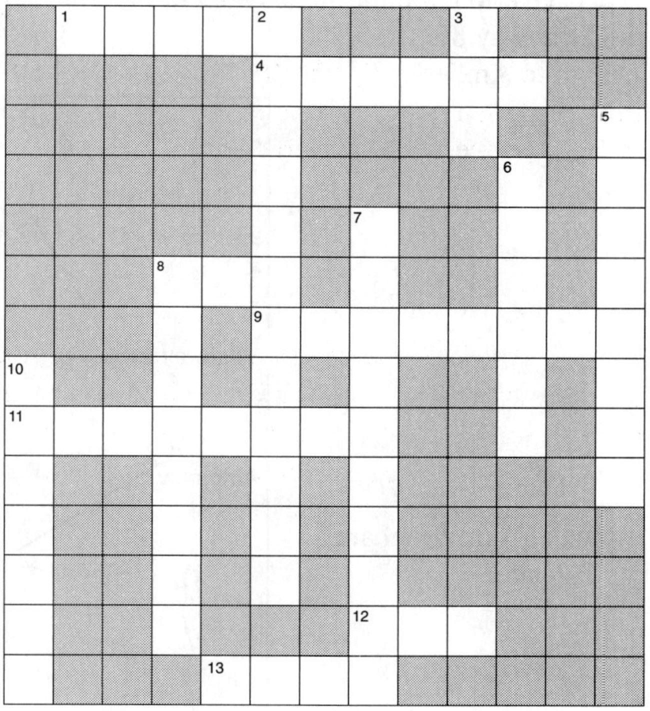

Across

1. A 90° angle is a __________ angle.

4. The tangent, sine, and cosine functions are __________ of side lengths in a right triangle.

8. Short for tangent ratio

9. Numerator of sine ratio

11. Denominator of tangent ratio

12. Short for sine ratio

13. Ratio of opposite over hypotenuse

Down

2. Mathematics of relations between the sides and angles of triangles

3. Short for cosine ratio

5. Mathematics of points, lines, surfaces, and solids

6. Ratio of adjacent side over hypotenuse

7. Longest side of a right triangle

8. Three-sided shape

10. Ratio of opposite over adjacent

1. The surface of this loading ramp is 264 cm long and the base is 245 cm long. Calculate the angle at which this ramp inclines, to the nearest degree.

Mark the known quantities on the diagram.

$\cos A = \frac{\square}{\square}$

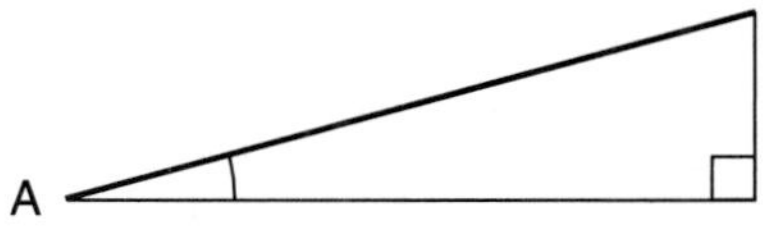

$\cos A =$ _______

$\angle A = \cos^{-1}($ _______ $)$

$\angle A \doteq$ _______°

Therefore, the ramp inclines at an angle of _______°.

continued ....

Name: ______________________________ Date: ______________

Section 7.3

2. To drive on the highway from Wingham, Ontario to Tiverton, you have to go northwest on Highway 86 to Amberley, then northeast on Highway 21. To fly directly to Tiverton, a pilot travels 46.9 km on a course at a 38° angle with Highway 86.

a) How far is it from Wingham to Amberley?

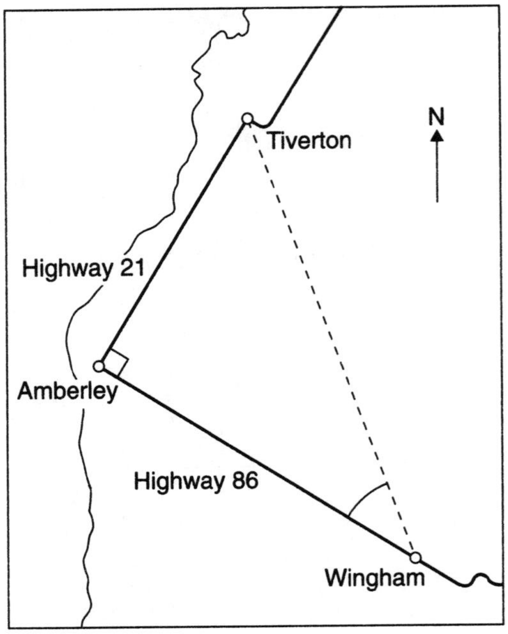

b) How far is it from Amberley to Tiverton?

c) Compare the driving distance from Wingham to Tiverton to the flying distance.

3. As part of his lifeguard training, Jeff practises throwing a lifeline to his partner. Jeff is standing on top of an 8.4-m cliff. He estimates that his partner's position in the water is 40° down from the horizontal. What length of lifeline does Jeff need?

Hint
First, find the complement of the 40° angle.

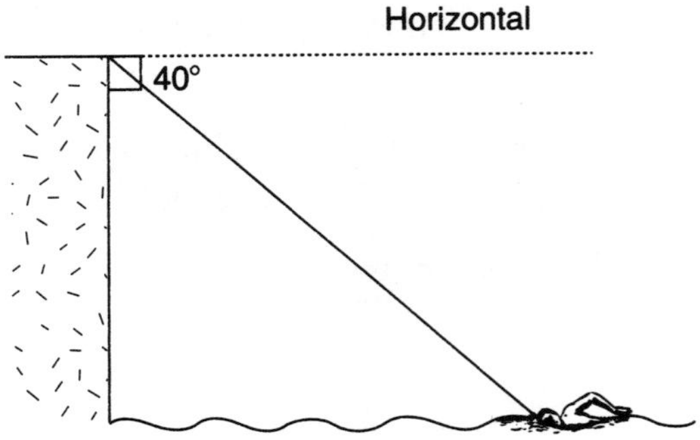

Name: ____________________ Date: ____________

7.4 Apply Trigonometry

Textbook pp. 274–277

Warm Up

1. Number Sense

Continue the pattern.

4, 2, 1, $\frac{1}{2}$, ______, ______, ______

Describe the pattern.

2. Mental Math/Estimating

Estimate $\frac{914}{1026}$ to the nearest tenth.

3. Proportional Reasoning

Express as unit rates.

\$3.99 for 12 pens

28 cm of snow in 8.0 h

4. Relations and Functions

Complete this table of values.

x	$y = -x + 4$	(x, y)
0		
1	3	(1, 3)
2		
3		

5. Algebra

A salesperson at an electronics store earns \$150 per week as a base salary plus 4% commission on all sales. A formula for the salesperson's weekly earnings is

A $E = 150 + 4s$
B $E = 150 + 0.04s$
C $E = 0.04(150 + s)$
D $E = 150 + \frac{0.04s}{100}$

6. Graphs and Tables

Use the table of values in question 4 to graph the linear function $y = -x + 4$.

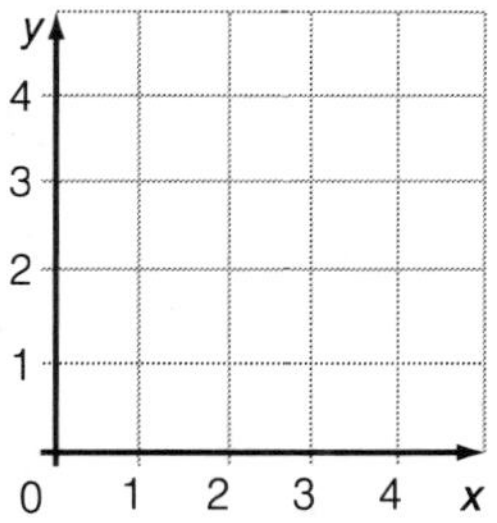

7. Math Literacy

The branch of mathematics that deals with the relations between the sides and angles of triangles is

______________________.

8. Previous Section

This diagram shows a metal brace welded to the square corner of a steel frame. How long is the brace?

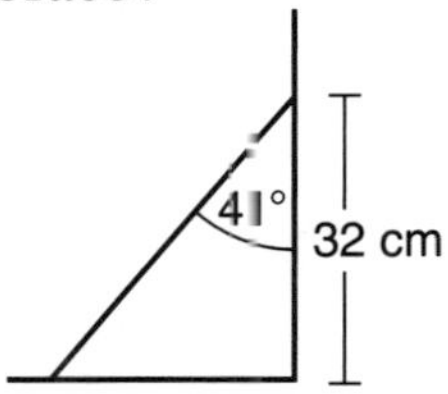

Name: ______________________ Date: ____________

Practise: Applying Trigonometry

Section 7.4

The angle between the horizontal and a straight line from the viewer to an object is an angle of elevation when the object is _________ the horizontal.
The angle between the horizontal and a straight line from the viewer to an object is an angle of

____

when the object is below the horizontal.

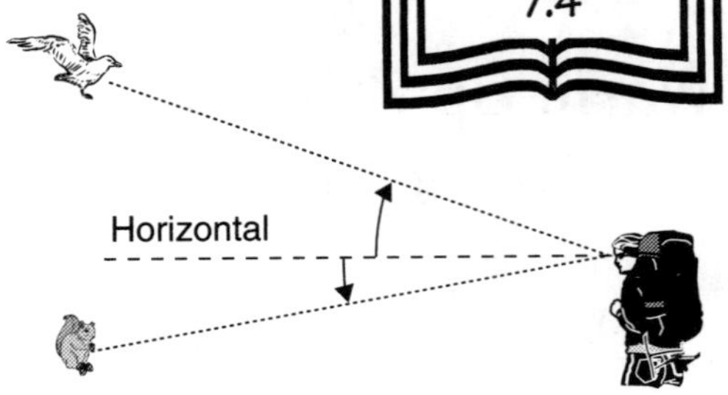

1. A chipmunk dug a tunnel at an angle of depression of 39°. The tunnel is 0.65 m long with a small den at the end. How far below the surface is the den?

Let _____ represent the depth of the den. Mark this depth and the known length on the diagram.

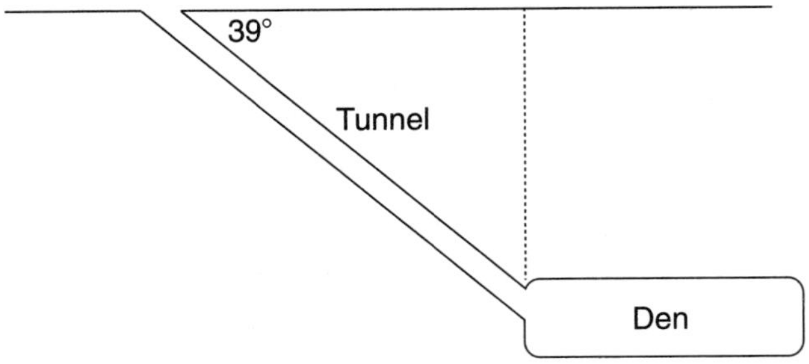

______ 39° = $\frac{\square}{\square}$

Therefore, the den is ________ ____ below the surface.

2. Cedar shingles may leak if used on a roof with a pitch of less than 1:3. Maia is about to reshingle a roof that slopes at an angle of 16°. Can she use cedar shingles for this roof?

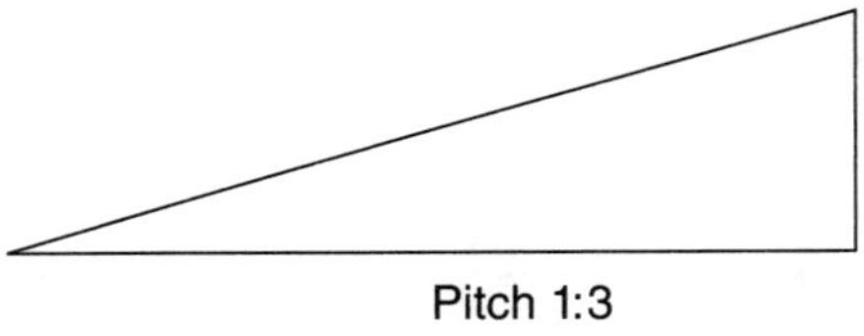

Hint
A roof with a pitch of 1:3 has a rise of 1 unit for a run of 3 units.

continued ....

Name: ______________________ Date: ______________

Section 7.4

3. A town stores sand for winter road maintenance in a cone-shaped building. At what angle does the side of the building meet the ground, to the nearest degree?

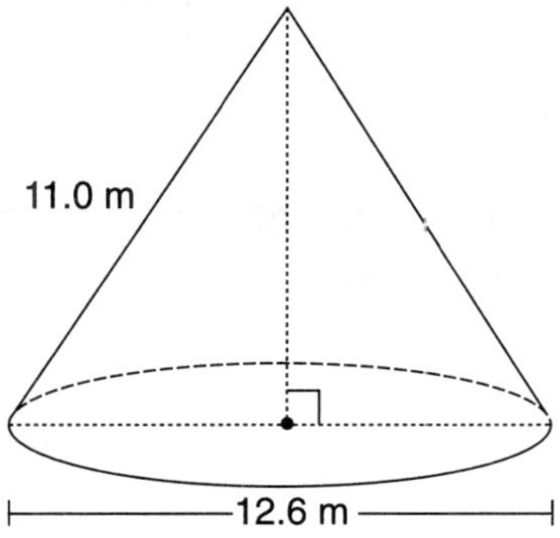

Hint
Divide the diameter by 2 to find the length of the base of the right triangle.

4. A repairman stands 3.4 m from a building and looks up at the antenna mounted at the edge of the roof. From his eye level, 1.8 m from the ground, the angle of elevation is 77°. The roof is 11.6 m from the ground. How tall is the antenna?

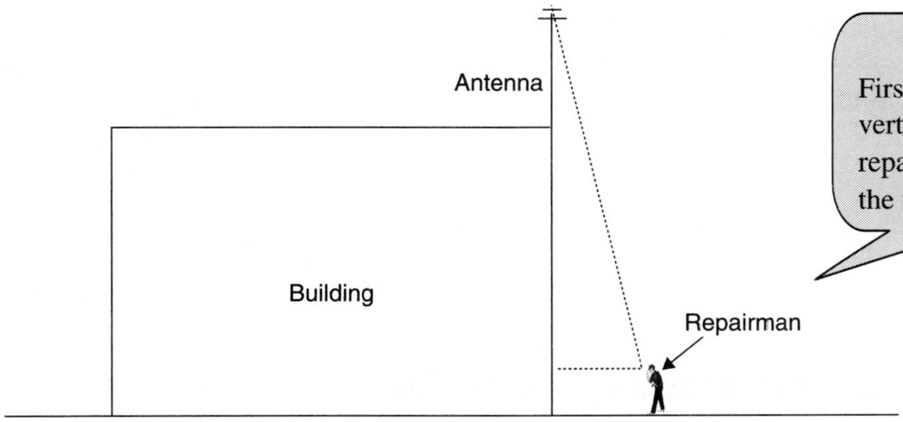

Hint
First, calculate the vertical distance from the repairman's eye level to the top of the building.

Name: ______________________________ Date: ______________

Chapter 7 Review

The date of the Chapter 7 test is ____________________.
Use these questions to check whether you are ready for this test.
For help preparing for the chapter test, see the study tips on pages x–xii.
In the questions below, round all numerical answers to one decimal place.

7.1 Explore the Tangent Ratio, textbook pages 250–258

1. a) Label the hypotenuse of ΔABC and the opposite and adjacent sides for ∠A.

b) Calculate tan A.

c) Find the measure of ∠A.

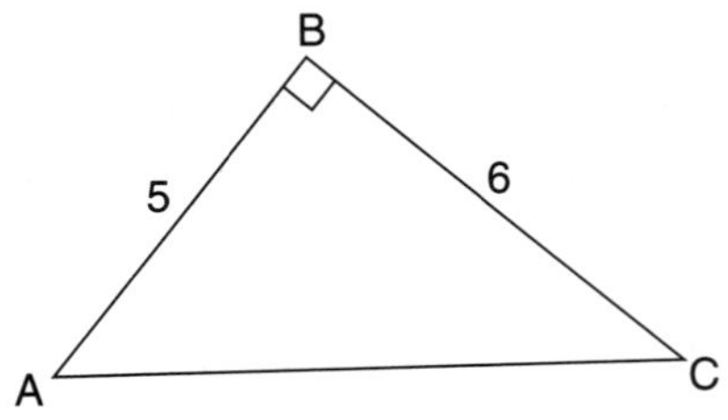

2. Rain from a storm cloud directly over the town of Arnstein is falling in Port Loring, 3.0 km to the west. The rain comes down at an angle of 40° to the ground. How high is the storm cloud?

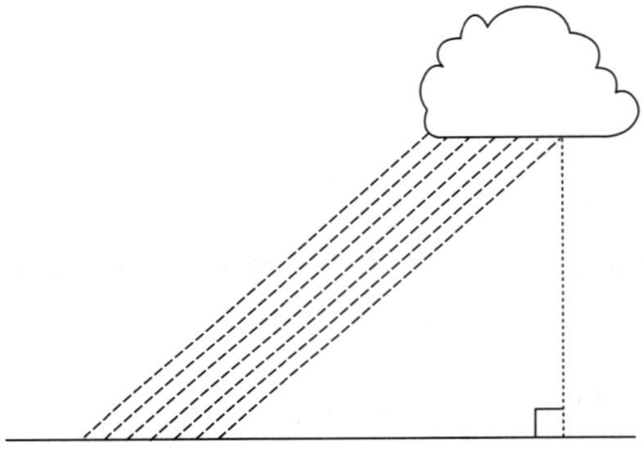

7.2 Explore the Sine Ratio, textbook pages 259–265

3. a) Label the hypotenuse of ΔDEF and the opposite and adjacent sides for ∠D.

b) Calculate sin D.

c) Find the measure of ∠D.

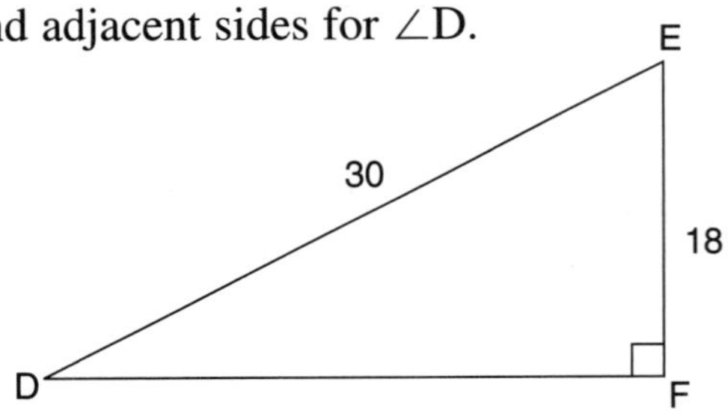

4. A ramp into an underground parking garage descends 2.4 m over its 20.0 m length. Determine the angle the ramp makes with the horizontal.

continued ....

Name: ____________________ Date: ____________

7.3 Explore the Cosine Ratio, textbook pages 266–273

5. a) Label the hypotenuse of ΔGHI and the opposite and adjacent sides for $\angle G$.

b) Calculate cos G.

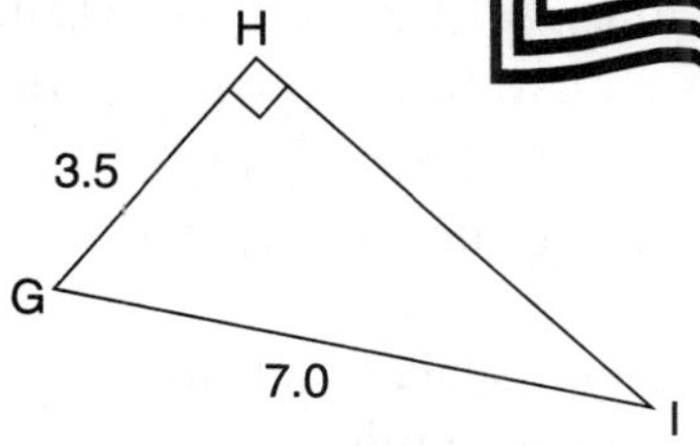

c) Find the measure of $\angle G$.

6. How deep is the water if this ship's anchor chain is 50.0 m long and the opening in the hull for it is 6.0 m above the water line?

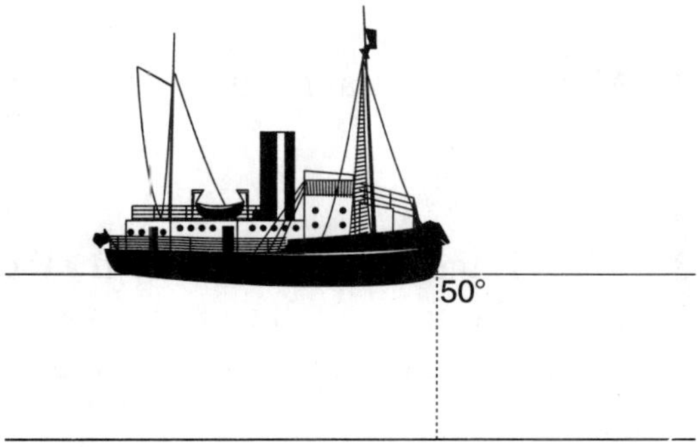

7.4 Apply Trigonometry, textbook pages 274–277

7. From the top of a hill 28.2 m high, the angle of elevation to the tip of a relay tower is 16.0°. The hilltop is 46.6 m from the tower. Determine the height of the tower.

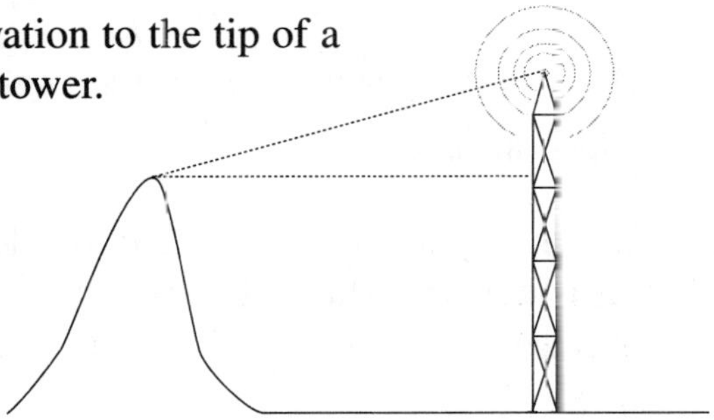

8. To make a neat corner for a railing, Susan cuts the ends of the boards at an angle.

a) How long is the diagonal cut for these boards?

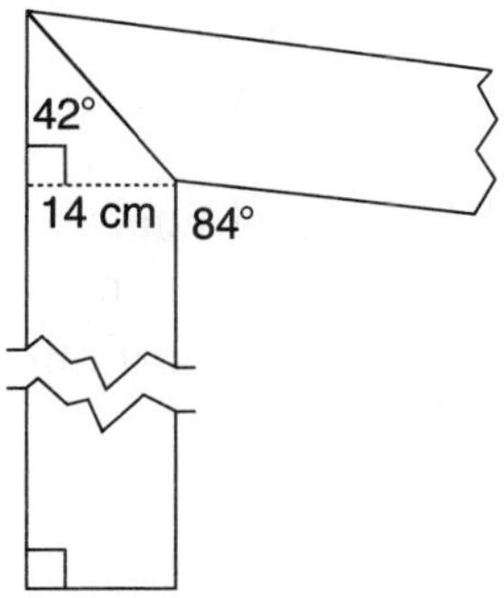

b) By how much is the outer edge of the left railing board longer than its inner edge?

Name: ______________________________ Date: ______________

Rich Problem: A Swim Meet

Chapter 7 Rich Problem

As swim manager for the Lake Vernon triathlon, you are designing a triangular course for the swim portion of the competition. The total distance should be within 1% of 1930 m (half the length of the Ironman swim). The last leg is to be exactly 500 m.

After sketching scale diagrams of several different designs, you chose this one.

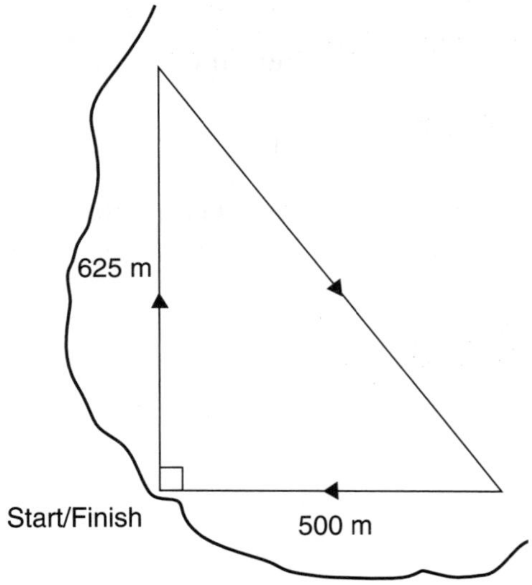

1. What is the scale of this diagram? (Hint: Use a ruler.)

2. Measure the total length of the course.

3. What is the acceptable range for the length of the course? Can you tell from your measurements whether the design is in this range?

4. Use a protractor to measure the angles at the turns.
Angle at first turn is _______°. Angle at second turn is _______°.

5. Use the Pythagorean Relation to calculate the length of the middle leg, to the nearest metre. Then, determine whether the total length of the course is close enough to 1930 m.

6. The race officials need to know how to lay out the ropes and buoys to mark the turns. Calculate the angles of the turns to the nearest tenth of a degree. Use your measurements from question 3 to check your calculations.

First Turn **Second Turn**

Name: ______________________ Date: ____________

CHAPTER 8 Quadratic Functions

Get Set

Answer these questions to check your understanding of the Get Ready concepts on pages 286–287 of the *Mathematics: Applying the Concepts 10* textbook.

Integers

1. Evaluate.

a) $-8 + (-12)$ **b)** $-8 - (-12)$ **c)** $-12 - (-8)$ **d)** $-8 \times (-12)$

Substitution

2. Find the value of y when $x = -2$.

a) $y = 2(x + 5)^2$ **b)** $y = 3x^2 - 4$ **c)** $y = -2(x - 3)^2 + 12$

Linear Functions

3. Complete the table, then graph the line represented by $y = -2x - 1$.

x	y
−2	
−1	
0	
1	
2	

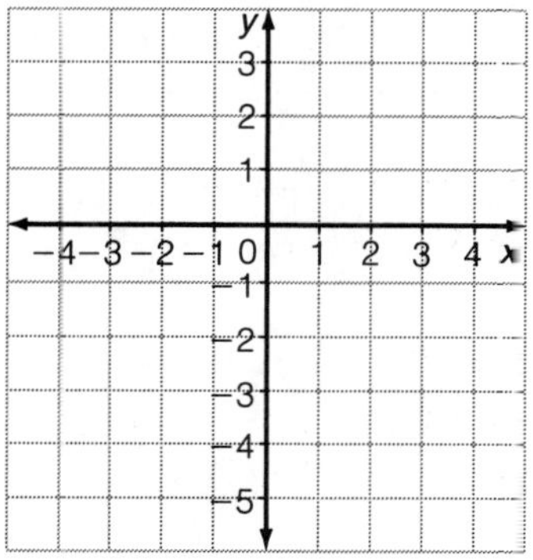

4. Complete this table.

	$y = 5x - 10$	$y = 9 + \frac{3}{4}x$	$3x + 2y = 18$
***y*-intercept**			
***x*-intercept**			

Translations and Reflections

5. Find the co-ordinates of the image of ΔXYZ if it is

a) translated 1 unit left

b) reflected in the x-axis

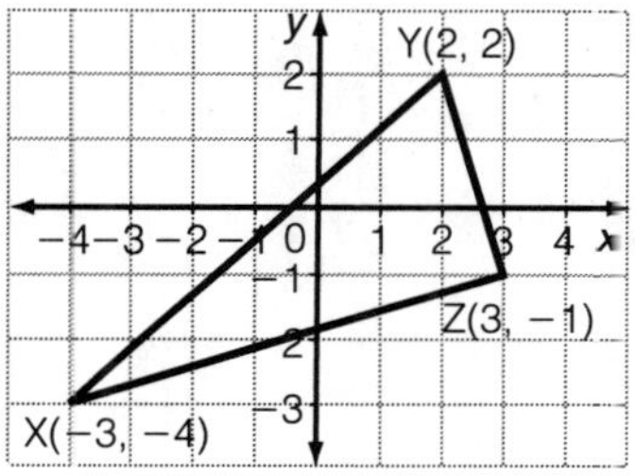

Name: ______________________________ Date: ______________

8.1 Introduce Quadratic Functions

Textbook pp. 288–292

Warm Up

1. Number Sense

What two numbers add to 5 and multiply to 6?

2. Mental Math/Estimating

If a 55-g serving of macaroni and cheese contains 9.8 g of fat, how much fat does a 220-g box contain?

3. Proportional Reasoning

If a metre stick casts a 20-m shadow, how tall is a tree that casts a 4-m shadow?

4. Relations and Functions

Trace the graph that represents a linear function.

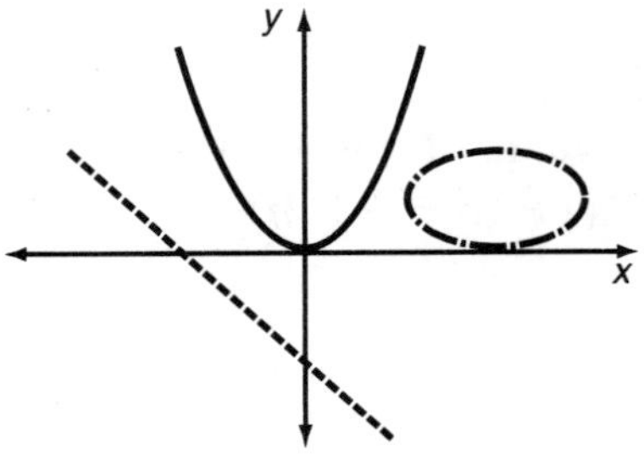

5. Algebra

Solve for x.

$$\frac{1}{2}x - 7 = 3$$

6. Graphs and Tables

This table shows the interest rates for a Canada Premium Bond that pays out simple interest each year.

Year 1	Year 2	Year 3	Year 4
2.45%	2.80%	3.00%	3.50%

How much more is the interest payment for a $1000 bond in year 4 than in year 1?

7. Math Literacy

The prefix *quad* means __________.
Define a word that starts with *quad*.

8. Previous Section

If a set of stairs has a grade (rise over run) of 0.75, what angle do the steps form with the ground?

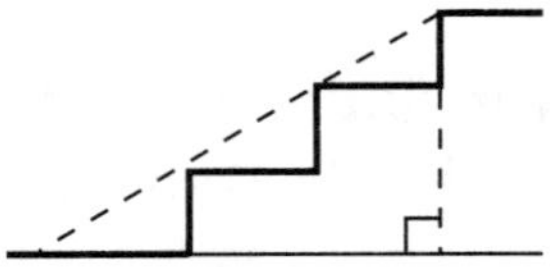

Name: ______________________ Date: ____________

Practise: Quadratic Functions

Section 8.1

The graph of a linear function is a __________ line, while the graph of a quadratic function is a ___-shaped curve called a __________________.

The simplest quadratic function is $y =$ ____.

A quadratic function has a maximum or _____________ value at its __________.

1. a) Circle the graphs that are parabolas.

Graph I

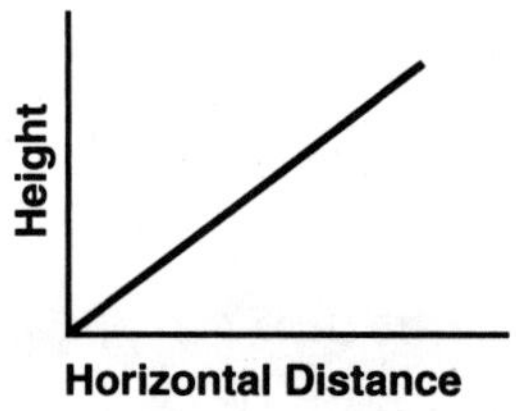

Graph II

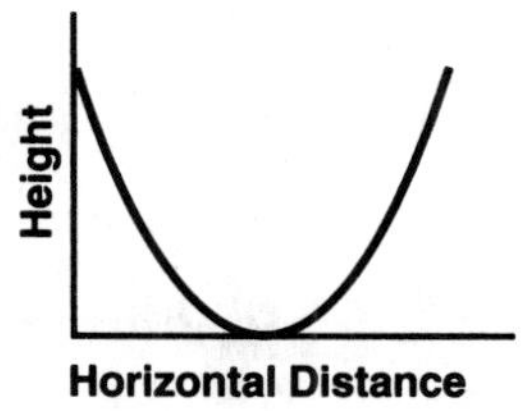

Graph III

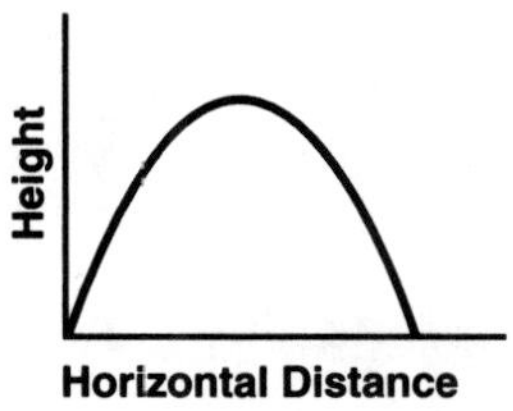

b) Which graph could represent the path of a newspaper thrown by a delivery person? Explain your reasoning.

2. This graph shows the height of a grasshopper as it jumps up and then comes back down to the ground.

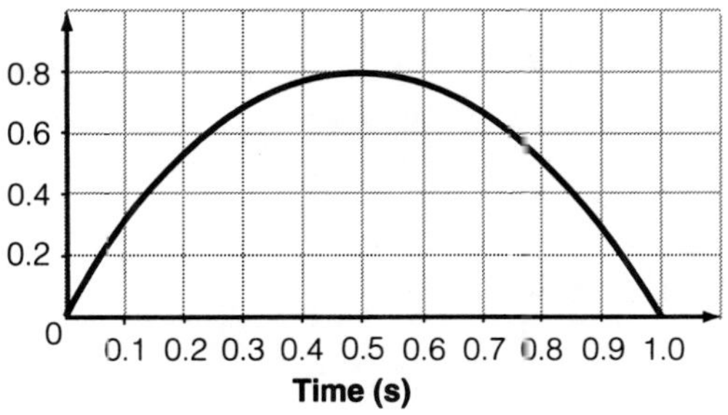

a) How high did the grasshopper jump?

b) How long was it in the air?

c) How high was the grasshopper at 0.75 s?

d) How long did it take to reach a height of 0.5 m?

Name: ______________________ Date: ______________

8.2 Quadratic Functions of the Form $y = ax^2$

Textbook pp. 293–299

Warm Up

1. Number Sense

What two numbers add to −5 and multiply to 6?

2. Mental Math/Estimating

Calculate mentally.

$152.8 \times 0.01 =$

$152.8 \div 0.01 =$

$152.8 + 0.01 =$

$152.8 - 0.01 =$

3. Proportional Reasoning

Solve for *a*.

$\frac{a}{3} = \frac{2}{9}$

4. Relations and Functions

Trace the graph that represents a quadratic function.

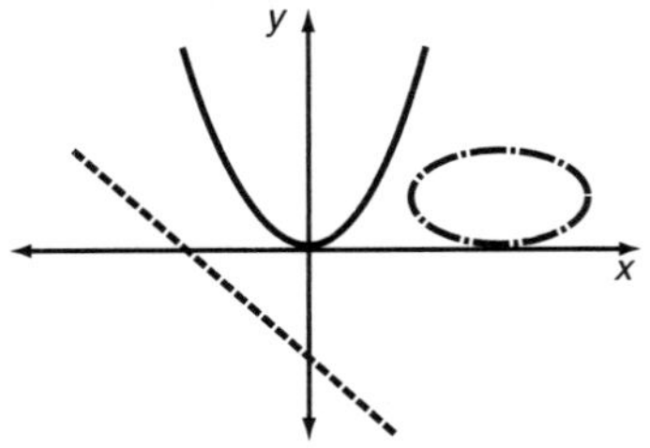

5. Algebra

Find y when $x = -3$.

$y = 2x^2$

6. Graphs and Tables

This graph shows the progress of a United Way fundraising drive.

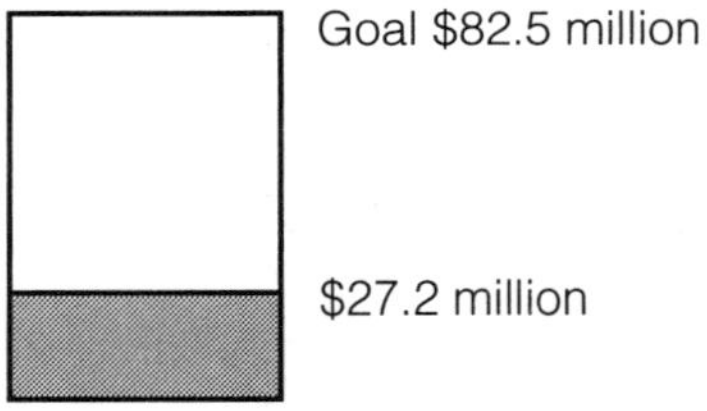

This drive still has to raise

$______________.

7. Math Literacy

If the number of employees at a company has tripled, then its staff has increased by a factor of ____.

8. Previous Section

The graph of $y = x^2$ has its vertex at the __________ of the Cartesian plane and is symmetric about the ___-axis.

Name: ______________________________ Date: ______________

Practise: Functions of the Form $y = ax^2$

Section 8.2

1. Put check marks in the appropriate boxes to complete this table.

	Features of Graph				
Equation	Opens upward	Opens downward	Narrower than $y = x^2$	Wider than $y = x^2$	Vertex at (0, 0)
$y = 2x^2$	✔		✔		✔
$y = 0.75\,x^2$					
$y = -3x^2$					
$y = 5.6x^2$					
$y = -\frac{5}{8}x^2$					

2. Write an equation for the quadratic function whose graph is the graph of $y = x^2$
   a) stretched vertically by a factor of 7

   b) compressed to half of its original height

   c) reflected in the x-axis, then stretched vertically by a factor of 3

3. The formula for the surface area of a sphere is $S = 4\pi r^2$, where r is the radius of the sphere.
   a) Complete this table. Then, graph the quadratic function.

Radius, r	Surface Area, S
1	
2	
3	
4	
5	

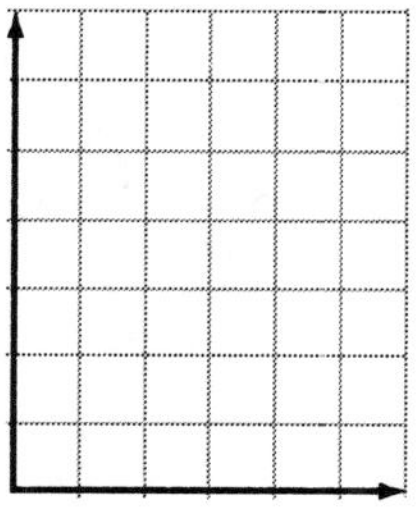

Hint
Many calculators have a π key that gives a value for π accurate to eight decimal places.

   b) The graph is half of a parabola. Why is there little point in showing the left half of the parabola for this quadratic formula?

   c) Calculate the surface area of a basketball that has a radius of 12 cm.

continued ....

Name: ______________________________ Date: ______________

Section 8.2

4. The entrance to a fairground has a 24-m high arch in the shape of a parabola with the vertex at the top. To design this arch, the architect used the equation $v = -0.06u^2$, where v is the vertical distance from the vertex and u is the horizontal distance from the vertex. Both distances are measured in metres.

a) How can you tell from the equation that the parabola opens downward?

b) Is the arch wider or narrower than one with the equation $v = u^2$? Explain.

c) Complete this table. Then, use the table to graph the shape of the arch.

d	v
−20	−24
−15	
−10	
−5	
0	
5	
10	
15	
20	

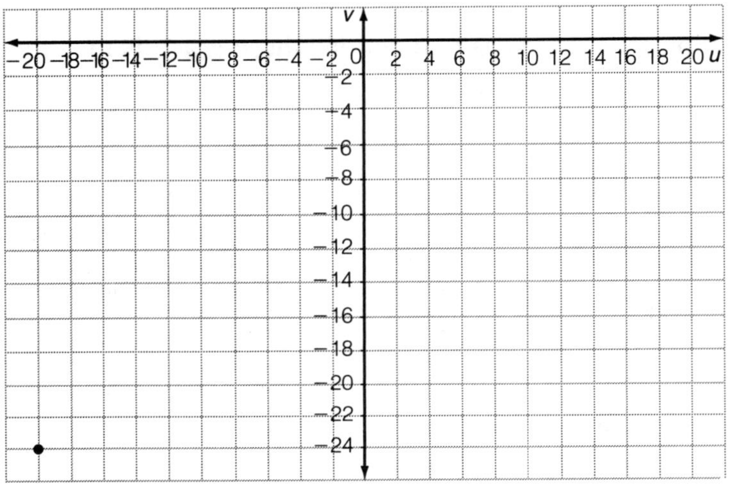

d) How wide is the arch at ground level?

> **Hint**
> Since the arch is 24 m high, the grid line for $v = -24$ represents ground level.

e) Use the equation to determine how high the arch is at a point 10 m in from where the arch meets the ground.

At a point 10 m in from where the arch meets the ground, u = ______ or ______.

$v = -0.06($ ______ $)^2$

v = ______

height above ground $= 24 + v$

$= 24 +$ ______

$=$ ______

> **Hint**
> Check your calculation by using your graph to estimate the height.

Name: ____________________ Date: __________

8.3 Quadratic Functions of the Form $y = x^2 + k$

Textbook pp. 300–304

Warm Up

1. Number Sense

Continue the pattern.

$\frac{1}{2}$, −1, 2, −4, ____, ____, ____

Describe the pattern.

2. Mental Math/Estimating

Evaluate mentally.

$x^2 + 5$, when $x = 1$

$t^2 - 2$, when $t = -2$

3. Proportional Reasoning

Find the before-tax price, *p*, of a sweatshirt that costs $80.49 including taxes in Sudbury.

$80.49 = p \times$ ______

4. Relations and Functions

For the quadratic function $d = 0.014s^2$, doubling *s* increases *d* by a factor of ____.

5. Algebra

Simplify by collecting like terms.

$x^2 + 3x - 7 + 2x^2 + 5x + 4$

6. Graphs and Tables

The graph of the distance travelled by a falling object is ***not***

A linear **B** nonlinear
C parabolic **D** quadratic

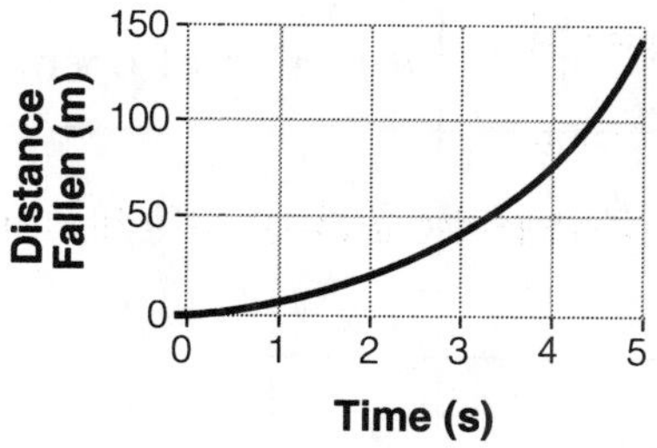

7. Math Literacy

ΔABC is a ________________ of ΔXYZ.

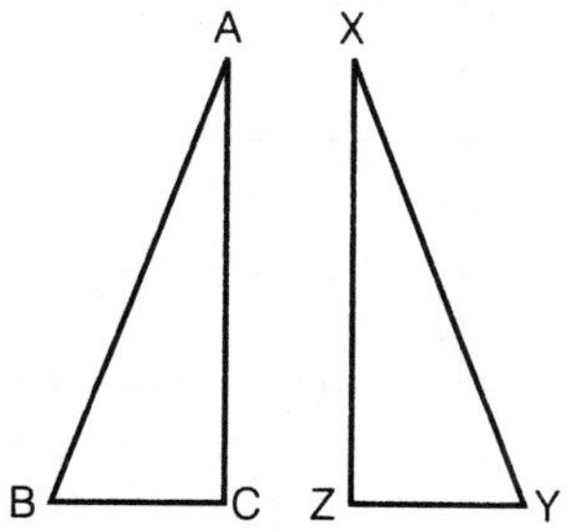

8. Previous Section

Circle the correct word in each set of brackets.

The graph of $y = -6x^2$ opens **(upward/downward)** and is **(wider/narrower)** than the graph of $y = x^2$.

Name: ____________________ Date: ____________

Practise: Functions of the Form $y = x^2 + k$

Section 8.3

1. Complete this table.

Equation	Vertex	y-intercept	Position Relative to Graph of $y = x^2$
$y = x^2 + 1$	(0, 1)	1	translated up 1 unit
$y = x^2 - 4$			
$y = x^2 + \frac{3}{2}$			
$y = x^2 - 7.8$			

2. Write an equation for

a) $y = x^2$ translated down 6 units.

b) a parabola opening upward with vertex (0, 10)

3. Complete this table comparing the graphs of pairs of quadratic functions.

Equations	Same	Different
$y = x^2$ $y = x^2 - 13$	shape direction of opening	vertex y-intercept
$y = x^2 + 4$ $y = -x^2 + 4$		
$y = x^2 - 8$ $y = \frac{1}{2}x^2 - 8$		
$y = 3x^2 + 9$ $y = 3x^2 - 9$		
$y = -2x^2 + 4$ $y = 2x^2 + 4$		

continued ....

Name: ______________________________ Date: ______________

Section 8.3

4. The shape of the main cable of this suspension bridge is a parabola. With the origin at the middle of the bridge's roadway, the equation for the parabola is $y = 0.00125x^2 + 40$.

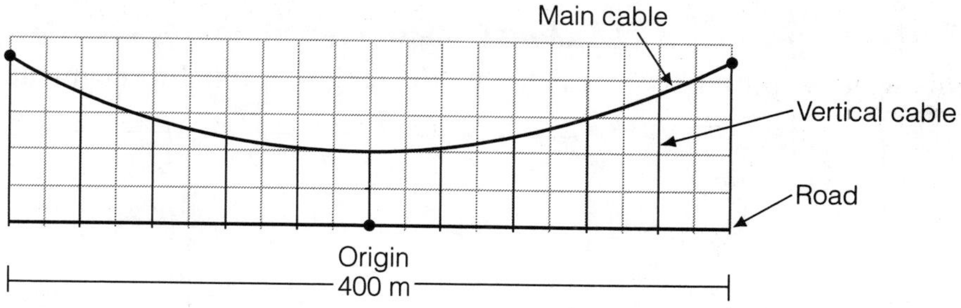

a) Find the length of the shortest vertical cable.

The bottom of the shortest vertical cable is at the origin, where $x =$ ____.

Therefore, $y = 0.00125(\_\_\_\_)^2 + 40$

$y = 0.00125 \times \_\_\_\_ + 40$

$y = \_\_\_\_ + 40$

$y = \_\_\_\_$

The shortest cable is ______ m long.

b) Find the length of the longest vertical cables.

The bridge is ______ m long. So, the lower ends of the two longest vertical cables are ______m from the origin.

Substitute this value for x into the quadratic equation, and solve for y:

Name: ______________________________ Date: ______________

8.4 Quadratic Functions of the Form $y = (x - h)^2$

Textbook pp. 305–311

Warm Up

1. Number Sense

What is wrong with this window setting?

```
WINDOW
 Xmin=0
 Xmax=100
 Xscl=10
 Ymin=0
 Ymax=-200
 Yscl=50
 Xres=1
```

2. Mental Math/Estimating

Estimate the length of this line segment.

3. Proportional Reasoning

In a right triangle, the ratio of the length of the opposite side to the length of the adjacent side for $\angle X$ is 1. What is the measure of $\angle X$?

4. Relations and Functions

As a hawk dives, its height is modelled by $h = 24 - t^2$, where h is the height, in metres, and t is the time, in seconds. How high is the hawk when $t = 4$?

5. Algebra

Write this equation in the form $Ax + By + C = 0$.

$$y = \frac{2}{3}x + 5$$

6. Graphs and Tables

What does this scatter plot tell you about the height of the newest building?

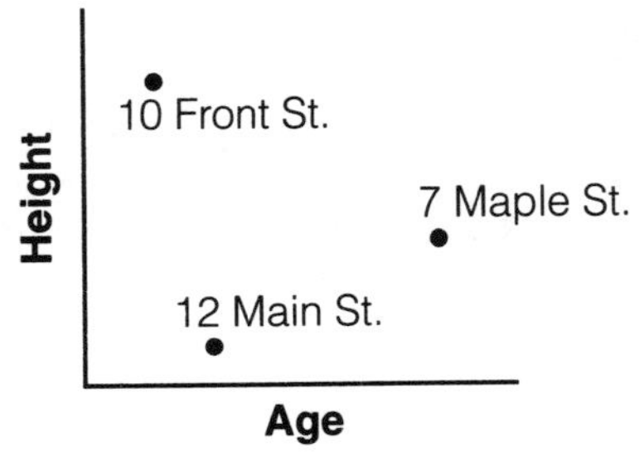

7. Math Literacy

Explain what a y-intercept is.

8. Previous Section

What is the maximum value of y for the function $y = -4.9x^2 + 25$?

Name: ______________________ Date: ____________

Practise: Functions of the Form $y = (x - h)^2$

Section 8.4

Hint
For a horizontal translation, the slide is opposite to the sign in the bracket.

1. Indicate the curve that corresponds to each quadratic function.

a) $y = (x + 5)^2$ _____

b) $y = (x - 5)^2$ _____

c) $y = (x - 1)^2$ _____

d) $y = (x + 1)^2$ _____

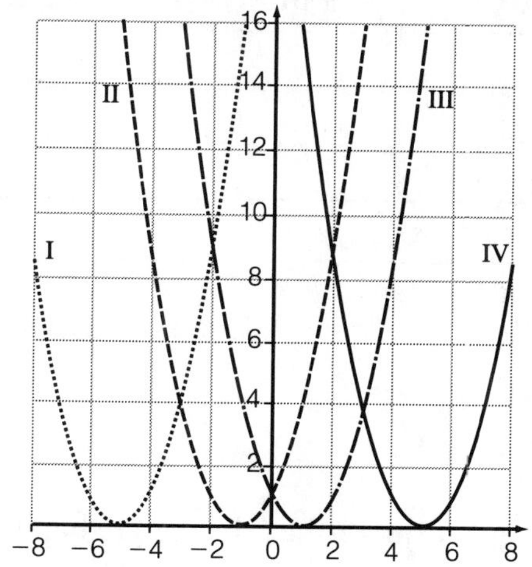

2. For the graph of $y = (x - 8)^2$,

a) give the co-ordinates of the vertex

b) find the x-intercept

c) describe the direction of opening

d) describe its shape relative to the graph of $y = x^2$

3. Place a check mark in each row to complete this table comparing the graphs of $y = x^2 + 9$ and $y = (x + 9)^2$.

Feature	Same	Different
Direction of opening		
Vertex		
x-intercept		
y-intercept		
Shape relative to $y = x^2$		

continued ....

Name: ______________________________ Date: ______________

Section 8.4

4. **a)** Complete this table.

Equation	Vertex	y-intercept	x-intercepts
$y = (x + 9)^2$			
$y = (x - 9)^2$			
$y = x^2 - 9$			
$y = x^2 + 9$			

b) Explain why the graph of $y = x^2 + 9$ does not have any x-intercepts.

5. This drawing of a flashlight reflector has the same shape as the graph of $y = x^2$.

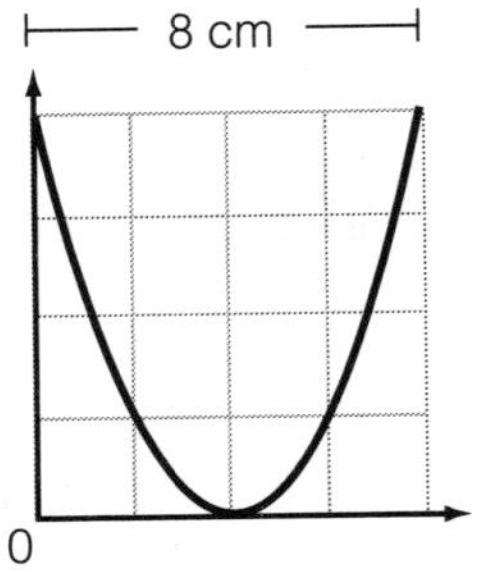

a) Find the co-ordinates of the vertex of the reflector.

b) Write the equation for the parabola in the drawing.

6. Write a quadratic function whose graph is a translation

a) 14 units to the left of the graph of $y = x^2$

b) 10 units to the right of the graph of $y = (x + 1)^2$

Hint
Picture where the vertex of the original graph is, then slide it the required distance.

7. Draw a line from each description to the corresponding equation.

a) the graph of $y = x^2$ translated down 4 units

b) the graph of $y = x^2$ stretched vertically by a factor of 4

c) the graph of $y = x^2$ translated right 4 units

d) the graph of $y = (x + 4)^2$ translated right 4 units.

$y = (x + 4)^2$

$y = (x - 4)^2$

$y = (x + 8)^2$

$y = x^2 + 4$

$y = x^2 - 4$

$y = x^2$

$y = 4x^2$

Name: ____________________ Date: ____________

8.5 Quadratic Functions of the Form $y = a(x - h)^2 + k$

Textbook pp. 312–317

Warm Up

1. Number Sense

Find two values for x that satisfy $(x + 1)^2 = 9$

2. Mental Math/Estimating

32.65×40.1 equals

A 130.9265
B 1309.265
C 13092.65
D 130926.5

3. Proportional Reasoning

Complete this Pythagorean Triple.

{9, 12, ____}

4. Relations and Functions

Which function is shown in this graph?

A $y = x^2 - 6$
B $y = (x - 6)^2$
C $y = x^2 + 6$
D $y = (x + 6)^2$

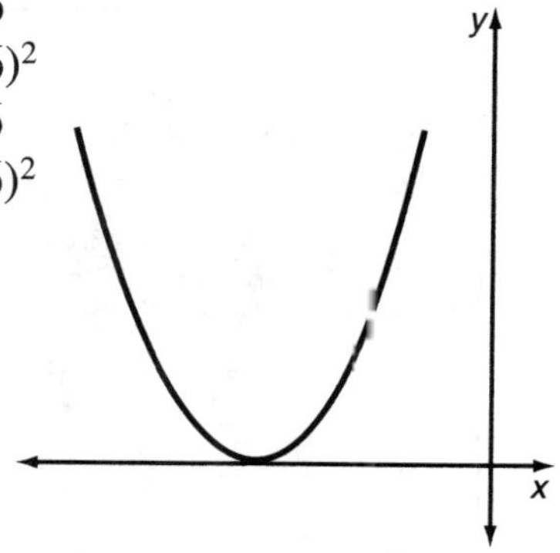

5. Algebra

Solve using the elimination method.

$2x + 3y = 12$
$2x + y = 4$

6. Graphs and Tables

Over a period of 25 years, the difference in fees on these two investments is about

$________.

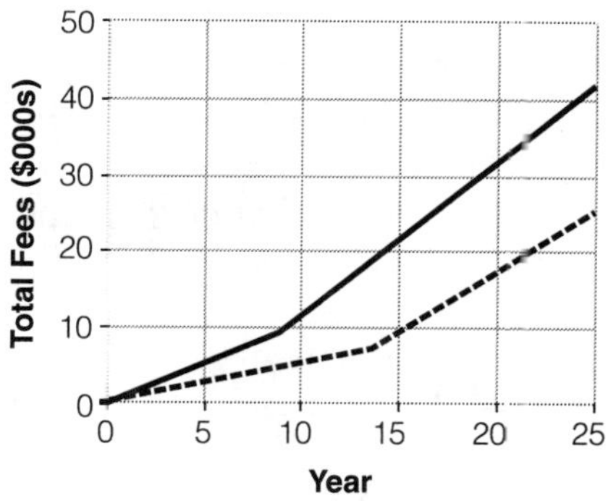

7. Math Literacy

A line running from corner to corner inside a rectangle is called a

____________________.

8. Previous Section

Circle the correct phrase in the brackets. The vertex of the graph of $y = (x - 9)^2$ is **(left of / right of / above / below)** the vertex of the graph of $y = x^2$.

Name: ______________________________ Date: ______________

Practise: Functions of the Form $y = a(x - h)^2 + k$

Section 8.5

1. Complete this table listing how the values of *a*, *h*, and *k* make the graph of the quadratic function $y = a(x - h)^2 + k$ different from the graph of $y = x^2$.

Transformation	Controlled by *a*, *h*, or *k*?
Translation up	*k*
Vertical compression	
Translation right	
Translation left	
Vertical stretch	
Translation down	
Reflection in the *x*-axis	

2. Complete this table.

Equation	Vertex	Direction of Opening	Shape Relative to Graph of $y = x^2$
$y = -5(x + 7)^2 - 8$	$(-7, -8)$	down	narrower
$y = 0.75(x - 4)^2 + 2$			
$y = (x + 12)^2 + 9$			
$y = -\frac{5}{8}(x - \frac{7}{9})^2$			
$y = 3x^2 - 5$			
$y = -(x - 8)^2 - 2$			

3. Indicate the curve that corresponds to each quadratic function.

a) $y = \frac{1}{3}x^2$ ____

b) $y = x^2 + 3$ ____

c) $y = 2(x - 3)^2 - 2$ ____

d) $y = (x + 6)^2 + 5$ ____

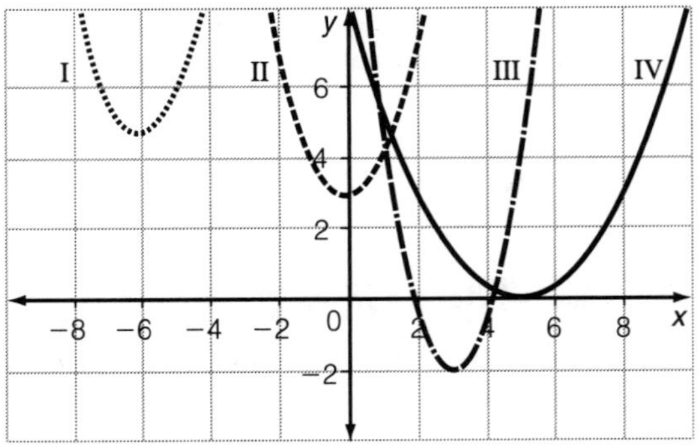

continued ....

Section 8.5

4. Complete this equation for the quadratic function with a graph that
- is three times as narrow as the graph of $y = x^2$
- has a vertex at (6, 4)
- opens downward

$y = \_\_(x \_\_ \_\_)^2 \_\_ \_\_$

5. Seen from above, an Everbright 400 bow window has a parabolic shape. The function that models this shape is $y = 0.25(x - 2)^2 - 1$, where x is the distance from the left side of the window and y is the distance out from the wall. All measurements are in metres.

a) Sketch a graph of the quadratic function.
- Mark a point at (0, 0).
- Mark a point at the vertex.
- Use the symmetry of a parabola to locate a second point on the x- axis.
- Join these three points with a smooth parabolic curve.

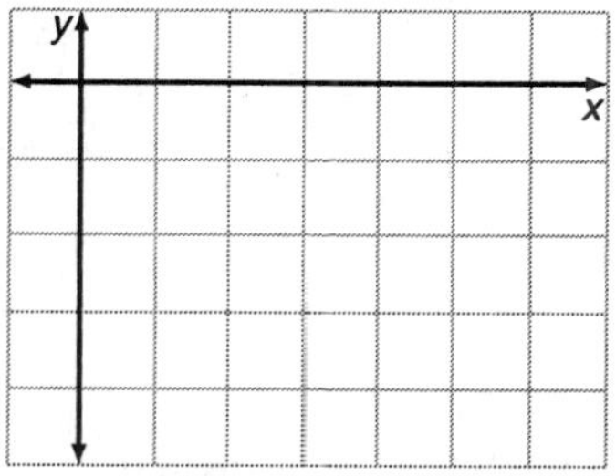

b) What is the maximum distance that the window sticks out from the wall?

Hint
A parabola has a maximum or minimum at its vertex.

c) How wide is the window?

6. The cross section of this designer umbrella can be modelled by the quadratic function $y = -\frac{1}{27}(x - 45)^2 + 75$, where x is the distance in from the edge of the umbrella cover and y is the distance up from its base. These distances are in centimetres.

a) Mark the co-ordinates of points A, B, and C on the diagram.

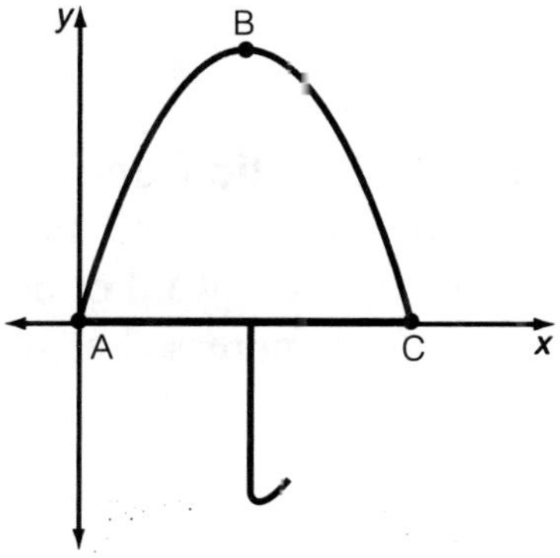

b) How wide is the umbrella at its base?

c) How tall is the umbrella (not counting the handle)?

Name: ______________________________ Date: ______________

Chapter 8 Review

Chater 8 Review

The date of the Chapter 8 test is ____________________.
Use these questions to check whether you are ready for this test.
For help preparing for the chapter test, see the notes on pages x–xii.

8.1 Introduce Quadratic Functions, textbook pages 288–292

1. Circle the graphs that could represent quadratic functions.

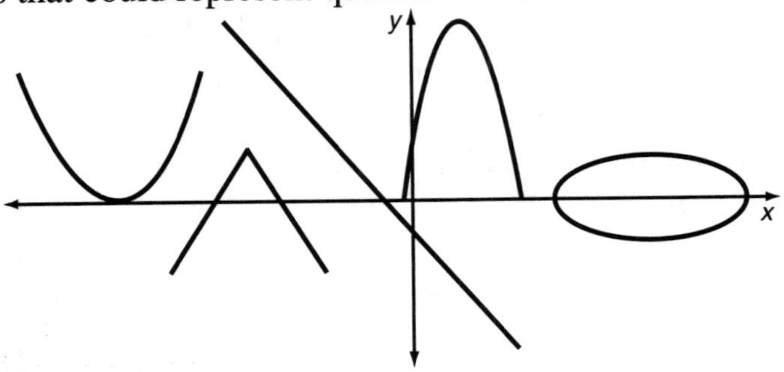

2. This diagram shows the cross section of an igloo a mathematics class built for their town's winter carnival.

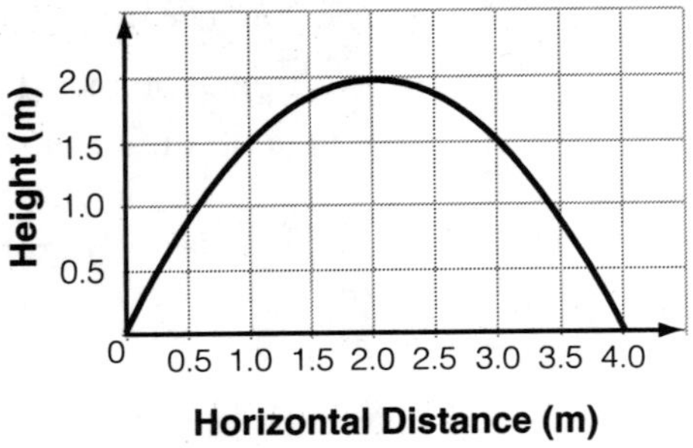

a) What is the maximum height of the igloo?

b) How close to the bottom of the wall can a 1.5-m tall child stand upright inside the igloo?

8.2 Quadratic Functions of the Form $y = ax^2$, textbook pages 293–299

3. For each quadratic function, indicate whether its graph

- opens upward or downward
- is compressed or stretched relative to the graph of $y = x^2$

a) $y = 4x^2$

opens ____________

compressed/stretched

b) $y = \frac{1}{6}x^2$

opens ____________

compressed/stretched

c) $y = -17x^2$

opens ____________

compressed/stretched

continued ....

Name: ______________________________ Date: ______________

Chapter 8 Review

4. If a falling object has little air resistance, the distance, d, it travels can be modelled with the quadratic function $d = 4.9t^2$, where d is in metres and t is the duration of the fall in seconds.

a) Complete this table. Then, graph the function.

Time, t (s)	Distance, d (m)
1	
2	
3	
4	
5	

b) How far does an object fall in the first 2.5 s?

c) Use your graph to estimate how long it takes an object to fall 100 m.

8.3 Quadratic Functions of the Form $y = x^2 + k$, textbook pages 300–304

5. Find the y-intercept and the coordinates of the vertex for each quadratic function.

a) $y = x^2 + 5$

y-intercept:

vertex:

b) $y = x^2 - 64$

y-intercept:

vertex:

c) $y = x^2 + 8.6$

y-intercept:

vertex:

6. The cross section of the chocolate drop in this diagram is parabolic. The equation of the curve is $y = -x^2 + 1$, where x and y are both measured in centimetres.

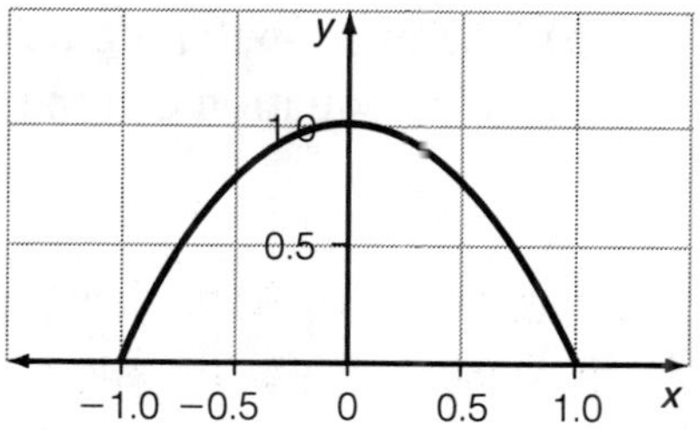

a) Find the y-intercept.

b) How thick is the chocolate drop?

c) Find the x-intercepts of the parabola.

d) How wide is the chocolate drop at its base?

e) How can you tell from the equation that the parabola opens downward?

Name: ______________________________ Date: ______________

8.4 Quadratic Functions of the Form $y = (x - h)^2$, textbook pages 305–311

7. For the graph of the quadratic function $y = (x - 7)^2$, list

a) the co-ordinates of the vertex: (____, ____)

b) the x-intercept: ________

c) the shape relative to the graph of $y = x^2$: ______________________

d) the position relative to the graph of $y = x^2$: ______________________

8. Write the equation for the graph of $y = x^2$ moved

a) 4 units to the right **b)** 17 units to the left

8.5 Quadratic Functions of the Form $y = a(x - h)^2 + k$, textbook pages 312–317

9. Circle the equations that represent quadratic functions.

a) $y = x^2 + 5$ **b)** $y = -x - 11$ **c)** $v = u^2$ **d)** $y = x^3$

e) $y = 7.8x^2$ **f)** $y = (x + 1)^2$ **g)** $y = 9(x + 4)^2 - 8$ **h)** $t = 2 - 5s$

10. A mathematics student volunteers as a clown at a children's hospital. He puts on make-up so that his lower lip looks like a parabola 8 cm wide. He wants to draw a diagram to help him get the make-up the same for every visit.

a) Find the co-ordinates of the vertex.

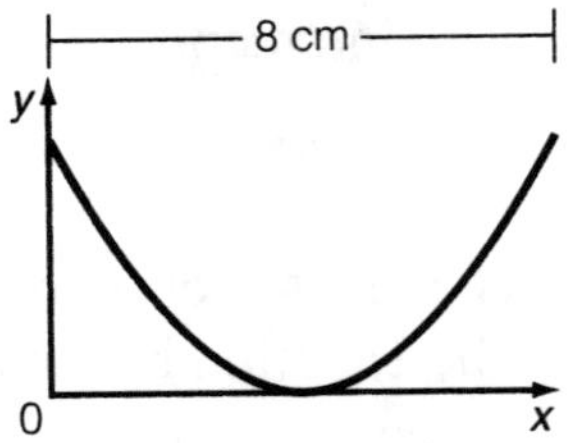

b) The make-up smile has a shape twice as wide as the graph of $y = x^2$. What equation can the student use to draw the diagram?

Name: ______________________ Date: ____________

Rich Problem: Designing a Sign

Chapter 8 Rich Problem

Norm's Fine Fast Foods has a huge, parabola-shaped letter "n" in front of the store. The space under this arch is 7.50 m high and 10.0 m wide. Norm has hired you to build a sign to hang inside this arch. Norm outlines how he wants the sign to look:

- The slogan "3 CAN DINE FOR $7.99" is to be centred on the sign.
- Each character will be 20 cm wide and 30 cm high. Spaces between words will also be 20 cm wide.
- The margins on all four edges of the sign will be 20 cm.
- The words can be on one or two lines.
- If the sign has two lines, the space between the lines will be 20 cm.
- To protect the sign from vandals, the sign will be mounted as high up as it will fit. The bottom of the sign must be at least 4.0 m above the ground.

1. a) Mark the vertex at the origin of the grid below.
b) Draw a horizontal line at the appropriate level to represent the ground.
c) Mark on the two points where the arch meets the ground. Label these two points with their co-ordinates.
d) Sketch a scale drawing of the parabola-shaped arch.

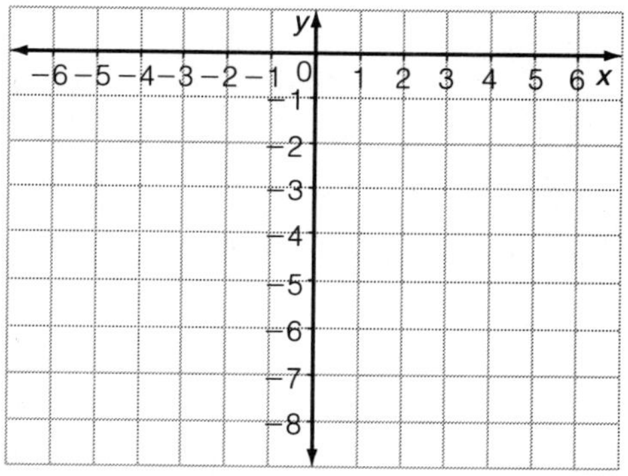

2. Since the vertex of the parabola is at the origin, the equation of the quadratic function has the form $y = ax^2$. Find the value of a for Norm's arch by substituting the coordinates for one of the end points into the equation.

continued ....

Name: ______________________________ Date: ______________

Chapter 8 Rich Problem

3. Calculate the width of a sign with the slogan all on one line.

4. a) How much of the sign will be to the right of the y-axis when you place the sign as high up as it will fit?

Hint
Convert all dimensions to the same units for your calculations.

b) Determine the x-coordinate of the top right corner of the sign.

5. Find the y-coordinate of the top right corner of the sign by substituting the x-coordinate into the equation for the arch.

6. Calculate the height of the sign.

7. How high above the ground will the bottom of the sign be?

8. Calculate the dimensions of a sign with the slogan on two lines. Split the slogan after the word "DINE."

9. How high above the ground will the bottom of the two-line sign be?

10. Will Norm be satisfied with both designs?

Name: ______________________ Date: ____________

CHAPTER 9 Algebraic Expressions

Get Set

Answer these questions to check your understanding of the Get Ready concepts on pages 324–325 of the *Mathematics: Applying the Concepts 10* textbook.

Polynomials

1. Expand.

a) $x(x + 8)$ **b)** $6(x + 5)$ **c)** $4x(2x - 3)$ **d)** $-6x(2 - 8x)$

2. Find the area of each rectangle.

a)

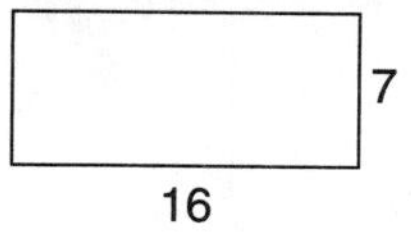

b)

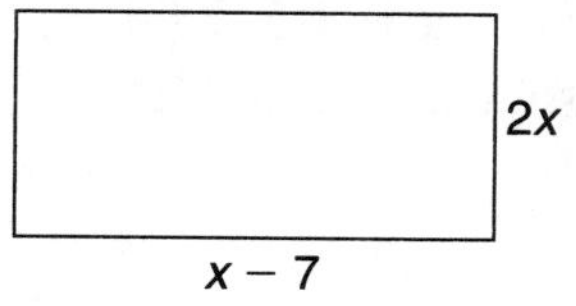

3. Simplify.

a) $3a + 2b - a + 5b + 4a - 3b$ **b)** $7x^2 + 5x + 4 - 3x^2 - 9x$

Factors

4. State three factors of

a) 20 **b)** 44 **c)** 81 **d)** −36

5. State the greatest common factor (GCF) of

a) 8, 20, and 12 **b)** 25, 75, and 55 **c)** $28x^2$ and $49x$ **d)** x^6, x^4, and x^3

6. Find two integers that have a product of

a) 15 and a sum of 8 **b)** −14 and a sum of 5 **c)** 81 and a sum of −18

Solving Equations

7. Solve.

a) $x + 7 = 0$ **b)** $2x = -8$ **c)** $5x - 4 = 0$ **d)** $12 + x = 0$

Name: ______________________________ Date: ______________

9.1 Multiply Two Binomials

Textbook pp. 326–329

Warm Up

1. Number Sense

A student's answer to "multiply negative 4 by positive 3" is 12. What error did the student make?

The correct answer is ________.

2. Mental Math/Estimating

A roll of wallpaper covers about 4.0 m^2. For a room with 50 m^2 of wall space, the number of rolls that you should order is

A 10 **B** 11
C 12 **D** 13

3. Proportional Reasoning

Goaltender Martin Brodeur had 7 shut-outs in his first 27 games of the 2003-2004 season. How many shut-outs could he expect in 70 games?

$$\frac{7}{27} = \frac{n}{70}$$

4. Relations and Functions

Which equation is not a quadratic function?

A $y = 2x - 9$
B $y = 2x^2 - 9$
C $y = 2(x - 9)^2$
D $y = 2(x - 9)^2 + 1$

5. Algebra

Solve for p.
$3p - 12 = 15$

6. Graphs and Tables

An astronomical unit (AU) is about 150 000 000 km.

Planet	Distance From Sun (AU)
Mercury	0.39
Earth	1.00
Jupiter	5.20
Pluto	39.44

Jupiter is about ________________ km from the sun.

7. Math Literacy

When you multiply two or more numbers together, the result is called a

_ _ _ _ _ _ _ _.

8. Previous Section

The graph of $y = \frac{2}{3}(x - 2)^2 + 6$ has its vertex at

A (–2, 6)
B (2, 6)
C (6, –2)
D (–6, –2)

Name: ______________________________ Date: ______________

Practise: Multiplying Two Binomials

Section 9.1

1. The expression $3x - 8$ is a *bi*nomial because it has ________ terms.
Write an example of a binomial that involves

a) an addition ____________ **b)** a negative term ____________

c) the letter w ____________ **d)** a multiple of a variable ____________

2. Expand each expression by multiplying the binomials.
Then, simplify by combining the like terms.

> **Hint**
> FOIL gives the order for multiplying the terms of two binomials:
> First terms
> Outside terms
> Inside terms
> Last terms

a)

$(x + 5)(x + 2)$

$= x(x) + x(\_\_\_) + 5(\_\_\_) + \_\_\_(\_\_\_)$

$= x^{\square} + \_\_\_x + \_\_\_ + \_\_\_$

$= \_\_\_ + \_\_\_ + \_\_\_$

b) $(a + 1)(3a + 4)$ **c)** $(2t - 5)(3t - 2)$ **d)** $(5a - 4)(6a + 1)$

e) $(7 + 2x)(2 - x)$ **f)** $(3y + 4)(3y - 4)$ **g)** $(2m + 9)(2m + 9)$

3. a) Find an expression for the area of this rectangle by multiplying the binomials that represent the length and the width.

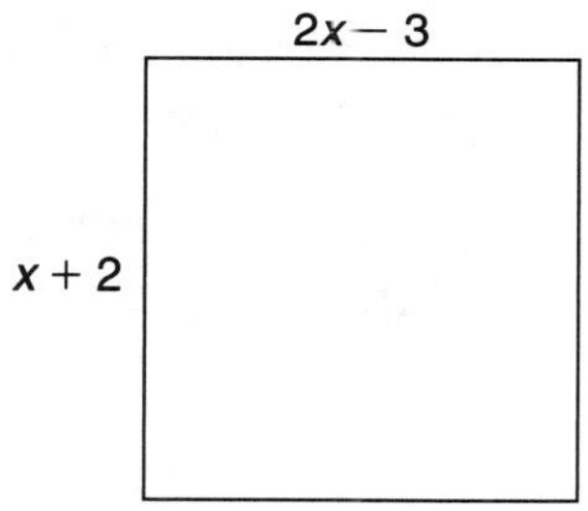

b) Evaluate your expression from part a) with $x = 7$.

c) Find the length and width of the rectangle when $x = 7$.

Length: Width:

d) Use the length and width from part c) to find the area of the rectangle. Compare this area to your answer for part b).

continued ....

Section 9.1

4. Shareen is a contractor who designs and builds garages. To provide a storage area, she makes the length of each garage 4 m longer than the width.

a) Shareen needs to know the area of a garage to estimate the cost of the flooring and roofing materials. Write and simplify a formula she could use to calculate the area of a garage w metres wide.

A = width × length

A = ___(___ + ___)

A =

b) Often when Shareen gives a quotation, her customer asks about the difference in the price for a larger or smaller garage. Write and simplify formulas for the area of a garage that is 2 m wider and one that is 2 m narrower.

Wider Garage

Width is w + ___

Length is (w +___) + ___ = ___ + ___

A = (___ + ___)(___ + ___)

A =

Narrower Garage

c) Test your formulas in part b) by calculating the areas when $w = 5$. Then, compare these results with areas calculated by finding the length and width first.

Wider Garage

Area using your formula:

A =

Area using length and width:

Width is w + ___

Length is (w + ___) + ___ =

A =

Narrower Garage

Name: ______________________ Date: ______________

9.2 Special Products

Textbook pp. 330–333

Warm Up

1. Number Sense

All even numbers are divisible by a factor of __________.

2. Mental Math/Estimating

A flyer is advertising a \$79.49 World Atlas for \$60 off. The percent savings is about

A 25% **B** 60%
C 75% **D** 133%

3. Proportional Reasoning

In right triangle PQR, the cosine ratio of ∠P is 0.5. The hypotenuse is __________ as long as the side __________ to ∠P.

4. Relations and Functions

A company's profit, *P*, is related to its revenue, *R*, and costs, *C* by the formula $P = R - C$. If the company is losing money, *R* must be __________ than *C*.

5. Algebra

Evaluate for $k = -4$.
$3k^2 + 8$

6. Graphs and Tables

This graph compares the change in readership over one year for four Toronto newspapers.

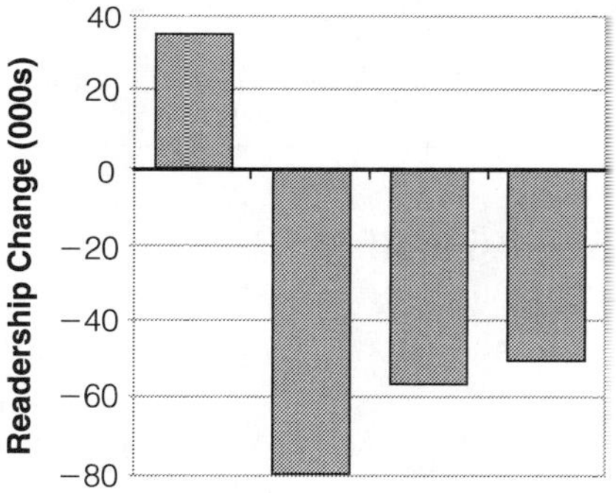

The total number of readers decreased by about __________.

7. Math Literacy

Label the sides of this right triangle in relation to ∠A.

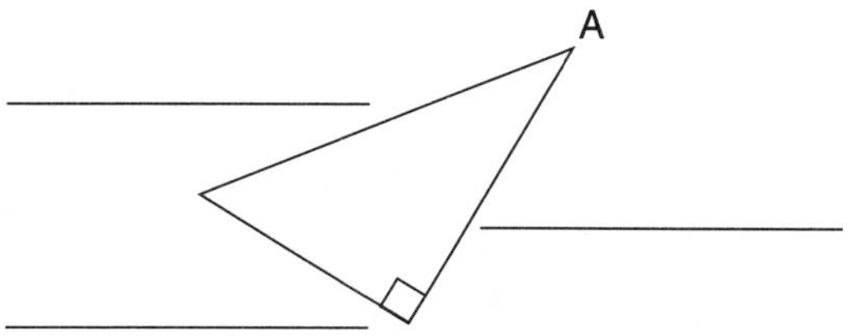

8. Previous Section

Expand and simplify.
$(2x - 5)(x + 4)$

Name: ______________________________ Date: ______________

Practise: Special Products

Section 9.2

1. Classify each expression as the square of a binomial (Sq), the product of the sum and difference of the same two terms (SD), or neither (N).

   a) $(5x - 2)(5x + 2)$ ____ **b)** $(2a - 9)^2$ ____ **c)** $(t + 3)(t - 3)$ ____

   d) $(4 + 7y)(4 - 7y)$ ____ **e)** $(3x - 5)(3x + 7)$ ____ **f)** $(9x - 1)(9x - 1)$ ____

2. Complete this table. (Hint: Both methods should give the same answer.)

	Square of a Binomial	Product of a Sum and Difference
Expand and Simplify	$(3x + 4)^2$ $= (\underline{\qquad})(\underline{\qquad})$ $= \underline{\quad}(3x) + \underline{\quad}(4) + \underline{\quad}(3x) + \underline{\quad}(4)$ $= \underline{\quad}x^2 + \underline{\quad}x + \underline{\quad}x + \underline{\quad}$ $= \underline{\quad} + \underline{\quad} + \underline{\quad}$	$(3x + 4)(3x - 4)$ $= \underline{\quad}(3x) + \underline{\quad}(-4) + \underline{\quad}(3x) + \underline{\quad}(-4)$ $= \underline{\quad}x^2 - \underline{\quad}x + \underline{\quad}x - \underline{\quad}$ $= \underline{\quad} - \underline{\quad}$
Use the Shortcut Pattern	$(3x + 4)^2$ $= (\underline{\quad})^2 + 2(\underline{\quad})(\underline{\quad}) + (\underline{\quad})^2$ $= \underline{\quad} + \underline{\quad} + \underline{\quad}$	$(3x + 4)(3x - 4)$ $= (\underline{\quad})(\underline{\quad}) + (\underline{\quad})(\underline{\quad})$ $= \underline{\quad} - \underline{\quad}$

3. Expand and simplify.

   a) $(x + 7)^2$ **b)** $(w + 8)(w - 8)$

   c) $(2y - 3)^2$ **d)** $(4a - 1)(4a + 1)$

continued ....

Name: ______________________________ Date: ____________

Section 9.2

4. Bertha, an interior designer, has worked out a pattern for tiling the floor of a hotel lobby for a client. Her design uses square tiles for the main colour. The tiles for the accent colours are also square, but they are 7 cm smaller. The border is made with rectangular tiles that are 2 cm longer and 2 cm narrower than the square tiles for the main colour.

a) Choose a letter to represent the length of a tile for the main colour.

Let ____ represent the length, in ________________, of a main tile.

b) Write and simplify an expression for the length, width, and area of each type of tile.

	Main Tile	**Accent Tile**	**Border Tile**
Length:			
Width:			
$A =$ ___ $\times$ ___			
$A =$ _____			

c) The tile that Bertha's client chooses for the main colour is 10-cm square. Complete this table for the tiles for the hotel lobby.

Measure	Main Tile	Accent Tile	Border Tile
Length (cm)	10	10 − ____ = ____	
Width (cm)	10		
Area using length × width (cm^2)	10 × 10 = _____		
Area using expression from part b) (cm^2)	$(\_\_\_\_\_)^2$ = _____		

Name: ______________________ Date: ______________

9.3 Expand and Simplify Polynomial Expressions

Textbook pp. 334–337

Warm Up

1. Number Sense

Continue the pattern.

0, −1, −4, −9, _____, _____, _____

Describe the pattern.

2. Mental Math/Estimating

The square of 10.25 is closest to

A 3 **B** 10

C 20 **D** 100

3. Proportional Reasoning

In right triangle ABC, the sine ratio of ∠A is 0.5. The side opposite ∠A is

__________ as long as the hypotenuse.

4. Relations and Functions

This scatter plot shows the change in temperature of Lake Waseosa during the fall. As the number of weeks increases,

the surface temperature ____________.

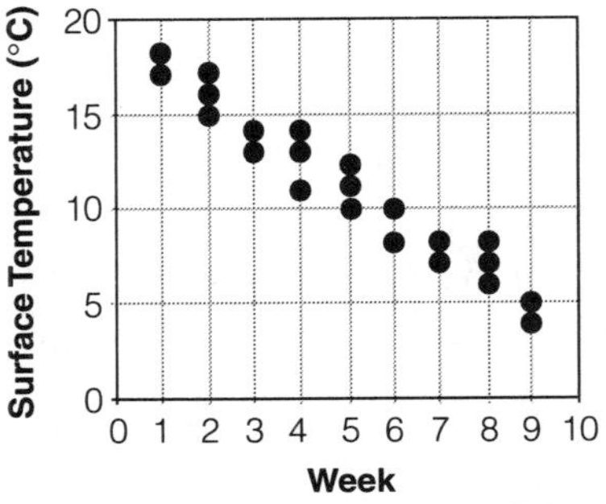

5. Algebra

Add.

$$\begin{array}{r} 3x^2 + 8x - 7 \\ x^2 - 5x - 1 \\ \hline \end{array}$$

6. Graphs and Tables

The lowest enrolment was _____ in the month of ______________.

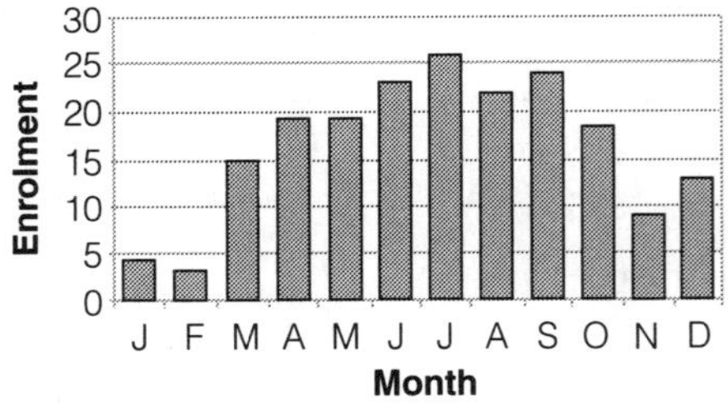

7. Math Literacy

The shape of the graph of a quadratic function is a **p** _ _ _ _ _ _ _.

8. Previous Section

The graph of $y = (x - 6)(x + 6)$ is

A a straight line

B two intersecting straight lines

C two parallel straight lines

D a parabola

Name: ______________________ Date: __________

Practise: Polynomial Expressions

Section 9.3

1. Expand and simplify.

a) $(-2x + 5)^2$

$= (\_\_\_\_)^2 + 2(\_\_\_\_)(\_\_\_\_) + (\_\_\_\_)^2$

$= \_\_\_\_ x^2 - \_\_\_\_ x + \_\_\_\_$

b) $-2(x + 5)^2$

$= -2[(\_\_\_\_)^2 + 2(\_\_\_\_)(\_\_\_\_) + (\_\_\_\_)^2]$

$= -2[x^2 + \_\_\_\_ x + \_\_\_\_]$

$= \_\_\_\_ x^2 + \_\_\_\_ x + \_\_\_\_$

c) Is $(-2x + 5)^2$ equivalent to $-2(x + 5)^2$?

Hint
- Follow BEDMAS: Perform the exponent operation, then multiply.
- Treat square brackets as you would round brackets.

2. Expand and simplify.

a) $(3x + 7) + 2(4x - 3)$

$= 3x + 7 \_\ \_\_\_\_\ \_\ \_\_\_\_$

$= \_\_\_\_ x + \_\_\_\_$

Hint
For the multiplication, think of "2 times $4x$ plus 2 times -3."

b) $(3x + 7) - 2(4x - 3)$

$= 3x + 7 \_\ \_\_\_\_\ \_\ \_\_\_\_$

$= \_\_\_\_ x + \_\_\_\_$

Hint
For the multiplication, think of "-2 times $4x$ plus -2 times -3."

3. Expand and simplify.

a) $(4a - 3)^2 + (3a - 1)(3a + 1)$

$= [(\_\_\_\_)^2 + 2(\_\_\_\_)(\_\_\_\_) + (\_\_\_\_)^2] + [(\_\_\_\_)^2 + (\_\_\_\_)(\_\_\_\_)]$

$= [\_\_\_\_ a^2 + \_\_\_\_ a + \_\_\_\_] + [\_\_\_\_ a^2 - \_\_\_\_]$

$= \_\_\_\_ a^2 + \_\_\_\_ a + \_\_\_\_$

b) $7(v + 6) - 4(8v + 3)$

c) $(4z + 5)(z - 4) + (3z - 7)(2z - 1)$

d) $(c - 6)(2c - 9) - 3(c + 4)^2$

e) $-5(2y + 7)(3y - 2) - (4y + 5)(4y - 5)$

continued ....

Name: ______________________________ Date: ______________

Section 9.3

4. a) Write an expression for the area on this floor plan. Then, expand and simplify the expression.

$A = (\_ + \_)(\_ + \_) + (\_ + \_)(\_ + \_)$

$A =$

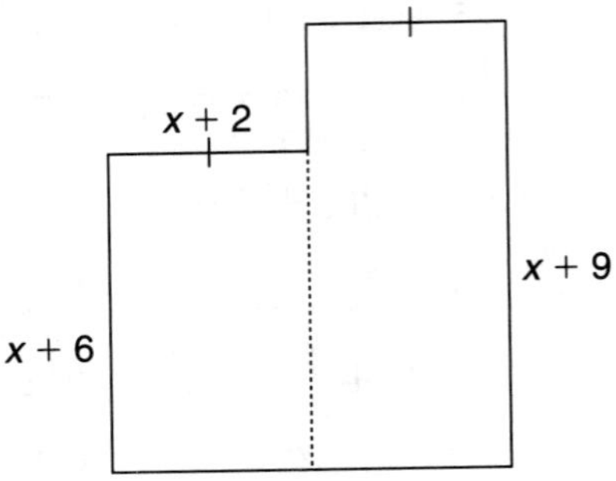

b) Write and simplify an expression for the perimeter of the floor in the plan.

c) Use the expressions in parts a) and b) to calculate the area and perimeter when $x = 5$.

Area **Perimeter**

5. A company that makes a variety of computer mice uses the same package design for the different types of mice. Each mouse is shipped in a rectangular box with sides that are 9 cm longer than the mouse and square ends that are 6 cm longer than the mouse.

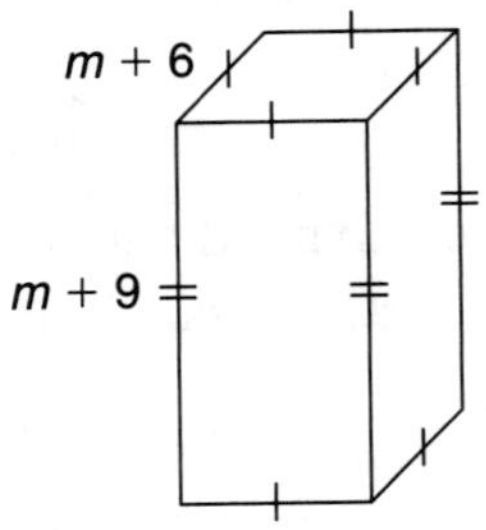

a) What does the variable m in the diagram represent?

b) Write and simplify an expression for the surface area of the outside of the box.

c) Find the surface area of the box for a mouse that is 12 cm long.

Name: ____________________ Date: ____________

9.4 Common Factors

Textbook pp. 338–341

Warm Up

1. Number Sense

How much time is between 9 A.M. and 4 P.M.?

2. Mental Math/Estimating

The distance from Toronto to Montreal is about 545 km. At an average speed of 90 km/h, the trip should take about

A 4 h **B** 5 h **C** 6 h **D** 7 h

3. Proportional Reasoning

For this triangle, the tangent ratio of ∠U is 0.5. Find tan V.

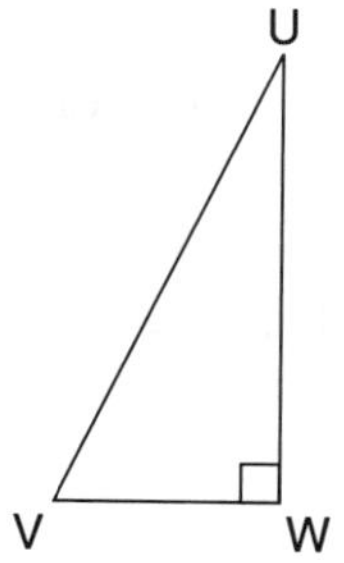

4. Relations and Functions

One construction company uses the formula $n = 5f + 45$ to estimate the number of labourers, n, needed for a building with f floors. If a building needs 90 labourers, how many floors does it have?

5. Algebra

Multiply, then collect like terms.

$(x + 4)(2x - 1)$

6. Graphs and Tables

What is wrong with this graph?

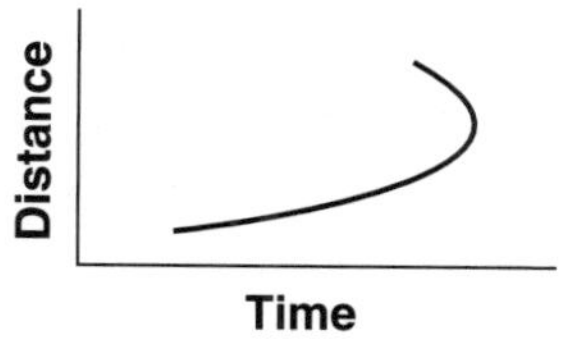

7. Math Literacy

The greatest number that divides evenly into each of a set of numbers is their

g _ _ _ _ _ _ _

c _ _ _ _ _

f _ _ _ _ _.

8. Previous Section

Write and simplify an expression for the area of the glass in this window.

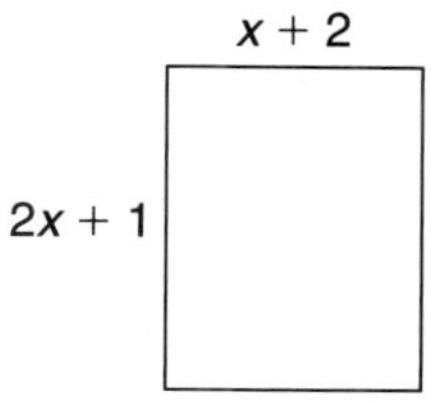

Name: ________________________________ Date: ______________

Practise: Common Factors

Section 9.4

Factoring is the opposite of ______________.

1. Find the greatest common factor (GCF) of
   a) 98 and 210

   $98 = 2 \times 7 \times$ ___

   common factors

   $210 = 2 \times 3 \times 5 \times$ ___

   ___ $\times$ ___ is the greatest number that divides evenly into both 98 and 210.

   Therefore, GCF is ____.

   b) x^5, x^3, and x^2

   $x^{\square}$ is the highest power of x that divides evenly into x^5, x^3, and x^2.

   Therefore, GFC is ____.

2. Write each expression as a product with the greatest common factor. Check by expanding.
   a) $9x^3 - 15$

   $=$ ___(___ $-$ ___)

   GCF of 9 and −15 is ___.
   The second term does not include the variable, so no common factor can include the variable.
   Therefore, GCF is ___.

   Check: ___(___ $-$ ___) $=$ ___ $-$ ___

   b) $25t^4 + 5t^3 + 10t^2$

   $=$ ___(___ $+$ ___ $+$ ___)

   GCF of 25, 5, and 10 is ___.
   GCF of t^4, t^3, and t^2 is ___.
   Therefore, GCF is ___.

   Check: ___(___ $+$ ___ $+$ ___) $=$ ___ $+$ ___ $+$ ___

   c) $4a^3 + 18a$

   $=$ ___ $(2a^3 + 9a)$

   $=$ ___ (___)$(2a^2 + 9)$

   $=$ ___ $(2a^2 + 9)$

   Check: ___$(2a^2 + 9) =$

   d) $v^5 + 7v^3 - 8v^2$

   Check:

   e) $16y^4 - 8y^3 + 24y$

   Check:

   f) $27m + 45n$

   Check:

continued ....

Name: ______________________________ Date: ______________

g) $5w^5 - 2w^4 + w^3$

Check:

h) $10x + 35x^2 - 20x^4$

Check:

4. Find an expression for the length of a rectangle that has a width of $6x$ and an area of $A = 30x^4 + 24x$.

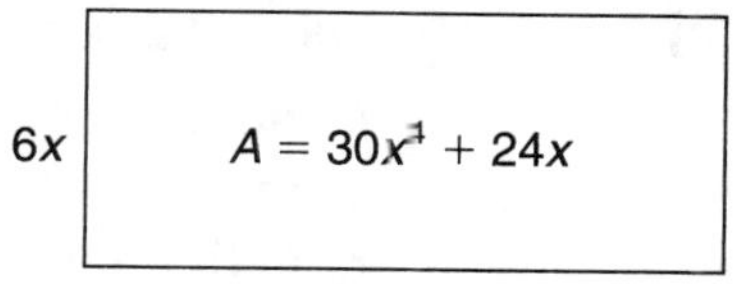

5. Find expressions for the dimensions of this rectangle given that the width is the greatest common factor of the area.

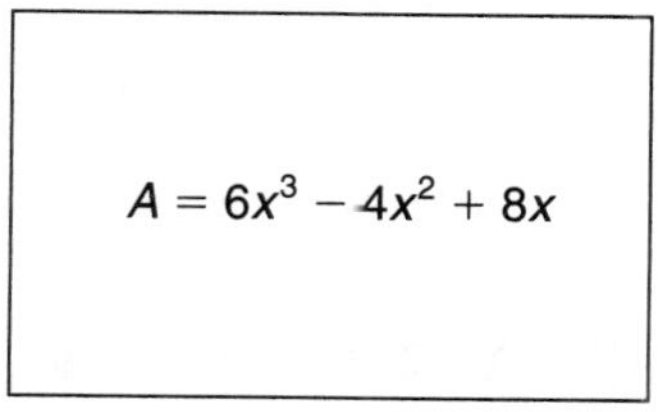

6. To design rectangular placemats, Lee first decides the area using the formula $A = 15s^2 + 18s$, where s is the width, in centimetres, of the widest band in the pattern of the fabric.

a) Find expressions for the length and width of the placemats given that the width is the greatest common factor of the area.

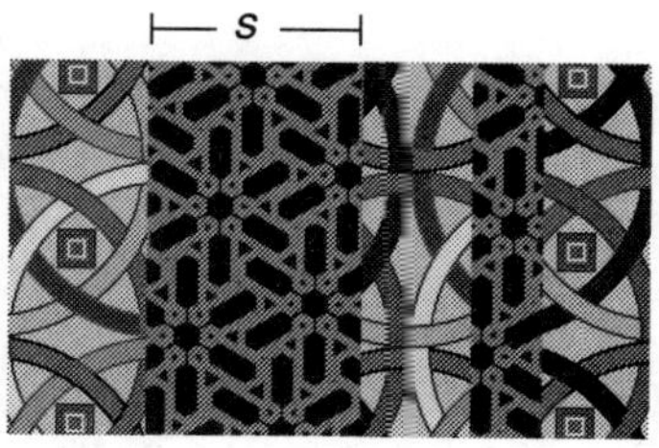

b) Confirm that the length and width are in the ratio of 2:1 when $s = 6$.

Name: ______________________ Date: ______________

9.5 Factors of a Difference of Squares

Textbook pp. 342–348

Warm Up

1. Number Sense

Circle the numbers that are perfect squares.

4 7 9 12 16 20 32 36 44

2. Mental Math/Estimating

A flyer advertises 6 boxes of facial tissues for $2.99. If there are 150 tissues to a box, then each tissue costs about

A $\frac{1}{4}$¢ **B** $\frac{1}{3}$¢ **C** $\frac{1}{2}$¢ **D** 1¢

3. Proportional Reasoning

Last year, Mamoud planted a square vegetable garden with an area of 16 m^2. This year, he doubled the length of each side of the garden. What is the area of his garden now?

4. Relations and Functions

The equation of this quadratic function is

A $y = 2x^2$
B $y = (x + 2)^2$
C $y = (x - 2)^2$
D $y = x^2 + 2$

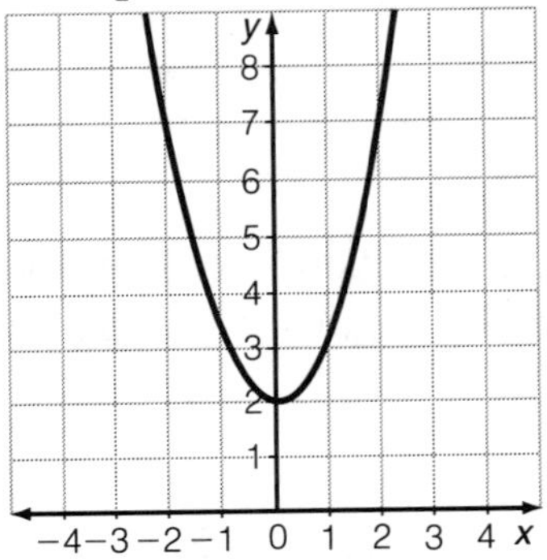

5. Algebra

For a half-day meeting, a hotel charges $225 for use of a conference room plus $5 per person for coffee service. Write an algebraic expression for the hotel's charges, *C*, for the meeting. Define the variable.

6. Graphs and Tables

This table summarizes a study of results from polygraphs ("lie-detectors").

Jury Verdict	Polygraph Reading	
	Innocent	Guilty
Innocent	63%	25%
Guilty	36%	75%

Of 100 people who appeared innocent on a polygraph, _______ were found guilty by a jury.

7. Math Literacy

The line through the middle of this parabola is an axis of

s _ _ _ _ _ _ _ _.

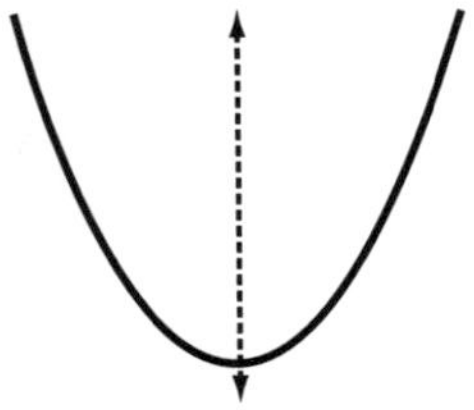

8. Previous Section

Find an expression for the length of this rectangle.

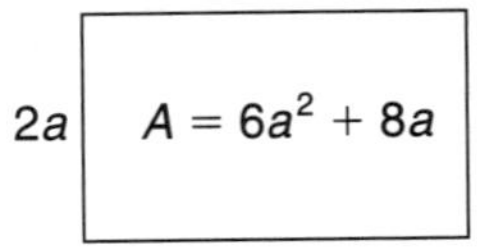

Name: ______________________________ Date: ______________

Practise: Factors of a Difference of Squares

Section 9.5

Factoring →

$a^2 - b^2 = (\_\_\_ + \_\_\_)(\_\_\_ - \_\_\_)$

← Expanding

1. Circle the expressions that are differences of squares.

a) $v^2 - 4$ **b)** $g^2 - 12$ **c)** $25 - h^2$ **d)** $9a^2 - 64$ **e)** $4y^2 + 25$

2. Factor fully. Check by expanding.

a) $81x^2 - 16$

$= (\_\_\_ + \_\_\_)(\_\_\_ - \_\_\_)$

Check: $(\_\_\_ + \_\_\_)(\_\_\_ - \_\_\_)$

$= \_\_\_\ \_\_\_\ \_\_\_$

b) $x^4 - 25$

$= (\_\_\_ + \_\_\_)(\_\_\_ - \_\_\_)$

Check:

Hint
$(x^a)^b = x^{ab}$

c) $2x^3 - 8x$

$= \_\_\_(\_\_\_ - \_\_\_)$

$= \_\_\_(\_\_\_ + \_\_\_)(\_\_\_ - \_\_\_)$

Check: $\_\_\_(\_\_\_ + \_\_\_)(\_\_\_ - \_\_\_)$

$= \_\_\_(\_\_\_ - \_\_\_)$

$= \_\_\_\ \_\_\_\ \_\_\_$

Divide each term by the GCF.

Factor the difference of squares.

d) $9s^2 - 49$

Check:

e) $z^2 - 81$

Check:

f) $75 - 48e^2$

Check:

g) $8y^5 - 2y^3$

Check:

continued ....

Name: ______________________ Date: ____________

Section 9.5

3. Since $x^2 - 9$ is a difference of squares, the equation $x^2 - 9 = (x + 3)(x - 3)$ is true for all values of x. Show that this equation is true for

a) $x = -3$

L.S. = (___)^2 − 9 **R.S.** = (___ + 3)(___ − 3)

L.S. = ___ − ___ **R.S.** = (___)(___)

L.S. = ___ **R.S.** = ___

L.S. ___ **R.S.**

b) $x = 0$

L.S. = (___)^2 − ___ **R.S.** = (___ + ___)(___ − ___)

L.S. = ___ − ___ **R.S.** = (___)(___)

L.S. = ___ **R.S.** = ___

L.S. ___ **R.S.**

c) $x = 3$

L.S. = **R.S.** =

L.S. = **R.S.** =

L.S. = **R.S.** =

L.S. ___ **R.S.**

d) $x = 50$

L.S. = **R.S.** =

L.S. = **R.S.** =

L.S. = **R.S.** =

L.S. ___ **R.S.**

4. Explain why $(t + 5)(t - 4)$ expands to a trinomial while $(t + 5)(t - 5)$ expands to a binomial.

Name: ______________________________ Date: ______________

9.6 Factors of Trinomials of the Form $x^2 + bx + c$

Textbook pp. 345–348

Warm Up

1. Number Sense

Solve for x.

$2^x = 16$

2. Mental Math/Estimating

A distance of 1 700 000 cm is

A 1.70 km　**B** 17.0 km

C 170 km　**D** 1700 km

3. Proportional Reasoning

Complete this proportion for a circle.

$\frac{\text{diameter}}{\text{circumference}} = \frac{1}{\square}$

4. Relations and Functions

The formula for the number of minutes, m, in n days is $m = 1440n$. The graph of this function is

A linear with a positive slope

B linear with a negative slope

C quadratic

D neither linear nor quadratic

5. Algebra

Evaluate for $x = 6$.

$y = x^2 - 6x + 9$

6. Graphs and Tables

This graph shows that a people with high stress levels take ____________ sick days if they exercise a lot.

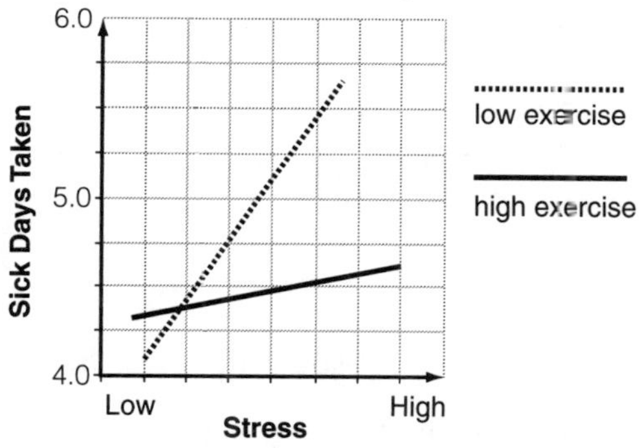

7. Math Literacy

An algebraic expression with three terms is a _ _ _ _ _ _ _ _ _ _ _ _ _.

8. Previous Section

The area of the front cover of your textbook could be represented by $A = x^2 - 4$. Write expressions for the length and for the width of the cover.

Name: ____________________ Date: ____________

Practise: Factors of $x^2 + bx + c$

Section 9.6

1. Factor $x^2 + 7x + 12$.

Find two numbers that add to 7 and multiply to 12:

Try $1 \times$ ___ $= 12$ $\quad 1 +$ ___ $=$ ___

$2 \times$ ___ $= 12$ $\quad 2 +$ ___ $=$ ___

$3 \times$ ___ $= 12$ $\quad 3 +$ ___ $=$ ___

Therefore, $x^2 + 7x + 12 = (x +$ ___ $)(x +$ ___ $)$.

2. Factor fully. Check by expanding.

a) $x^2 + 13x + 40$

Find m and n such that $m + n =$ ______ and $m \times n =$ ______.

The product, _____, is positive, so m and n are either both ________________

or both ________________.

The sum, ________, is positive, so m and n are both ________________.

Try $1 \times$ ___ $=$ ___ $\quad 1 +$ ___ $=$ ___

$2 \times$ ___ $=$ ___ $\quad 2 +$ ___ $=$ ___

$4 \times$ ___ $=$ ___ $\quad 4 +$ ___ $=$ ___

$5 \times$ ___ $=$ ___ $\quad 5 +$ ___ $=$ ___

So, m is ___ and n is ___.

$x^2 + 13x + 40 = (x$ ___ ___ $)(x$ ___ ___ $)$

Check: $(x$ ___ ___ $)(x$ ___ ___ $) =$

b) $x^2 + 6x - 16$

Find m and n such that $m + n =$ ____ and $m \times n =$ ____.

The product, _____, is negative so only one of m and n is ______________.

The sum, _____, is positive, so the number closer to 0 must be ______________.

Try $-1 \times$ ___ $=$ ____ $\quad -1 +$ ___ $=$ ___

$-2 \times$ ___ $=$ ____ $\quad -2 +$ ___ $=$ ___

So, m is ___ and n is ___.

$x^2 + 6x - 16 = (x$ ___ ___ $)(x$ ___ ___ $)$

Check: $(x$ ___ ___ $)(x$ ___ ___ $) =$

continued ....

Name: ______________________________ Date: ______________

Section 9.6

c) $a^2 - 14a + 45$

Here, $m + n =$ _____ and $m \times n =$ _____.

The product, _____, is _______________, so m and n are either both _______________ or both _______________.

The sum, _____, is _______________, so m and n are both _______________

Try $-1 \times$ _____ $=$ _____ $-1 + ($_____$) =$ _____

$-3 \times$ _____ $=$ _____ $-3 + ($_____$) =$ _____

$-5 \times$ _____ $=$ _____ $-5 + ($_____$) =$ _____

So, m is ___ and n is ___.

$a^2 - 14a + 45 = (a$ __ ___$)(a$ __ ___$)$

Check: $(a$ __ ___$)(a$ __ ___$) =$

d) $x^2 + 17x + 72$

Check:

e) $w^2 + 3w - 10$

Check:

f) $t^2 - 4t - 32$

Check:

g) $x^2 - 10x - 11$

Check:

5. A company makes clipboards with areas given by $A = p^2 - p - 42$, where p is the length, in centimetres, of the paper the clipboard is designed to hold.

a) What expressions for length and width is the company likely using?

b) Use two different methods to find the area of the clipboard when $p = 28$.

Substitute Into Area Formula **Find Area From Length and Width**

Name: ______________________ Date: ______________

9.7 Solve Quadratic Equations by Factoring

Textbook pp. 349–352

Warm Up

1. Number Sense

Two brothers are aged 6 and 5. How old will the younger one be when his older brother's age has tripled?

2. Mental Math/Estimating

If your heart beats 68 times per minute, the number of beats in a day is about

A 1000 **B** 10 000
C 100 000 **D** 1 000 000

3. Proportional Reasoning

At 80 km/h, how long will it take to drive 20 km?

4. Relations and Functions

The relation in this graph is

A linear **B** piecewise linear
C quadratic **D** parabolic

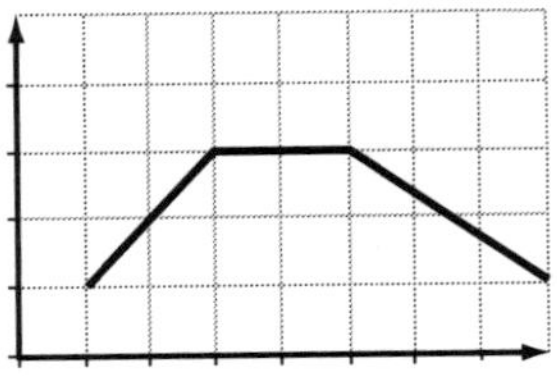

5. Algebra

Find the volume of this cylinder, to the nearest unit.

$V = \pi r^2 h$

$V =$

$V =$

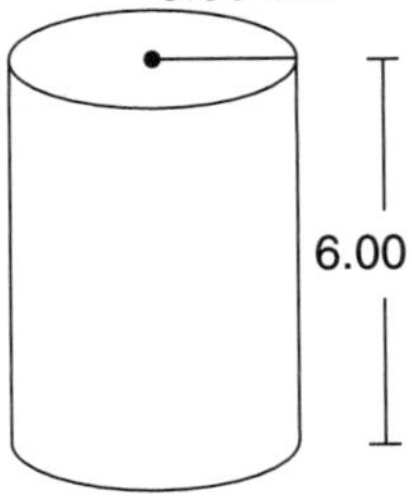

6. Graphs and Tables

This table shows the time it takes various planets to orbit the sun.

Planet	Orbit Period (years)
Mercury	0.34
Earth	1.00
Jupiter	11.86
Pluto	243

Pluto takes about ______ times longer than Jupiter to orbit the sun.

7. Math Literacy

Complete these two definitions of *vertex*:

- a _________ where two _________ of a polygon meet
- the _________ where a parabola meets its _______ of symmetry

8. Previous Section

Factor this trinomial.

$x^2 - 4x - 12$

Name: ______________________________ Date: ______________

Practise: Solving Quadratic Equations

Section 9.7

If $ab = 0$, then $a =$ ____, or $b =$ ____, or $a = b =$ ____.

1. For each statement, circle T for true or F for false.

a) If $mn = 0$, then m could be a number not equal to zero. T F

b) If $mn = 0$, then n could be a number not equal to zero. T F

c) If $mn = 0$, then m and n could both be numbers not equal to zero. T F

d) If $mn = 0$, then m and n could both be zero. T F

e) If $mn = 8$, then m could equal 0 or n could equal 0. T F

f) If $mn = 8$ then either m must equal 8 or n must equal 8. T F

2. Solve each equation.

a) $(x + 2)(x + 5) = 0$

Either $x + 2 =$ ____ or $x + 5 =$ ____.

Therefore, $x =$ ____ or $x =$ ____.

b) $(a + 7)(a - 4) = 0$

Either ____ $= 0$ or ____ $= 0$.

Therefore, $a =$ ____ or $a =$ ____

3. Solve by factoring. (Hint: Quadratic equations often have two solutions.)

a) $x^2 + 9x + 18 = 0$

(________)(________) = 0

Either ________ $= 0$ or ________ $= 0$.

Therefore, $x =$ ____ or $x =$ ____.

b) $y^2 - 12y + 27 = 0$

(________)(________) = 0

Either ________ $= 0$ or ________ $= 0$.

Therefore, $y =$ ____ or $y =$ ____.

c) $t^2 - 6t - 16 = 0$

d) $v^2 + 6v - 40 = 0$

e) $x^2 - 36 = 0$

f) $u^2 + 8u + 16 = 0$

g) $2y^2 - 28y + 90 = 0$

h) $4x^2 - 36 = 0$

Hint
If the x^2 term has the form ax^2, look for a common factor or a difference of squares.

continued ....

Name: ______________________________ Date: ______________

Section 9.7

4. Solve by rearranging the equation, then factoring.

a) $a^2 + 7a = 30$

Subtract to make the right side 0: $a^2 + 7a -$ ____ $= 30 -$ ____

Simplify: $a^2 + 7a -$ ____ $= 0$

Factor: $(a +$ ____ $)(a -$ ____ $) = 0$

Therefore, either ________ = 0 or ________ = 0.

Solve the linear equations: $a =$ ____ or $a =$ ____

b) $x(x + 5) = 36$

Expand the left side: ____ + ____ = 36

Subtract to make the right side 0: ____ + ____ − ____ = 36 − ____

Simplify: ____ + ____ − ____ = 0

Factor: (________)(________) = 0

Therefore, either ________ = 0 or ________ = 0.

Solve the linear equations: $x =$ ____ or $x =$ ____

c) $s(s - 3) = 28$

d) $3z^3 = 75z$

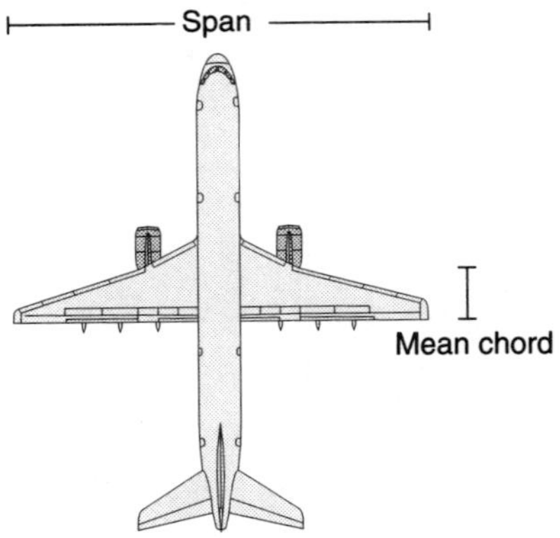

5. On an airplane, the distance across a wing is called the chord, and the distance from tip to tip of the wings is the wing span. An aircraft designer wants the wings to have a total area of 84 m^2 and a span, s, 25 m longer than the mean chord, c.

a) Write expressions for the wing area and span that the designer wants.

b) The formula $A = cs$ gives a reasonable estimate of the area of the wings. Substitute to eliminate s from this formula.

c) How long should the designer make the mean chord?

Hint
The chord length must be a positive number.

Name: ______________________ Date: ____________

Chapter 9 Review

The date of the Chapter 9 test is ______________________.
Use these questions to check whether you are ready for this test.
For help preparing for the chapter test, see the study tips on pages x–xii.

9.1 Multiply Two Binomials, textbook pages 326–329

1. Expand and simplify.

a) $(x + 8)(x + 3)$ **b)** $(4y + 2)(y - 3)$ **c)** $(3z - 5)(2z - 1)$

2. Michel's new calculator is 2 cm wider than the length of its display and 3 cm longer than twice the length of the display.

a) Select a letter to represent the length of the display. Then, write expressions for the length and width of the calculator.

b) Write and simplify an expression for the area of the top of the calculator.

9.2 Special Products, textbook pages 330–333

3. Expand and simplify. Use the shortcut patterns if you wish.

a) $(5a - 8)^2$ **b)** $(2x - 7)(2x + 7)$

9.3 Expand and Simplify Polynomial Expressions, textbook pages 334–337

4. Write an expression for the area of the roof of this building. Expand and simplify the expression.

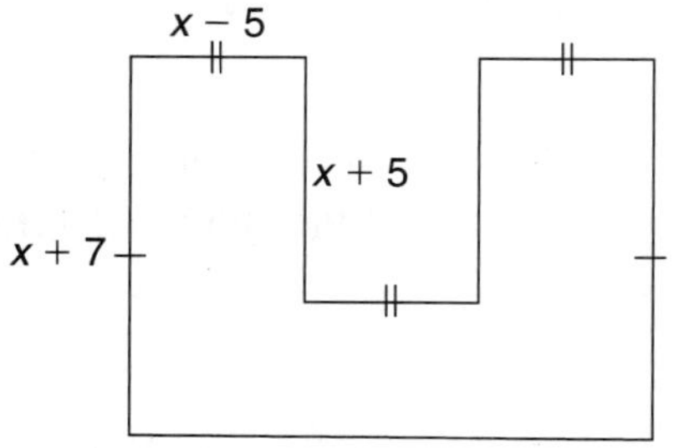

continued ....

Name: ______________________________ Date: ______________

9.4 Common Factors, textbook pages 338–341

5. Factor each expression by finding the greatest common factor.

a) $21t^2 - 49t - 28$

b) $12x^4 + 8x^3 - 16x^2$

9.5 Factors of a Difference of Squares, textbook pages 342–344

6. Factor fully. Check by expanding.

a) $a^2 - 121$

Check:

b) $16x^2 - 25$

Check:

9.6 Factors of Trinomials of the Form $x^2 + bx + c$, textbook pages 345–348

7. Factor each expression.

a) $w^2 + 15w + 26$

b) $x^2 + 2x - 35$

c) $y^2 - 12y + 27$

d) $z^2 - 9z - 36$

9.7 Solve Quadratic Equations by Factoring, textbook pages 349–352

8. Solve each quadratic equation by factoring.

a) $x^2 + 10x + 25 = 0$

b) $t(t + 6) - 10 = 62$

9. René has enough plywood to build a rectangular dock with an area of 24 m^2. He wants the width of the dock to be 5 m less than its length.

a) Write an expression for the area of the dock.

b) Solve the quadratic equation to determine the length of the dock.

Name: ______________________________ Date: ______________

Rich Problem: Cargo Container

Chapter 9
Rich Problem

You have been asked to help design a cargo container for use on ocean-going freighters. The container will

- be a rectangular prism (box shape) 3 m high
- have three identical openings, each 2 m longer than its height
- be 2 m wider than the length of an opening
- be 8 m longer than twice the length of an opening
- have a surface area of 300 m^2 excluding the doors on the openings

Your job is to calculate the dimensions of the container and the openings.

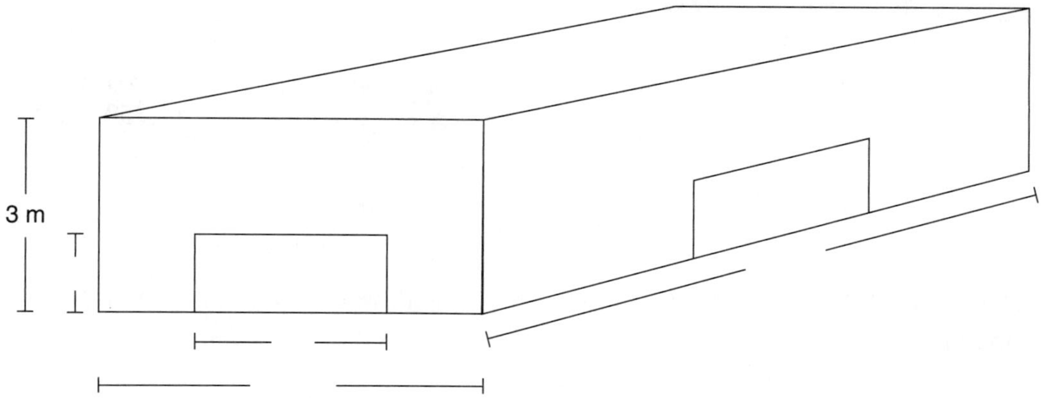

1. a) Select a letter to represent the length of an opening: _____ .

b) Write an expression for each of these dimensions, and mark them on the diagram.

Height of an opening: ________

Width of the container: ________

Length of the container: __________

c) Complete the table. Simplify the expressions for the areas.

	Front End	Right Side	Top	Open
First Dimension (m)	3	3		
Second Dimension (m)				
Area (m^2)				

continued ....

Name: ______________________ Date: ______________

Chapter 9 Rich Problem

2. Write and simplify an expression for the surface area of all six sides of the container less the area of the three openings.

$A = 2(\_\_\_\_\_\_) + 2(\_\_\_\_\_\_) + 2(\_\_\_\_\_\_\_\_) - 3(\_\_\_\_\_\_)$

Hint
Opposite sides of the container are the same size.

3. How long must you make the openings to get the surface area of the container to be 300 m^2?

$\_\_\_\_\_\_ + \_\_\_\_\_\_ + \_\_\_\_\_\_ = 300$

Hint
$4 \times 52 = 208$

4. Use your answer to question 3 to calculate the length and width of the container and the height of the openings.

Length of container:

Height of an opening:

Width of container:

5. Use the expression for the surface area of the container to complete this table of values. Then, plot the values and sketch a graph of the function.

Length of Openings (m)	Surface Area (m^2)
0	
1	
2	
3	
4	
5	

6. Explain how you know from the graph that the surface area of the container increases as the length of the openings increases, even though the openings are getting larger.

Name: ______________________________ Date: ______________

CHAPTER 10

Solving Problems: Quadratic Functions

Get Set

Answer these questions to check your understanding of the Get Ready concepts on pages 362–363 of the *Mathematics: Applying the Concepts 10* textbook.

Multiplying Polynomials

1. Expand and simplify.

a) $(x - 3)(x + 7)$ **b)** $(2t + 5)^2 - 6t$ **c)** $(4f + 1)(4f - 1)$

Finding *y*-intercepts

2. Find the *y*-intercept for each function.

a) $y = 7x - 13$ **b)** $y = 2x^2 + 8$ **c)** $y = (x + 11)^2 + 2$ **d)** $y = x^2 - 9x - 3$

Factoring

3. Write each expression as the product of two binomials.

a) $x^2 + 12x + 27$ **b)** $y^2 - 81$ **c)** $v^2 - 9v - 10$ **d)** $u^2 + 8u + 16$

Solving Equations

4. Solve by factoring.

a) $x^2 + 9x + 20 = 0$ **b)** $x^2 - 5x + 6 = 0$ **c)** $x^2 - 36 = 0$

Vertices of Parabolas

5. Give the coordinates of the vertex of each function.

a) $y = (x - 9)^2 + 4$ **b)** $y = -9(x + 1)^2$ **c)** $y = 2x^2 - 6$ **d)** $y = 3(x - 7)^2 - 15$

Name: ______________________ Date: ______________

10.1 Relate Roots and Intercepts

Textbook pp. 364–368

Warm Up

1. Number Sense

What two numbers add to 16 and multiply to −36?

2. Mental Math/Estimating

A stadium has seating for 45 156 fans. There were 8922 empty seats at a recent game. Estimate the attendance at this game, to the nearest 1000.

3. Proportional Reasoning

If gasoline costing 72.9¢/L increases in price by 10%, what will the new price be? Round to one decimal place.

4. Relations and Functions

Jared is paid $10 per hour plus $100 per week for being on call. An equation for this function is

A $p = -10h - 100$
B $p = 100h + 10$
C $p = 10h + 100$
D $p = -10h + 100$

5. Algebra

Expand and simplify.
$(3m - 4)(2m + 1)$

6. Graphs and Tables

This table lists the number of years a $10 000 investment will last with various interest and payment rates.

Annual Payment ($)	Interest Rate			
	6%	7%	8%	9%
900	18	22	28	—
1000	15	17	20	26
1100	13	14	16	19

What interest rate will give $1000 per year for 20 years?

7. Math Literacy

The distance between the origin of the Cartesian plane and the point where a line or curve meets an axis is an

_ _ _ _ _ _ _ _ _.

8. Previous Section

Solve by factoring.
$v^2 - 81 = 0$

Name: ______________________________ Date: ____________

Practise: Roots and Intercepts

Section 10.1

For the graph of a quadratic function in the factored form $y = a(x - s)(x - t)$, the ___-intercepts are s and t.

1. This graph shows a quadratic function.

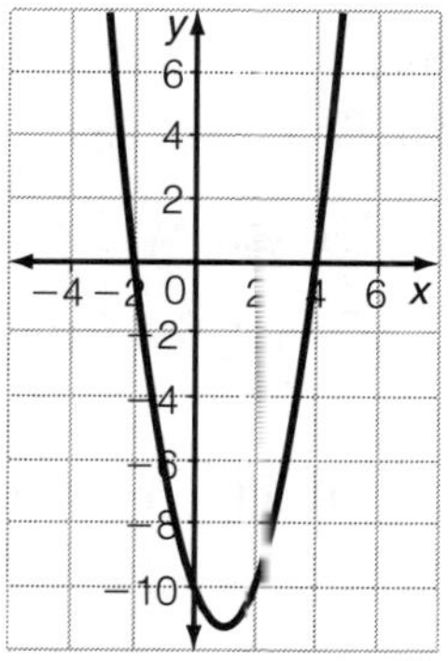

a) State the y-intercept of the function.

b) State the x-intercepts of the function.

c) Why are these x-intercepts also called *zeros* of the function?

2. **a)** Describe the graph of the quadratic function $y = x^2 - 15x + 50$.

The graph is a ______________ that opens ______________. It has the same width as the graph of $y =$ ____, and its y-intercept is ______.

b) Write $y = x^2 - 15x + 50$ in factored form.

If the factors are written as $(x + m)(x + n)$, then $m + n = -15$ and $mn =$ _____.

Therefore, both m and n must be ________________.

Try -2 and ____: $m + n =$ _____

-5 and ____: $m + n =$ _____

Therefore, the factored form of $y = x^2 - 15x + 50$ is $y =$ ________________.

c) Find the roots of $x^2 - 15x + 50 = 0$.

Hint
The roots have the same values as the x-intercepts.

d) Check your answer to part c) by substituting each root into the original equation.

For $x =$ ____,

L.S. $= (\_\_)^2 - 15(\_\_) + 50$ **R.S.** $= 0$

L.S. $=$ ____ $-$ _____ $+ 50$

L.S. $=$ ____

Does **L.S** $=$ **R.S**? ____

For $x =$ ____,

L.S. $=$

continued ....

Name: ______________________________ Date: ______________

Section 10.1

3. a) Describe the graph of the quadratic function $y = -x^2 + 5x + 14$.

b) Write $y = -x^2 + 5x + 14$ in factored form.

Divide by the common factor: $y = -1(\_\_\_^2 \_\_\_ 5x \_\_\_ 14)$

Factor the trinomial: $y = -1(x \_\_\_ \_\_\_)(x \_\_\_ \_\_\_)$

c) Find the roots of $x^2 + 5x + 14 = 0$.

4. Complete this table.

Equation	$x^2 - 2x - 8 = 0$	$x^2 - 64 = 0$	$x^2 + 13x + 36 = 0$
Factored Form	$(x + \_\_)(x - 4) = 0$	$(x + \_\_)(x - \_\_) = 0$	
Roots	$x = \_\_\_$, $x = 4$	$x = \_\_\_$, $x = \_\_\_$	
Related Function	$y = x^2 - \_\_\_ - \_\_\_$	$y =$	
x-intercepts	___ and 4	___ and ___	
y-intercept			

5. This graph shows the path of water from a hose at the top of a ladder on a fire truck. The equation for this path is $h = -0.1d^2 + d + 7.5$, where h is the height above the ground, in metres, and d is the horizontal distance from the fire truck, also in metres.

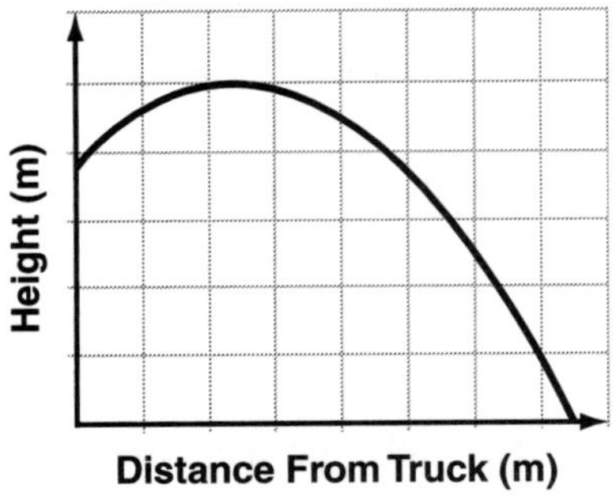

a) State the *y*-intercept. __________

b) What does the *y*-intercept represent in this situation?

c) Find the *d*-intercepts by factoring $h = -0.1d^2 + d + 7.5$.

Hint
First divide out the negative common factor.

d) How far from the fire truck will the water reach?

Name: ______________________________ Date: ______________

10.2 Standard and General Forms of a Quadratic Equation

Textbook pp. 369–374

Warm Up

1. Number Sense

Continue the pattern.

0, 3, 12, 27, ___, ___, ___

Describe the pattern.

2. Mental Math/Estimating

Estimate how many hours a person with a full-time job works in a year.

3. Proportional Reasoning

If a car travels 1 km in 1 min, its speed is ______ km/h.

4. Relations and Functions

A function with the equation $y = ax^2 + bx + c$ is *not* quadratic if

A a is negative
B $a = 0$
C $b = 0$
D $c = 0$

5. Algebra

Factor $x^2 - 2x - 15$.

6. Graphs and Tables

CDN$1000 is equivalent to about ________ British pounds.

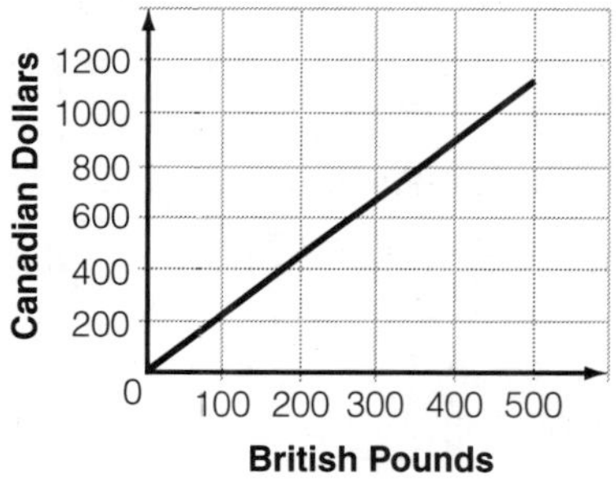

7. Math Literacy

A **r** ___ ___ ___ of the quadratic equation $x^2 + bx + c = 0$ is a **z** ___ ___ ___ of the function $y = x^2 + bx + c$.

8. Previous Section

Find intercepts of the graph of $y = x^2 - 2x - 15$. (Hint: Use your answer to question 5.)

x-intercepts:

y-intercept:

Name: ________________________________ Date: ______________

Practise: Forms of a Quadratic Equation

Section 10.2

For the graph of a quadratic function in the *standard* form $y = a(x - h)^2 + k$, the vertex is (___ ___).

For the graph of a quadratic function in the *general* form $y = ax^2 + bx + c$, the y-intercept is ____.

1. For each function, state the vertex of its graph.

a) $y = (x - 3)^2 + 5$ **b)** $y = 2(x - 10)^2 + 45$ **c)** $y = -9(x + 1)^2 - 1$

2. For each function, state the y-intercept of its graph.

a) $y = x^2 - 4x + 5$ **b)** $y = 25x^2 - 16$ **c)** $y = -0.5x^2 + 2x - 2.5$

3. For each function, state the x-intercepts of its graph.

a) $y = (x + 4)(x + 7)$ **b)** $y = (x - 6)(x - 2)$ **c)** $y = 3(x + 2)(x - 11)$

4. The standard form for a quadratic equation is also known as the *vertex form*. Explain why.

5. Find the vertex, y-intercept, and x-intercepts for the function $y = 2(x - 1)^2 - 18$. Then, use these values to sketch the graph of the function.

The equation is in ______________ form.

Therefore, the vertex is (___, ___).

Expand the equation to find the y-intercept:

$y = 2(x^2 - $ ___ $x +$ ___ $) - 18$

$y = 2x^2 -$ ___ $x +$ ___ $- 18$

$y = 2x^2 -$ ___ $x -$ ___

The y-intercept is ____.

Factor the general form of the equation to find the zeros:

$y = 2(x^2 -$ ___ $x -$ ___ $)$

$y = 2(x -$ ___ $)(x +$ ___ $)$

Therefore, the zeros are _____ and _____.

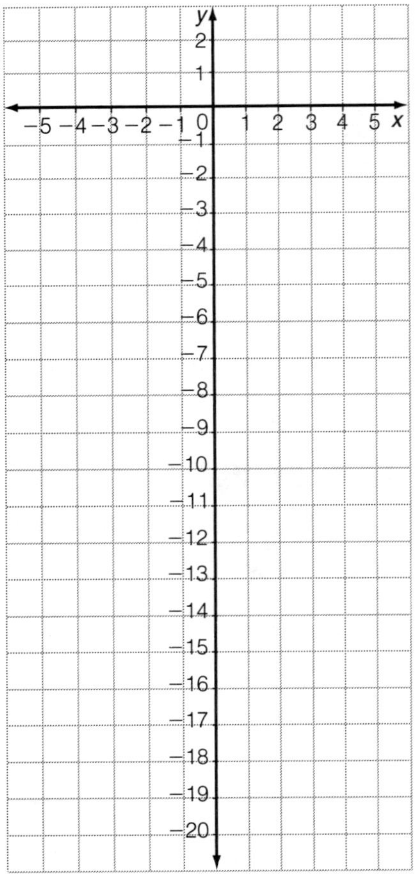

continued...

Name: ______________________ Date: ______________

Section 10.2

6. Determine the vertex, the y-intercept, and the x-intercepts for each function.

a) $y = (x - 4)^2 - 9$

vertex: (___, ___)

Expand to general form:

$y = x^2 -$ ___$x +$ ___ $- 9$

$y = x^2 -$ ___$x +$ ___

The y-intercept is ______.

Now, factor the equation:

$y = (x$ ___ ___$)(x$ ___ ___$)$

The x-intercepts are ___ and ___.

b) $y = -2(x - 3)^2 + 50$

vertex: (___, ___)

$y = -2(x^2$ ___ ___x ___ ___$) + 50$

7. This rope swing hanging from a tree branch forms a parabola. With the origin at the left end of the swing, the equation for the shape of the rope is $y = (x - 15)^2 - 225$, where both x and y are measured in centimetres.

a) Give the coordinates of the vertex of the swing.

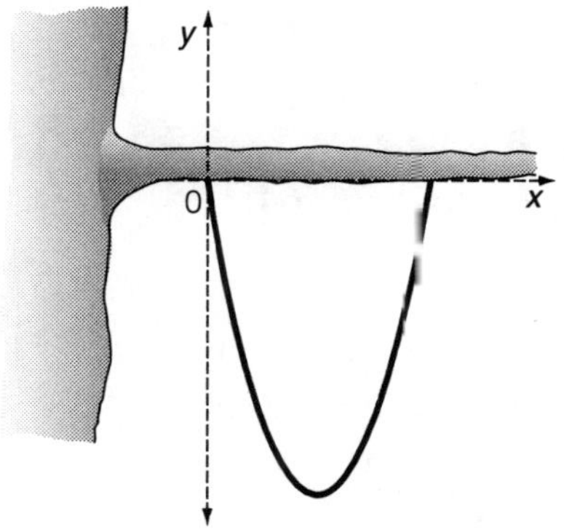

b) How far does the swing hang down from the tree branch?

c) Rewrite the function in general form.

d) Rewrite the function in factored form.

e) State the zeros of the function.

f) How far apart are the ends of the rope?

Name: ______________________ Date: ______________

10.3 Approximate Intercepts Graphically to Solve Problems

Textbook pp. 375–380

Warm Up

1. Number Sense

Most licence plates in Ontario have four letters followed by three numbers. How many licence plates start with AKFP?

2. Mental Math/Estimating

For a person with a stride of 0.8 m, the number of steps in 1 km is about

A 1000 **B** 1200
C 1600 **D** 2000

3. Proportional Reasoning

Use a Pythagorean Triple to find the length of side BC.

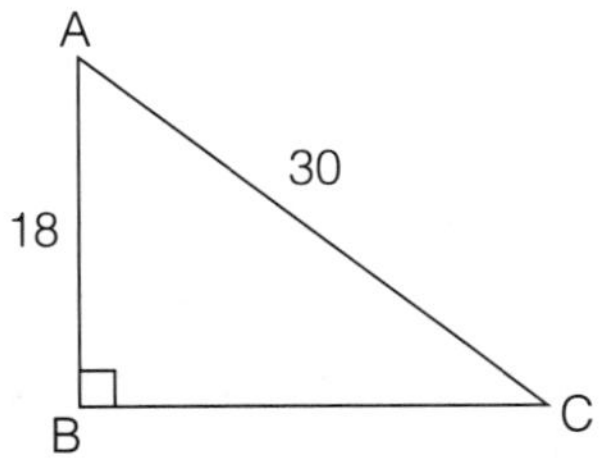

4. Relations and Functions

Which function does not have the same y-intercept as the others?

A $y = -2x + 4$
B $y = x^2 - x - 4$
C $y = -2x - 4$
D $y = -4(x + 1)^2$

5. Algebra

Factor $x^2 - 64$.

6. Graphs and Tables

This table shows how long one type of battery backup can run various devices.

Device	Power (W)	Time (h)
Telephone	5	40
Stereo	10	20
Work light	15	13.3
Fan	20	10
Computer	25	8

This battery can power a 100-watt load for about ____ h.

7. Math Literacy

An approximate value is ___________ to the actual value.

8. Previous Section

Find the vertex and y-intercept for $y = 3(x - 3)^2 - 7$

vertex:

y-intercept:

Name: ______________________________ Date: ______________

Practise: Approximating Intercepts Graphically

Section 10.3

1. Circle the correct item in each bracket.

   a) The graph of $y = ax^2 + bx + c$ is a (**circle / line / parabola**).

   b) The function $y = ax^2 + bx + c$ is in (**factored / general / standard**) form.

   c) The y-intercept of the graph is (a / b / c).

   d) The graph opens upward if a is (**negative / positive / zero**).

   e) The x-coordinate of the vertex is ($-b$ / $\frac{-b}{2a}$ / $\frac{-a}{2b}$).

2. a) For the quadratic function $y = 3x^2 - 12x + 2$, find the direction of opening of its graph, the y-intercept, and the x-coordinate of the vertex.

   For this function, a = ___, b = ____, and c = ____.

   Since ____ is positive, the parabola opens ____________________.

   The y-intercept is _____.

   The x-coordinate of the vertex is $\frac{-\square}{\square} = \frac{-(\quad)}{(\quad)(\quad)}$

   $=$

   b) Graph the function on a graphing calculator or by hand. Use your answers to part a) to help choose window settings or complete the table of values. Then, sketch the graph.

   To show the y-intercept on the graph, set **Ymin** < ____ < **Ymax**.

   Since a parabola is symmetric about a line through its __________, the x-coordinate of the vertex should be about halfway between **Xmin** and _______.

x	y
0	
1	
2	
3	
4	

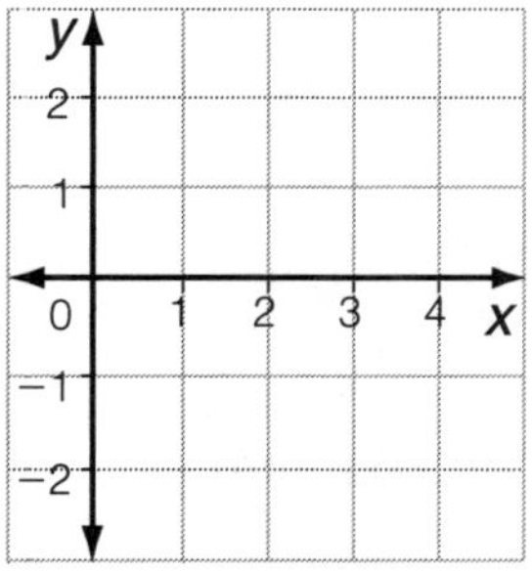

   c) Use the graph to find the zeros of the function, to one decimal place.

Hint
For help with graphing calculator functions, see page 377 of the textbook.

continued ....

Name: ______________________________ Date: ______________

Section 10.3

3. Complete this table. Use a graphing calculator to find the zeros, to one decimal place.

Equation	$y = 2x^2 - 24x - 27$	$y = -x^2 + 6x - 7$	$y = 0.5x^2 - 44x + 75$
Value of *a*			
Value of *b*			
Value of *c*			
Direction of opening			
***y*-intercept**			
***x*-coordinate of vertex**			
Zeros			

4. During an egg-toss game, Nazir pitches an egg that follows a path described by $h = -0.31d^2 + d + 1.5$, where h is the egg's height above the ground, in metres, and d is the horizontal distance from Nazir, also in metres.

a) Graph this path on a graphing calculator. Display only the first quadrant. Adjust the window settings to show the y-intercept, vertex, and one of the zeros. List your window settings below, and sketch the graph.

```
WINDOW
 Xmin=
 Xmax=
 Xscl=
 Ymin=
 Ymax=
 Yscl=
 Xres=
```

b) Explain why negative values of h and d do not apply to this situation.

c) How high was the egg when Nazir released it?

d) Find the maximum height the egg reaches, to the nearest centimetre.

e) If Nazir's partner misses catching the egg, how far from Nazir will it be when it hits the ground, to the nearest centimetre?

Name: ______________________ Date: ______________

10.4 Use Graphs to Solve Projectile Problems

Textbook pp. 381–387

Warm Up

1. Number Sense

Books are often made by binding together sets of 16 pages, known as *signatures*. How many signatures are in a 208-page book?

2. Mental Math/Estimating

In October 2003, Canada's national debt was about \$511 billion, and the population was about 31.6 million. Divided equally, each citizen's share of this debt is about

A \$16
B \$160
C \$1600
D \$16 000

3. Proportional Reasoning

A batting average is the ratio of the number of base hits a baseball player makes to the number of times at bat. In 1941, Ted Williams had a batting average of 0.406 for 456 times at bat. How many base hits did he get that year?

4. Relations and Functions

The graph of the relation between the number of math classes you have had and the number of Warm Up questions left to do has

A positive slope
B negative slope
C zero slope
D positive slope at first, then negative

5. Algebra

Evaluate for $t = 3$.
$h = -4.9t^2 + 60t$

6. Graphs and Tables

In 2002, Canadians gave ______________ more to charities than in 1999.

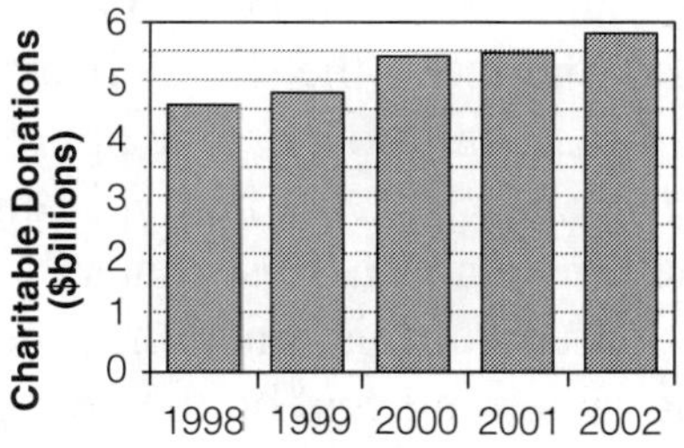

7. Math Literacy

Binomials have _______ terms, trinomials have _______ terms, and a __________________ has only one term.

8. Previous Section

Find the y-intercept and x-coordinate of the vertex for the graph of $y = 2x^2 + 16x - 8$.

y-intercept:

x-coordinate of vertex:

Name: ______________________ Date: ____________

Practise: Graphs of Projectile Problems

Section 10.4

1. This graph shows two typical projectile paths. Draw a line to join each phrase in the left column below with the corresponding item in the right column.

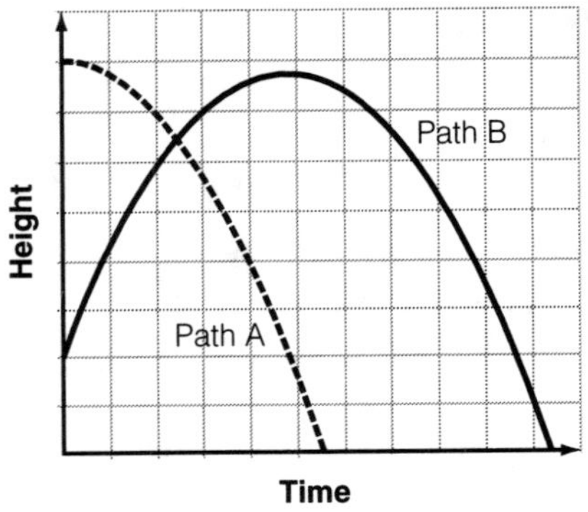

a) height of projectile when $t = 0$	zero
b) shape of projectile path	x-coordinate of vertex
c) motion downward at increasing speed	y-coordinate of vertex
d) motion upward, then downward	x-intercept
e) maximum height of projectile	y-intercept
f) time when height is greatest	parabola
g) time when projectile hits the ground	Path A
h) height when projectile hits the ground	Path B

2. In 2003, Sultana Frizell of Perth, Ontario set a Canadian high school record for shot put. She threw the shot, a heavy metal ball, over 15 m. The path of her record-breaking throw can be approximated by the function $h = -4.9t^2 + 8.2t + 1.8$, where h is the height above the ground, in metres, and t is the time elapsed, in seconds.

   a) Sketch a graph of this function, using either a graphing calculator or the table of values and grid on the next page. List your window settings if you use a graphing calculator.

```
WINDOW
 Xmin=
 Xmax=
 Xscl=
 Ymin=
 Ymax=
 Yscl=
 Xres=
```

continued ....

Name: ______________________________________ Date: ______________

Section 10.4

Time, t (s)	Height, h (m)
0	
0.4	
0.8	
1.2	
1.6	
1.8	

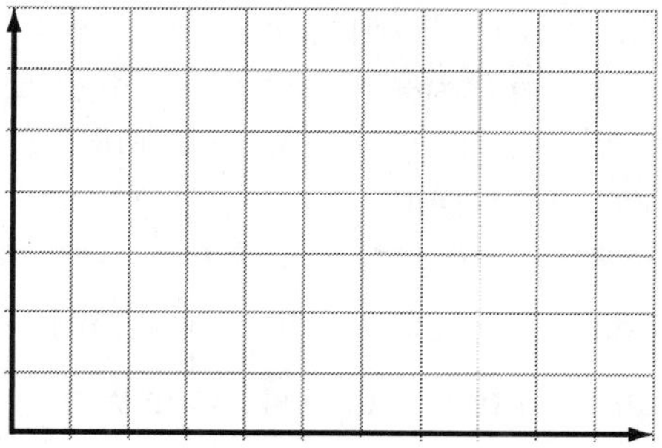

b) How high was the shot when it left Sultana's hand?

On the graph, the initial height of the shot is represented by the ____ -intercept.

Therefore, the shot was ____ m from the ground when Sultana released it.

c) What maximum height did the shot reach?

The maximum occurs at the ________ of the parabola.

Therefore, the maximum height is the ____ -coordinate of this point, or ____ m.

Hint
Use **TRACE** to find the coordinates of points on the graph.

d) When did the shot reach its maximum height?

The ____ -coordinate of the ____________ represents the time the shot reached its maximum height. From the graph, this time was about ____ s.

e) How long was the shot in the air?

The ____ -intercept shows when the shot hits the ground.

Therefore, the shot was in the air for ____ s.

f) Add the line $y = 3$ to your graph. Then, use this line to find the time interval when the shot is higher than 3 m.

Hint
Use **TRACE** or **CALC/5: intersect** to find the coordinates of points where the line intersects the parabola.

continued ....

Name: ______________________ Date: ______________

Section 10.4

3. Alice dropped a stone from a bridge 56.8 m above a river. At the same time, Barry threw a stone straight down from the bridge. A reasonable model for stones thrown from this bridge is $y = -4.9t^2 - v_0t + 56.8$, where y is the stone's height above the river in metres, v_0 is the stone's initial downward speed in metres per second, and t is the time since the stone was released, in seconds.

a) Write an equation for the height above the river of Alice's stone.

At the instant when Alice releases her stone, it is not moving. So, $v_0 =$ _____.

Therefore, the equation for Alice's stone is $y = -4.9t^2 +$ _____.

b) The initial speed of Barry's stone is 6 m/s. Write an equation for the height above the river of Barry's stone.

c) Whose stone do you think hit the water first? Explain your reasoning.

d) Sketch a graph of both functions, using either a graphing calculator or this table of values and grid. List your window settings if you use a graphing calculator.

```
WINDOW
 Xmin=
 Xmax=
 Xscl=
 Ymin=
 Ymax=
 Yscl=
 Xres=
```

	Height, *h* (m)	
Time, *t* (s)	**Alice's Stone**	**Barry's Stone**
0		
0.5		
1.0		
1.5		
2.0		
2.5		
3.0		

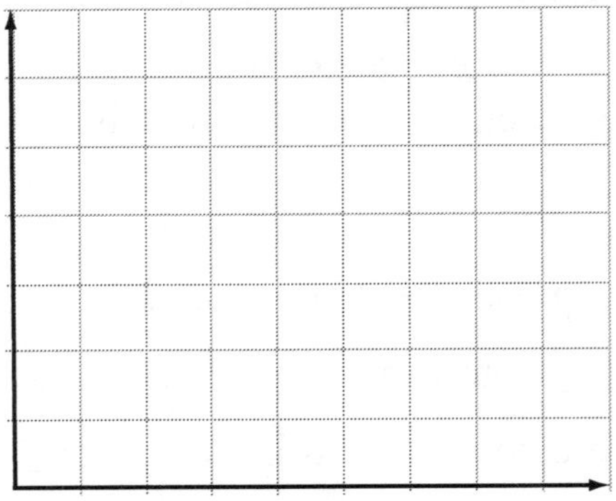

e) How long did it take Alice's stone to hit the water?

f) How long did it take Barry's stone to hit the water?

Name: ______________________________ Date: ______________

Chapter 10 Review

The date of the Chapter 10 test is ______________________.
Use these questions to check whether you are ready for this test.
For help preparing for the chapter test, see the study tips on pages x–xii.

10.1 Relate Roots and Intercepts, textbook pages 364–368

1. Jeannie's view of a fireworks display is partially blocked by a billboard. From her point of view, the path of one of the fireworks corresponds to $h = -d^2 + 7d - 10$, where h is the apparent height, in metres, of the firework above the billboard and d is the horizontal distance, in metres, from the left edge of the billboard. How far to the right of the top left corner of the billboard does the firework

   a) first appear?

   b) disappear?

10.2 Standard and General Forms of a Quadratic Equation, textbook pages 369–374

2. **a)** State the vertex of the graph for the function $y = 3(x + 6)^2 - 48$.

   b) Rewrite $y = 3(x + 6)^2 - 48$ in general form. What does the constant term in the general form represent?

   c) Find the x-intercepts of $y = 3(x + 6)^2 - 48$ by rewriting in factored form.

3. For the first part of its flight, Tom's paper airplane follows a parabolic path described by $h = 0.25(d - 2)^2 + 0.5$, where h is the height above the floor and d is the horizontal distance from Tom, both in metres.

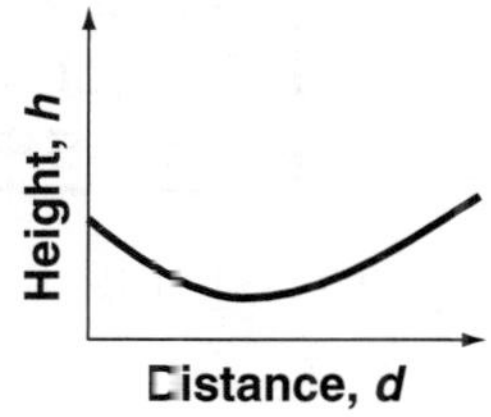

   a) How high above the floor was the plane when Tom launched it?

   b) How close to the floor did the plane get during the parabolic part of its flight?

continued ....

Name: ____________________ Date: ____________

Chapter 10 Review

10.3 Approximate Intercepts Graphically to Solve Problems, textbook pages 375–380

4. a) Find the y-intercept and the x-coordinate of the vertex for $y = 2x^2 + 9x - 6$.

b) Graph $y = 2x^2 + 9x - 6$ on a graphing calculator. List the window settings you use and sketch the graph.

```
WINDOW
 Xmin=
 Xmax=
 Xscl=
 Ymin=
 Ymax=
 Yscl=
 Xres=
```

c) Use the calculator to find the x-intercepts and the coordinates of the vertex.

10.4 Use Graphs to Solve Projectile Problems, textbook pages 381–388

5. For a movie, a stuntman jumps from the roof of a tall building. The stuntman's height, h, in metres, above the landing net is given by $h = -4.9t^2 + 86.4$, where t is the time, in seconds, since he jumped.

a) How far below the roof is the landing net?

b) Graph the function on a graphing calculator. List the window settings you use and sketch the graph.

```
WINDOW
 Xmin=
 Xmax=
 Xscl=
 Ymin=
 Ymax=
 Yscl=
 Xres=
```

c) What is the stuntman's height above the net 1.2 s after he jumps?

d) A camera is filming from a window that is 42.3 m above the landing net. When will the stuntman pass this camera?

e) Describe how you could use **CALC/5:intersect** to find the answer to part d).

Name: ______________________________ Date: ______________

Rich Problem: Quadratic Coaster

Chapter 1
Rich Problem

You are working for a company that is making custom steelwork for a new amusement park. The designer of the roller coaster wants the track at the bottom of the first drop to have a parabolic shape with the dimensions shown in this drawing.

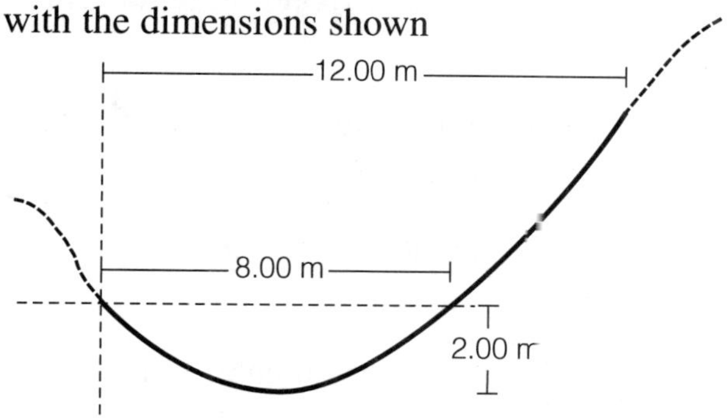

You have to prepare detailed measurements for bending the track to the required shape. If you can find the equation for the parabola, you can use a spreadsheet or a computer-aided design (CAD) program to calculate all the measurements.

1. a) Place the origin at the left end of the parabolic track. Then, find the coordinates of the other point where the track crosses the *x*-axis. Mark these coordinates on the diagram.

b) Mark the coordinates of the vertex on the diagram.

Hint
A parabola is symmetric about a vertical axis through the vertex.

2. The standard form of a quadratic function is $y = a(x - h)^2 + k$.

a) What do h and k represent in this equation?

b) What are the values of h and k for the parabolic track?

c) Substitute these values into $y = a(x - h)^2 + k$.

For the parabolic track, $y =$

d) Substitute the coordinates for one of the points on the parabola into the equation. Then, solve for a.

$y = a(x - \_\_\_)^2 + \_\_\_$

Hint
Pick the point with the coordinates that will make the calculation easiest.

e) Write an equation for the parabolic track. Then, expand and simplify this equation so that it is in general form.

continued ....

Name: ______________________ Date: ______________

Chapter 1 Rich Problem

3. The track will cost thousands of dollars to make, so you want to check that your equation is right. You know that quadratic equations can also be written in the factored form $y = a(x - s)(x - t)$.

a) What do s and t represent in this equation?

b) What are the values of s and t for the parabolic track?

c) Substitute these values into $y = a(x - s)(x - t)$.

For the parabolic track, $y =$

d) Substitute the coordinates of the vertex into this equation and solve for a.

e) Substitute this value for a into the equation from part c). Then, rewrite the equation in general form.

f) Does the equation in part e) match the equation you found in question 2?

4. **a)** How high is the right end of the parabolic track above the left end?

b) How high is the right end of the parabolic track above the vertex?

Key Equations

Chapter 1 Proportional Reasoning

Cross multiplying is a shortcut for multiplying both sides of a proportion by both of the denominators.

If $\frac{a}{b} = \frac{c}{d}$, then $a \times d = b \times c$.

$$\text{Unit rate} = \frac{\text{first quantity}}{\text{second quantity}}$$

$$\text{Percent} = \frac{\text{first number}}{\text{second number}} \times 100 \qquad \text{Percent change} = \frac{\text{change in the quantity}}{\text{original value}} \times 100$$

$$\text{Scale} = \frac{\text{diagram measurement}}{\text{actual measurement}}$$

Chapter 2 Equations and Formulas

Solving an Equation: To cancel a term or factor in an equation, perform the opposite operation on both sides of the equation.

Transposing a Term: Transposing is a shortcut for adding or subtracting the same term on both sides of an equation. The sign of the transposed term changes. If $x + a = b$, then $x = b - a$.

Clearing Fractions: Multiply by the least common denominator.

Chapter 3 Linear Functions

If a point (x, y) is on a line, the coordinates of the point will satisfy the equation of the line.

Slope of a Line: $m = \frac{\text{rise}}{\text{run}} = \frac{\text{difference in } y\text{-values}}{\text{difference in } x\text{-values}} = \frac{y_2 - y_1}{x_2 - x_1}$

Slope and *y*-intercept Form: $y = mx + b$, where m is the slope of the line and b is the y-intercept.

Standard Form: $Ax + By + C = 0$, where A, B, and C are integers, and A and B cannot both equal zero.

Chapter 4 Piecewise Linear Functions

$a < b$ means "a is less than b."

$a > b$ means "a is greater than b."

$a \leq b$ means "a is less than or equal to b."

$a \geq b$ means "a is greater than or equal to b."

Chapter 5 Systems of Linear Equations

The solution for a system of two equations must satisfy both of the equations.

Chapter 6 Similar Triangles

Similar Triangles

If $\Delta ABC \sim \Delta PQR$, then
$\angle A = \angle P$, $\angle B = \angle Q$, and $\angle C = \angle R$.

Also, $\frac{AB}{PQ} = \frac{BC}{QR} = \frac{AC}{PR}$, or $\frac{c}{r} = \frac{a}{p} = \frac{b}{q}$.

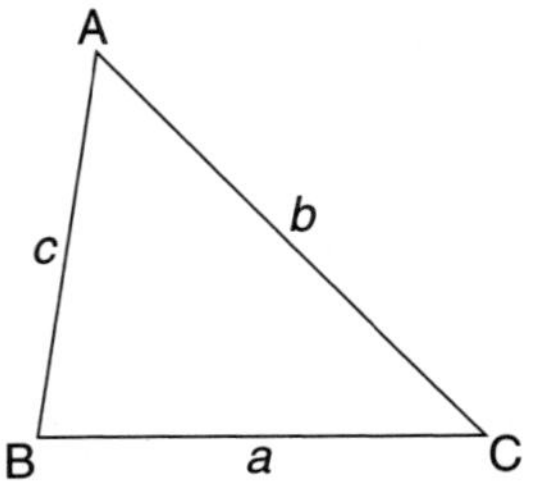

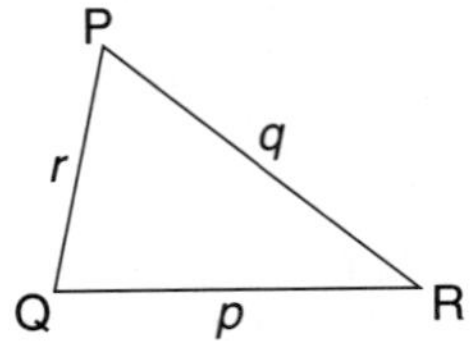

Pythagorean Relation

In ΔABC, with $\angle C$ a right angle,
$AB^2 = AC^2 + BC^2$, or $c^2 = a^2 + b^2$.

If $c^2 \neq a^2 + b^2$, ΔABC cannot be a right triangle.

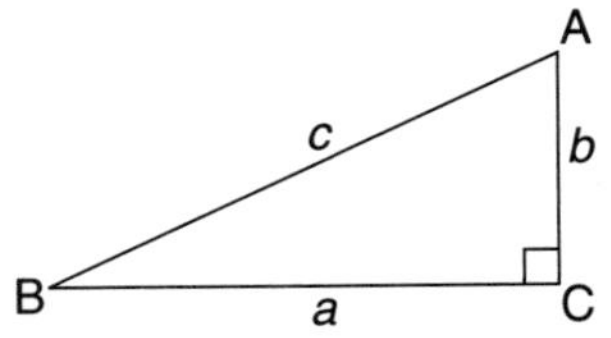

Pythagorean Triples

$\{a, b, c\}$ are a Pythagorean Triple if a, b, and c are natural numbers and $c^2 = a^2 + b^2$.

Chapter 7 Trigonometry

Trigonometric Ratios

For the angles in a right triangle, tangent ratio $= \frac{\text{opposite}}{\text{adjacent}}$

sine ratio $= \frac{\text{opposite}}{\text{hypotenuse}}$

cosine ratio $= \frac{\text{opposite}}{\text{adjacent}}$

In ΔABC, with $\angle C$ a right angle,

$\tan A = \frac{BC}{AC} = \frac{a}{b}$ $\quad$ $\tan B = \frac{AC}{BC} = \frac{b}{a}$

$\sin A = \frac{BC}{AB} = \frac{a}{c}$ $\quad$ $\sin B = \frac{AC}{AB} = \frac{b}{c}$

$\cos A = \frac{AC}{AB} = \frac{b}{c}$ $\quad$ $\cos B = \frac{BC}{AB} = \frac{a}{c}$

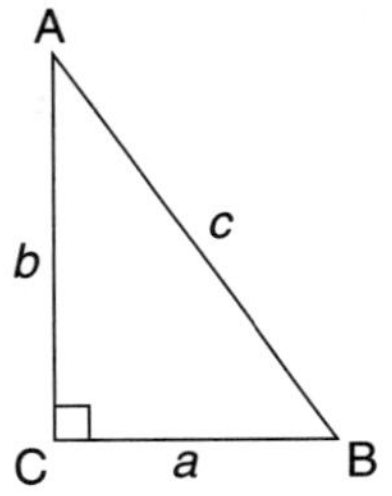

Finding an Angle Measure From a Trigonometric Ratio

If $\tan x = y$, then $x = \tan^{-1} y$.
If $\sin x = y$, then $x = \sin^{-1} y$.
If $\cos x = y$, then $x = \cos^{-1} y$.

Chapter 8 Quadratic Functions

Basic Quadratic Function: $y = x^2$

Graph is a parabola opening upward with vertex at (0, 0).

Transformed Quadratic Function: $y = a(x - h)^2 + k$, where $a \neq 0$

Graph is a parabola that

- opens upward if $a > 0$ and opens downward if $a < 0$
- is narrower than the graph of $y = x^2$ if $a > 1$ or $a < -1$
- is wider than the graph of $y = x^2$ if $-1 < a < 1$
- has its vertex at (h, k)

Chapter 9 Algebraic Expressions

Product of Two Binomials

$(a + b)(c + d) = ac + ad + bc + bd$ (Note: ac means $a \times c$.)

Square of a Binomial

$(a + b)^2 = a^2 + 2ab + b^2$

Product of the Sum and Difference of Two Terms

$(a + b)(a - b) = a^2 - b^2$

Factoring

$x^2 - y^2 = (x + y)(x - y)$

$x^2 + bx + c = (x + m)(x + n)$, where $m \times n = c$ and $m + n = b$

Solving Equations

If $(x + a)(x + b) = 0$, then either $x = -a$ or $x = -b$.

Chapter 10 Solve Problems: Quadratic Equations

Quadratic Functions

Standard Form: $y = a(x - h)^2 + k$

Vertex is (h, k).

General Form: $y = ax^2 + bx + c$

y-intercept is c, and x-coordinate of vertex is $\frac{-b}{2a}$.

Factored Form: $y = a(x - s)(x - t)$

x-intercepts (zeros) are s and t.

Solving Quadratic Equations

The roots of the equation $ax^2 + bx + c = 0$ are the zeros of the function $y = ax^2 + bx + c$.

Height of a Projectile

A reasonable approximation for the height, y, of a projectile is $y = -4.9t^2 + v_0 t + h$, where t is the time in seconds, v_0 is the initial upward speed in metres per second, and h is the initial height in metres.

Notes

Use this page to record information that you need often. List items such as

- page numbers for key concepts and examples you found helpful
- instructions for your calculator
- tips for solving problems
- addresses for web sites on mathematics